# Pedagodzilla

Exploring the Realm of Pedagogy

Mark Childs

Rebecca Ferguson

Michael Collins

& Elizabeth Ellis

*Pedagodzilla: Exploring the Realm of Pedagogy* © 2024 by Childs, Ferguson, Collins, Ellis is licensed under Attribution-NonCommercial-NoDerivatives 4.0 International https://creativecommons.org/licenses/by-nc-nd/4.0/

First edition, 2024

ISBN: 9798320499055

Imprint: Independently published

*This book is dedicated to all the podcast guests who've joined us in our pop-culture perambulations and to all the listeners who have kept us coming back to the microphones.*

*Any errors are the fault of ghosts.*

# CONTENTS

Dramatis personae ............................................ iii

Chapter 1: Introduction: I am Pedagodzilla – hear me roar! ........................................................................ 1

**Part 1: The Foothills of Foundations**

Chapter 2: How do spooky Muppets guide Scrooge through transformative learning? ................................... 11

Chapter 3: Come Dunning with me, Kruger! How do you know if what you are serving up is any good? ... 29

Chapter 4: How do ontology and epistemology help you eliminate Jar Jar Binks with headcan(n)ons? Part 1 ........................................................................ 45

Chapter 5: Yeah, but do ontology and epistemology help you eliminate Jar Jar Binks with headcan(n)ons? Part 2 ........................................................................ 63

Chapter 6: Mapping the Realm of Pedagogy .... 75

**Part 2: The Plateaux of Paradigms**

Chapter 7: How does behaviourism help players catch 'em all in *Pokémon Go*? ................................... 87

Chapter 8: Was Yoda an effective supply teacher (and would he have been better if he'd used Barak Rosenshine's ten principles of instruction)? ........................................ 107

Chapter 9: How does *The Hitchhiker's Guide to the Galaxy* help Arthur Dent take a cognitive load off? ...... 127

Chapter 10: How does Julie Andrews escape the Nazis with active learning? .................................................. 143

Chapter 11: How does problem-based learning help Buffy the Vampire Slayer...er, slay vampires? .............. 159

Chapter 12: Does Neo really experience experiential learning in *The Matrix*? .................................................. 179

Chapter 13: How can you make constructivism amount to more than a hill of beans? ................................ 197

## Part 3: The Basin of Bonds

Chapter 14: How does social constructivism enable the Fellowship of the Ring to find the path to success? ...................................................................... 219

Chapter 15: How does Arnie keep his skin on through situative learning in the movie *Predator*? ........... 241

Chapter 16: From n00b to l33t. How communities of practice provide a route into *World of Warcraft* . 259

Chapter 17: How did the Apollo 13 crew use constructionism to return safely to Earth? ....... 277

Epilogue: Journey's end or there and back again ...................................................................... 297

# DRAMATIS PERSONAE

### Markzilla
A Zilla who likes a coffee, a snooze, and a good debate about epistemology. Played by Dr Mark Childs, instigator and lead author.

### Mikezilla
A Zilla with a heart full of adventure and a head full of floof. Played by Mike Collins, who did a bit of writing, the scrappy illustrations, and even scrappier book layout.

### Beckzilla
A Zilla who knows her way around the realms of Pedagogy and a Poké Ball. Played by Prof Rebecca Ferguson, academic lead and co-author.

### Lizzilla
A Zilla with chameleonic skin and a penchant for Rococo furniture. Played by Elizabeth Ellis, whose invisible hand as editor is anywhere you don't see a massive mistake.

### Supporting Zillas
A collection of fabulous Zillas who contributed to the original recordings and outlines of the chapters. Some atomic powers.

**CHAPTER 1:**

# INTRODUCTION: I AM PEDAGODZILLA – HEAR ME ROAR!

*Mark Childs*

It begins not with a whisper, but with a blather:

> '*Hello, and welcome to* Pedagodzilla, *the podcast that takes the monstrously impenetrable world of pedagogic theory, research and observation and makes sense of it through the far more enjoyable lens of geeky games, books, film, TV, and comics. In each episode we're going to take a concept, a model, a theory, and just about anything to do with education, really lazily slap an analogy over the top in order to make it real, and then tell you how you can use it in your own practice.*'

That was Mike Collins' introduction to the very first episode of season one of *Pedagodzilla*, way back in March 2019. The idea behind the *Pedagodzilla* podcast was a very simple one – two or more people talk about an aspect of learning and teaching, explore it through the lens of popular culture, then situate that learning within practice.

The result ended up being enormously popular – by education podcast standards anyway – and by the time we took a break from releasing monthly episodes in September 2021 we were heading towards 20,000 downloads. We have listeners on nearly every continent (still waiting for those elusive Antarctica hits) and the episodes have been used in teaching programmes and graduate schools as learning resources. We've even guest starred on other education podcasts.

Who is 'we'? We is Mike Collins – the man with a microphone and impostor syndrome incarnate – and Mark Childs – the man with a PhD in education and a National Teaching Fellow. And throughout the life of the podcast, we have been joined by a wide range of colleagues who have contributed their own education perspectives and love of pop culture.

The beginnings of the podcast were serendipitous. We both worked in Learning Design at The Open University (OU) and had just been to a reading group, looking at Paul Kirschner's paper on urban myths in education (Kirschner and van Merriënboer, 2013). Mike was heading towards a podcasting booth with some more reading in hand – his plan being to talk it through to himself and record it so he could embed it more firmly in his memory. Mark was walking around with a mug of coffee. We bumped into each other, explained what we were up to, and decided it made a lot more sense to record our thoughts as a dialogue. Mike would find it easier to get the ideas straight in his head, and Mark would have a warm place to drink his coffee.

The first conversation, about communities of practice, evolved into a pop-cultural link because of a paper by Oliver and Carr (2003) which was Mark's main touchstone for the topic. The pop-cultural lens of *World of Warcraft* turned out to be a great way to explore the issues, for two reasons. The first was that both Mike and Mark were using an educational concept that they knew something about, and the other was that they had the chance to talk about (in this case) a game they'd both played, albeit with different degrees of success.

That narrative has continued ever since – *Pedagodzilla* is the story of Mike's journey to learning more about pedagogy and Mark getting to offload all his pent-up geekiness. The reality is, it's a lot of fun. Particularly during the pandemic, meeting up and talking about all things teachery and geekery was a lifeline. And, by extension, it proved to be a lifeline for hundreds of listeners as well. In short, we'd be doing this even if no-one were listening. The fact that people are is an amazing bonus.

Our biggest thanks go to the special guests who've kept the show so varied and interesting. It would be a full-time job adapting all of the episodes we've produced so far, and the collection gathered in this book is just a fraction of the topics we've covered. The contributors to the episodes covered in this book are:

- Paul Astles
- Becky Cohen
- Olivia Rowland
- Mark Williams

Together – plus Elizabeth and Rebecca, they are the Zillas.

# About the book

Rather than compile a 'book of the podcast', which would have been a series of transcripts, we chose instead to create a digital written resource, pulling together the pop culture and the pedagogy in a more coherent way. Beginning with a transcript of a particular episode, we have developed a more discursive, but still to some extent scholarly, output. There were far too many episodes to include them all in one book, so for this first volume we've focused on the Big Concepts in teaching and learning, with some preliminary chapters on why they're important. Our plan is to follow this up with more volumes and perhaps eventually catch up with the podcasts.

As the concepts chosen were those Mike selected to inform his own understanding, when grouped together they form a relatively solid introduction to pedagogy. As a guide, Mark knows enough to give a good general overview, but not so much that the explanations get bogged down in nuances. We're offering these as an entertaining way to get up to speed with broad-stroke explanations of most of the basic ideas about education, and they are not intended to be comprehensive.

The guide to pop culture is even more scattergun, as we've obviously selected based on our own personal preferences (or those of the Zillas) and talked predominantly about our own perspectives on them. There are many, many still to talk about. As far as our geek obsessions go, we've barely scratched the surface.

It's also been pointed out (by Rebecca, the third major creative force behind the book) that we make a lot of pop-culture references without fully explaining them. We made a conscious decision early on that we'd unpack only the bits that a reader would really need to know to understand what we're talking about – this also keeps us honest when we start to lose ourselves in our fandoms. This has been helped in no small part by Elizabeth Ellis, who took on the unenviable role of editor, and whose discerning eye and steadfast dedication to clarity guided our enthusiastic, if occasionally chaotic, chapters into a coherent narrative.

We hope this doesn't feel as if we're excluding anyone, but we acknowledge this is heavily targeting an audience who share our cultural references.

We've also organised the chapters, so that they read as a coherent whole.

*Part 1* is the introduction, with a rationale for why we think learning about pedagogy is important, what it is, how a little learning about learning can be detrimental and how it can transform people if you get it right. We introduce some of the basics, such as the ontology and epistemology of approaches to education and how these have led to the different approaches discussed in the rest of the book.

*Part 2* is a series of chapters focusing on two different approaches to education – those drawing chiefly on positivist approaches to learning (like how the brain works) and those associated with constructivism (interpreting how learners make sense of the world) – together with the strengths and weaknesses of each. We have chapters on approaches that draw on the positivist end of things, on constructivist approaches, and also on whether 'virtual' counts as experience. We wrap the section up with a chapter comparing neurological and constructivist approaches.

*Part 3* looks at learning approaches that are concerned with interactions with society, the environment, and other contexts. We wrap this all up in our final chapter, which is our plan for what comes next. This was a journey for us, so we've presented the chapters as a journey here too, with twists, challenges, and dead ends along the way.

## A note on authorship

Due to the origins of the chapters in their episode form, attributing authorship has been a challenge. For that reason, we have adopted the following convention.

The person who did most of the keyboard tapping comes first in the list of authors. As the episodes are mainly Mike's brainchild with some input from Mark, most chapters should be attributed to both.

The episode guest usually follows afterwards, unless they have written the chapter. Or are Rebecca, who saved our bacon by writing a lot of the chapters.

Hopefully, that's fair and collegiate for everyone.

## How to read this book

Move your eyes from side to side and turn the pages. Hah, no, random *Monty Python* reference notwithstanding, we're offering the following explanation and suggested routes.

So that these read like book chapters rather than transcripts, we've adopted a single authorial voice rather than multiple ones, though there were points where the difference in opinion or experience between individuals was worth preserving, so we kept those in too. Where we've switched to personal perspectives, a little Zilla head accompanies the text.

> *Like this! My perspective here is that podcasting is a heck of a lot easier than writing and not mucking up the typesetting.*
> *~Mikezilla*

A link to the original podcast episode is included as a QR code at the end of each chapter, and in two cases there is an empty void where the episode hasn't (at time of publication of this book) been edited and published yet.

For people who are completely new to some of the concepts, we recommend starting with Chapter 6: Mapping the Realm of Pedagogy, which lays out the basic concepts, then flicking through looking for the Mikezilla interjections. For a more in-depth introduction, read the chapters on behaviourism, active learning, and social constructivism. If you have more background knowledge and just have specific things you're interested in or confused by, dipping into individual chapters works fine too, they're all written to be read as standalone pieces. However, the chapters are ordered to convey a journey through the subject, so if you're up for it, start at the very beginning (we've heard it's a very good place to start).

To convey a sense of that journey, we've written a short narrative around the chapters, explaining where we are in the process of learning about learning, and what the next chapter involves. We've written this from the perspective of three explorers. Meet the Zillas: Markzilla, Mikezilla and Beckzilla, including cameos from other Zillas in some chapters.

*And thus begins the tale of the Zillas, and their exploration of the realms of pedagogy. With a song in their hearts, and a healthy supply of coffee and biscuits they depart...*

# The secret origins (and references) of *Pedagodzilla*

Kirschner, P.A. and van Merriënboer, J.J.G. (2013) Do learners really know best? Urban legends in education, *Educational Psychologist*, 48:3, 169-183, DOI: 10.1080/00461520.2013.804395

Oliver, M. and Carr, D. (2009) Learning in virtual worlds: Using communities of practice to explain how people learn from play, *British Journal of Educational Technology*, Special Issue: Out of This World: 3-D MUVEs, 40:33, 444-457. Available at https://bera-journals.onlinelibrary.wiley.com/toc/14678535/2009/40/3

# PART 1
## THE FOOTHILLS OF FOUNDATIONS

*In which our Zillas learn how to transform themselves with a little knowledge, how a little knowledge can be a dangerous thing, and how to decide what is and isn't knowledge in the first place. All to prepare for their epic adventure across the Realm of Pedagogy.*

**CHAPTER 2:**

# HOW DO SPOOKY MUPPETS GUIDE SCROOGE THROUGH TRANSFORMATIVE LEARNING?

*Mike Collins and Mark Childs*

*Mikezilla and Markzilla arrive in a strange new country, the Realm of Pedagogy. Completely lost, they look around in bewilderment. 'Why are we here?' they ask, shrugging at each other (they do this a lot). A voice booms from the mist: 'Indeed, why are you here? Because on this journey you will learn about learning! But first, you must prepare yourselves to be transformed by that learning. For what is a journey if it does not result in your own inner journey?' The Zillas nod wisely, as if they understand any of this. Then! The mist clears. The landscape opens up. They see their first hint of what lies ahead: Mezirow's ten phases of Transformative Learning.*

This is the starting point for the metanarrative of our Zillas on their learning journey though a fantastical pedagogical world. If this were a Disney movie, they wouldn't hit transformative learning until near the end of Act 2 (apotheosis), but as it's such a critical part of characterising and understanding your own and others' learning journeys, it fits in best here, nice and early, as part of the groundwork.

As you make your way through your own pedagogic learning journey, and (on a smaller scale) this book, you may well find your existing views challenged. You may consider your experiences in new lights and contexts. These experiences may come together to transform what you know, and ultimately how you interact with the world. They may also help you understand why people often struggle to change their understanding. This is, in essence, transformative learning, which will be explored in this chapter through the lens of *The Muppets*, and the question: **How do spooky Muppets guide Scrooge through transformative learning?**

## *The Muppets* and *The Muppet Christmas Carol*

Jim Henson's Muppets and, by extension, *Sesame Street*, fall into the *Harry Potter* and *Star Wars* style of pop-culture Swiss army knives i.e. they can be applied to any pedagogy you care to point them at, and therefore should be used sparingly.

*The Muppets* is the single best family comedy/variety show staffed exclusively by semi-professional puppets and monsters, and headed up by an earnest and conscientious frog. They were the brainchild of Jim Henson, an accidental puppeteer who had foam-based characters getting up to mischief as early as 1955 with *Sam and Friends*, before hitting it big with *Sesame Street* in 1969, and then hitting it even bigger with *The Muppet Show* in

1976, bringing together decades-worth of characters and ideas in a glorious chaotic mess of fun, farce and muppetational madness.

The core characters of the show, including (but not limited to) Kermit the Frog, Fozzie Bear, Rizzo the Rat, The Great Gonzo, Miss Piggy, Statler and Waldorf, became pop-culture icons in their own right. As the show exploded to international success, big-screen movies inevitably followed: *The Muppet Movie*, *The Great Muppet Caper*, *The Muppets Take Manhattan*, and then absolutely nailing it with *The Muppet Christmas Carol* in 1992.

*The Muppet Christmas Carol* is a musical comedy retelling of the classic Charles Dickens story, *A Christmas Carol (1843)*, in which infamous grinch Ebenezer Scrooge – moneylender, miser and awful employer – is visited on Christmas Eve by the ghosts of his former business partners, and then by three spirits. They show him how his past has shaped his relationship with Christmas, how his Christmas cruelties are propagating outwards to affect the lives of his employees and family and, finally, how in the future his sour ways will leave him dead, alone, and unmourned.

What a sad tale this would be, if it weren't for transformative learning! As Scrooge is confronted by the realities of his life, he has a series of epiphanies, and resolves to change his miserly ways. Giant turkeys are purchased, everyone has a singalong, and the credits roll.

Why, you may ask, choose to focus on the Muppets' take on the story rather than Dickens' original text? Three reasons:

1. *The Muppet Christmas Carol* is something of a Christmas classic movie, beloved and seen by many as one of the rotational movies to watch in the run-up to Christmas each year. This level of exposure makes it a wonderfully relatable pop-culture lens, compared to the original text.
2. As retellings of the story go, it's one which stays relatively faithful to the original.

3. Muppets are brilliant and, given half a chance, the rest of this book would be about how much we love them.

There's a lot to love about the Muppets' take on the story. As with the other Muppet movies, the characters in the story are played by the characters from the Muppets cast. Kermit the Frog plays a heartfelt Bob Cratchit, Miss Piggy his wife, Fozzie Bear is Fozziwig (a take on the original Fezziwig) – and they are all very much themselves, performing two steps removed from the talented puppeteers beneath them. Their personalities shine through the roles, skating beautifully along the line between skit and a serious retelling of the story. The Muppets are their usual chaotic, effervescent selves, adding colour and humour to the story, and at the core of that story is Michael Caine, who plays Ebenezer Scrooge dead straight down the middle. A steely-eyed portrayal of the character and story – but situated within a world of Muppet madness.

Foam and fleece foolishness aside, the key story beats we need to answer our question are:

- The context: Scrooge is a 'squeezing, wrenching, grasping, scraping, clutching, covetous, old sinner' (Dickens, 1843). We see his rottenness demonstrated in relationships with employees, family and the community.
- Scrooge is confronted by the ghosts of his late business partners, Marley and Marley, suffering and burdened by chains forged during their life through their avarice and greed. They warn him that he will be visited by three spirits, that he is heading down a similar path to them – and that this is his chance of redemption. They do this through a very catchy song.
- Scrooge is visited by the Ghost of Christmas Past – a horrifying china-doll puppet, coming in at second place as

spookiest puppet in the movie. The ghost transports him to the past, where he sees himself growing up. First as a boy in school, abandoned there by his parents. Next as a young professional fussing about costs at Fozziwig's party, and meeting his love interest. Finally, he sadly parts ways with her – their relationship having not panned out, due to his miserly ways.[1]

- Scrooge is returned to his room to reflect, and then visited by the Ghost of Christmas Present – a jolly spirit who takes him to visit his own family, where Scrooge's unpleasantness is being ridiculed, and then to Bob Cratchit's family home, where Bob and his froglet/piglet children and wife live in poverty, and yet still manage to pull together Christmas spirit and generosity.

- Scrooge returns once more to his bed, before being summoned by the spookiest Muppet in the movie – the Ghost of Christmas Yet to Come – a silent, grave-cloth draped wraith. This final spirit takes Scrooge to a future where the town celebrates the death of an unloved and unmissed miser. Scrooge is horrified to discover that the person in question is him, and begs the spirit for one last chance to redeem himself.

- Scrooge is returned to his bed and, magically, it is now Christmas morning. He leaps out of bed 'as light as a feather, as happy as an angel, as merry as a schoolboy' (Dickens, 1843) – throws money at a passing urchin to buy a massive turkey, and sets about sharing his wealth with the community. He is a man transformed, and from then on, Dickens writes,

---

[1]. Useless trivia: There's a song that was cut from the original showing of the movie that properly conveys this plot point, which in the original otherwise leaves you guessing. It's been re-added to more recent cuts, and once you've watched it you'll see why it was cut. Bless Michael Caine, he hasn't got a singer's pipes.

'it was always said of him, that he knew how to keep Christmas well, if any man alive possessed the knowledge'.

And so, with Scrooge's transformation from grinch to pillar of the Christmas community identified, we can segue neatly into a discussion of transformative learning.

## Mezirow's transformative learning

Transformative learning is a learning theory that describes how people use critical self-reflection to consider and challenge their own beliefs, either changing their thinking and world-views gradually over time or suddenly in response to lightbulb moments and dilemmas. The meat of the theory is ten phases that learners go through during a transformative learning experience.

Jack Mezirow (1994) outlined the different elements while conducting research with adult women who successfully studied in public universities. His work has stood the test of a few decades – he began work on it in the 1970s, and published major works on it in the 1990s. Since then, original articles and case studies have built on his early work.[2]

As we dig into transformative learning, it's worth bearing in mind that, presented as an adult learning theory, it interweaves a professional context with deeper changes to understanding and schema[3], the networks of interconnected understanding, thoughts, ideas, memories and associations that learners develop to remember, navigate and use what they know. While this is great in the context of the original research, we have found that it

---

2. Some folk call it an adult learning theory, or andragogy, which is in turn an excellent example of pedantagogy. But we digress.
3. We'll go into these in a little more detail in Chapter 13 on BeanDad and constructivism.

is also wonderfully useful for giving a narrative to the process of changing, thinking and understanding.

We also need to clarify some of the language associated with it, namely 'objective understanding' and 'frames of reference'.

Transformative learning occurs within the context of the learner. Every learner has a body of experiences they've accumulated through life, things that they've done, that have happened to them, that they've heard about, read about, seen, smelt, touched and so on. These experiences make up their objective understanding (Mezirow, 1994).

Learners understand and interpret these experiences through their frames of reference: cognitive and emotional lenses through which they process objective experience. These might include a person's biases, political leanings, preconceptions – essentially any mental shorthand used to process and shape objective experiences into expectations, perceptions and feelings. These interpretations, in turn, affect how people react to behaviour, experiences and stimuli. Frames of reference are initially shaped by a person's upbringing and build (or transform – more on this shortly) over time as they are subjected to new objective experiences.

With that out of the way, let's get to the exciting bit – the phases of transformative learning (Mezirow, 1997). Remember how we said earlier that there were ten? Well, there are only six you really need to bother with for now:

1. **Disorienting dilemma.** The catalyst for transformation. When presented with an experience, a learner's objective understanding and assumptions do not match previous experience, causing a 'disorienting dilemma'. Despite the name, this dilemma can range from a small incongruity (unexpected data in a test, a surprising response to an email), to something large and disruptive (a hero disgraced, a barking cat, a law of physics challenged).

2. **Self examination.** Following the disorienting dilemma, the learner carries out a self-test of their beliefs and understandings, reflecting on how past experiences may or may not connect to the dilemma.
3. **Critical assessment.** The learner assesses their past assumptions, reviews those assumptions critically, and checks their validity. Accepting that some previously held assumptions may be wrong or incomplete opens up the potential to assimilate new (and previously incompatible) information. This is the stage where frames of reference begin to transform, based on the new understanding, integrating the new experiences.
4. **Recognition of shared experiences.** A look inward is followed by a look outward. Have others had their understanding similarly challenged? Have they shared similar transformations?
5. **Exploration of options for new behaviour.** With their new understanding in hand, the learner explores how it may impact interactions, actions and relationships. Essentially, how they will apply the updated frame of reference going forwards.
6. **Planning a course of action.** The learner looks to implement changes to behaviour based on the new frame of reference.

The other four phases (7-10) deal with how learners integrate the transformed frames of reference, try out new roles, build their confidence and ultimately translate this into different actions, where the transformation becomes observable by all the cool behaviourists watching. While it would be good to discuss this here, these are also steps learners go through in Kolb's experiential learning, which we'll be covering in depth in Chapter 12. So, for now, let's just focus on the key bit – the transformation itself. This is enabled by:

- **Critical reflection** – being an autonomous thinker
- **Rational disclosure** – being able to have a rational discussion (as an individual, or with others) around thoughts and beliefs
- **Centrality of experience** – understanding the experiences of oneself and others, how they have reacted, and what brought them to where they are.

You might observe this transformation process in a range of contexts, including (but not limited to):

- **Instrumental Learning** – in which an individual challenges their assumptions scientifically. 'Here's what I think – can I prove it empirically?'
- **Communicative Learning** – in which two or more people try to understand each other's differing purposes, values, beliefs and feelings, and in doing so create a new understanding. This meanders towards social constructivism, which we cover in Chapter 14.
- **Disruptive Learning** – in which life events, challenges and dilemmas conspire to force people to re-examine and reframe their understanding.

Ultimately, as with many learning theories, the core of transformative learning is pretty simple. New information, events and discussions can challenge existing understanding and ways of thinking. By engaging in rational, critical reflection you can examine your ways of thinking in relation to new objective knowledge and understanding. By seeing where these fit with your current modes of thinking, you will see where those frames of reference need to change to incorporate that new thinking. You then make a conscious effort to apply that updated frame of reference going forwards.

You may notice that this is dependent on the learner being capable of, and willing to, engage in rational critical reflection. We'll address some of the considerations this introduces later in the chapter.

> *This isn't the most sophisticated piece of pedagogy, but it really resonated with me, as it perfectly describes some 'ah-hah!' moments I've had since I first started learning about pedagogy. In fact, reading up about this originally prompted my own small transformative learning experience. Until we did this topic, I'd never really stopped to consider the distance travelled in my own understanding of pedagogy. Working through the phases, I was happily surprised to find I knew a damn sight more than I thought I did (still scratching the surface, but one is more than zero) – which prompted a shift in confidence on my part to engage in hurly-burly pedagogic discussion.* ~Mikezilla

> *There's a connection to self-regulation learning theory here as well. Zimmerman and his colleagues (2009) divide self regulation up into a forethought phase (task analysis and self-motivation beliefs), a performance phase (self-control and self-observation), and a self-reflection phase (self-judgement and self-reaction). When you come to think about it in more detail, it's more complicated than that because you're doing all those things at most stages. On the other hand, if you can't do those things then you're reliant on a teacher doing them for you, which is very restrictive in terms of learning.* ~Beckzilla

## The answer

To answer our question **How do spooky Muppets guide Scrooge through transformative learning?** we need to separate out Scrooge's context and the transformative learning steps that a procession of spooky Muppets takes him through.

First, we establish the context. Scrooge's frames of reference at the beginning of the movie centre on his own greed and self interest. His habits of mind are to be miserly and penny pinching in every aspect of his life, and his points of view cause him to look down on those who either do not share his worldview, or who are poor. The behaviours we as audience and Gonzo as narrator observe that result from these frames of reference include him being a tight-fisted taskmaster with his employees, ill-tempered with his nephew, and dismissive towards charity. Later on in the movie we learn about the objective understanding that initially shaped this.

Most importantly, Scrooge doesn't like Christmas! Is this Scrooge being 150 years ahead of the progressive curve and rejecting materialism and overconsumption, or is he just a festive buzzkill? Let's step through his transformative learning journey to find out, starting with his disorienting dilemma.

Scrooge is, in fact, subjected to several disorienting dilemmas (Phase 1) during his magic-filled night, none more disruptive than the initial encounter with the ghosts of Marley and Marley. This encounter challenges him not only with the concept that magic and ghosts operate within his ordered world, but that his own soul is destined for a miserable eternity, as demonstrated by his similarly miserly and enchained peers. The subtext here is that Scrooge's actions to date have never taken into account his post-death fate, and he now finds it thrust before him.

His visit to the past, while disorienting, presents him with no dilemma – but his visit to the present and, in particular, to the house of Bob Cratchit exposes the sad reality of the impact of his miserliness. Due to his poor pay, Bob and his family live a meagre existence, and Tiny Tim (somehow sadder as a coughing froglet) limps towards death's door. Based on his solitary existence, we assume that this is the first time that Scrooge has found himself face-to-face with the consequences of his actions. Interestingly, adjusted for inflation, Bob's salary of 15 shillings a week (an allegory for destitution) equates to a salary of around £34,000, well above the current UK average wage.

Finally, in his visit to the future, Scrooge confronts his own unloved and unmourned death (and the discovery that Tiny Tim has also died[4]). The tearful fear this inspires on his part could have the behaviourists arguing that this would have been the only dilemma he actually needed to be confronted with, but that would have made for a shorter movie (and sidestepped the intrinsic nature of the transformation).

This prompts self examination (Phase 2). Scrooge's trip to the past, combined with his disorienting experience, guides him through the experiences that shaped him. Abandoned at boarding school as a child, drilled in business and hard work, he exists separate from the community of his family and peers. His breakup with Belle snuffed out his last connection, leaving him bitter. He looks inwards and outwards for what we must assume is the first time in his life.

And thus begins a critical assessment (Phase 3) of Scrooge's assumptions. These are critically reviewed (with help from the ghosts) throughout his journey. His initial response to charity for the homeless who would rather die than submit to the workhouse is, 'If they would rather die, they'd better do it, and decrease the surplus population'. This is turned on its head as

---

4. 180-year-old spoiler alert

he is confronted with the imminent mortality of Tiny Tim. 'If he be like to die, he had better do it, and decrease the surplus population,' chides the Ghost of Christmas Present (Dickens, 1843).

Because this is a Christmas movie, Scrooge also finds his assumptions about the frivolity and waste he associates with Christmas have been misplaced. He has ignored the celebration of love shared within the community. As an invisible observer he is, for the first time, able to enjoy being part of Christmas.

The analogy with *A Christmas Carol* becomes temporarily wobbly as we approach the recognition of shared experiences stage (Phase 4). While we can assume that this is not the triumvirate of spirits' first rodeo, Scrooge is the only person in the movie with a story arc. Consider it more of a comment on the economies of storytelling in children's cinema than a criticism of the theory itself. We can assume that on Boxing Day, Scrooge sits down with Bob and a bottle of brandy, and recounts his spooky adventure and transformation – and that they share stories of times their own worldviews have shifted throughout their lives. Bob crossed the species threshold after all.

The analogy gets back on a transformative track with the exploration of new roles and actions (Phase 5). We see Scrooge doing this in real time throughout the movie, and then putting his new roles into action in the following phase. Reflections like 'such a meagre feast' at the Cratchits' Christmas spread indicate the wheels are beginning to turn. As the Ghost of Christmas Present passes, Scrooge begins to handle his new understanding of Christmas, and to consider what it means for him.

Finally, based on this transformation of his frames of reference, Scrooge develops a plan of action (Phase 6). On Christmas morning he springs out of bed and, in a flurry of revelation, sets out to put his new understanding of Christmas, generosity and community to work. He throws open his window, chucks money at a rabbit, compliments it, and then instructs it to purchase an enormous turkey.

He sets out into the world, donates to charity, is given his first Christmas gift (Beaker's scarf) confirming the validity of his new understanding (be horrid to the world, and it will hate you right back, be kind and generous, and the world will give you a scarf). Finally, he brings the whole town to Bob Cratchit's home, showers him with food, gives him a pay rise and mollifies Miss Piggy. He and the community all sit down to a slap-up Christmas dinner and a singalong. Even better, the narrator informs us that Tiny Tim does not die, hooray!

So then, to summarise the answer to our question, **How do spooky Muppets guide Scrooge through transformative learning?** A triumvirate of spirits conspires to instigate transformative learning. They confront Scrooge with a disorienting dilemma of ghostly goings-on, the impact of his actions, the threat of his mortality, and damnation. Shaken by this, Scrooge is guided in forming new understandings around Christmas, generosity and community, and then sets out to act on them on Christmas morning. Our spooky Muppets act as facilitators and metacognitive nudgers.

'Transformative! I'm as happy as an angel!'

A very grumpy angel

## Tips for practice

So, what can you pull from Scrooge learning how to celebrate Christmas that helps your practice?

The first thing to consider is the importance of (and dependency on) critical reflection. We'll be coming back to this in subsequent chapters, because it's such an important aspect of learning and teaching. Transformative learning hinges on learners being willing and able to reconsider their own frames of reference in relation to new information, as well as being willing to make changes based on their new understanding. Critical reflection as a skill and process can be taught (Perry, 2018), but having the guts to hold a mirror up to your own thinking is an act of humility which some folk just won't have.

By giving learners the metacognitive tools they need to engage in critical reflection, you're setting them up for an easier time with transformative learning – not only in the evolution of their own understanding in their particular field – but also as they progress through life and the many disorienting dilemmas it presents. Along the way, you're likely to want to play the part of the Christmas ghosties yourself, and guide learners in transforming their understanding. As you do so, just be aware that you can't win them all – the objective experiences and frames of reference of some learners will have resulted in a closed-loop cognitive system unequipped, unable[5] or unwilling to self-check, re-examine and change.

Another thing to draw from this is awareness of the fourth phase 'Recognition of shared experiences'. As with our other chapters in this section, it's worth considering that learning

---
5. Discussing reflection, and the barriers folk may face when engaging with it could fill a whole other book, but physical and mental disabilities, neurodivergence and the good old travails of life can all throw unintentional and unwanted spanners in the works of the transformative learning process.

journeys are a personal experience, where context and content can change – but the mechanics of the observable process are there if you look. If you're wrestling with a new idea that threatens to wobble your worldview then give yourself a pat on the back – by matching your actions to your frames of reference, and reinterpreting them as you encounter new understanding, you're adopting a scientific and academic mindset. This will give you greater understanding of your own life and learning experiences going forwards, and greater empathy for those you see at different phases. It's a look both outwards and inwards that allows us, like Scrooge, to reexamine our understanding of others, our role in the community, and the love we share.[6]

# Bah! References!

Dickens, C. (1843) *A Christmas Carol. In Prose. Being a Ghost Story of Christmas*. Chapman & Hall, London. Available at: https://www.gutenberg.org/cache/epub/46/pg46-images.html

Mezirow, J. (1994) Understanding transformation theory. *Adult Education Quarterly*, 44:4, 222-232.

Mezirow, J. (1997) Transformative learning: theory to practice. *New Directions for Adult and Continuing Education*, 74, 5-12.

Perry, J., Lundie, D. and Golder, G. (2019) Metacognition in schools: what does the literature suggest about the effectiveness of teaching metacognition in schools?, *Educational Review*, 71:4, 483-500, DOI: 10.1080/00131911.2018.1441127

---

6. What a schmaltzy way to end a chapter. If you've seen the movie, and the cult debate around the cut material, you might appreciate that it too ends on 'the love we share', except as a choral refrain for a song that was cut from the original. Neeeerd.

Zimmerman, B. J., & Moylan, A. R. (2009) Self-regulation: where metacognition and motivation intersect. In D. J. Hacker, J. Dunlosky & A. C. Graesser (Eds), *Handbook of Metacognition in Education*, 299-315, Routledge.

Scan the QR code to listen to the podcast episode

## CHAPTER 3:

# COME DUNNING WITH ME, KRUGER! HOW DO YOU KNOW IF WHAT YOU ARE SERVING UP IS ANY GOOD?

*Rebecca Ferguson, Paul Astles, Mike Collins*

Mikezilla and Markzilla emerge from their exploration of transformation, ready for the journey that lies ahead and prepared for how it will change them. They're learning about education. They've been to school, they've been to university. Sitting in lectures for hours on end must surely have given them all they need to know. But standing in their path is another Zilla.

This is Paulzilla. He waves a menu at them frantically. 'No, no,' he says. 'There's more, much more. You've just made the error that so many make. You know a little bit, but you don't know enough to know how little you know.' He opens his menu. 'Let me tell you about the Dunning-Kruger effect.'

This chapter tackles a British institution – the TV series *Come Dine with Me* – and a much-loved psychological concept, the Dunning-Kruger effect. It tells the story of people who don't know where their ability level is for something, and links this with a perennial question for educators: **How do you know whether what you are serving up is any good?**

## *Come Dine with Me*

In the popular TV series *Come Dine with Me*, in order to be judged the perfect dinner party host during a one-week contest, participants take it in turns to cook for and entertain the rest of the group. Their rivals, meanwhile, snoop around the house, make snide remarks about each other's cooking, home and lifestyle, and award each other points. The winner each week is the participant awarded the most points. The host on the final day opens the envelope to read out the results and the winner collects the £1000 prize. Overall, the show is so much more than the sum of its parts. It's wonderful – and not just in the opinion of one of the Zillas. Running on Britain's Channel 4 since 2005, with umpteen snippets available on YouTube, it has been described multiple times as a British institution. It's one of those shows that is cheap to produce but covers all the basic human connections and emotions, making for truly crap, and therefore truly exceptional, British TV. Audiences love seeing people failing spectacularly and being awful to each other.

We have often been perplexed by the show's undefined marking criteria. What is the difference between a 1 and 2, or a 4 and 5? There is no clarity on this point. Meals could just as easily be categorised as 'good', 'bad' or 'indifferent' and the outcome would be the same. (This perplexity can be applied to assessment in general. Why bother giving subjective percentage outcomes in cases when pass or fail would probably be sufficient? More on this later.)

To date, no one has ever achieved the programme's perfect score of 40 – the nearest was 39 in Liverpool 2006, with three guests awarding a perfect 10 and the fourth marking their host down for serving water in glass bottles. At the other end of the scale, in Wolverhampton 2009, one competitor was awarded just 7 points in total after swearing at his guests, throwing a starter out of the window, and delaying the meal for so long that there was talk of ringing for a takeaway. Again, there are parallels with educational assessment – why offer an apparent range of marks from 0-40, when the actual range is 7-39? In an educational setting, why present a scale that goes up to 100%, if nobody is ever awarded that perfect mark?

The most interesting part – and the best television – is not when a competitor is the perfect host and the perfect cook but rather when some parts of the evening fail spectacularly! One of the most famous moments in the show came at the end of a week when the host on the final day had to announce that his bitter rival had triumphed and accompanied the announcement with a, 'Dear Lord, what a sad little life, Jane. You ruined my night. Completely. So you could have the money. But I hope now you spend it on getting some lessons in grace and decorum, because you have all the grace of a reversing dump truck without any tyres on.'

A recurrent feature of the show is the inability of low-scoring contestants to recognise how badly things are going, paired with an overestimation of their own competence. As time ticks away, with his guests becoming restive, and one dish a complete write-off, the lowest-scoring-ever contestant says, 'I'm still gonna win it, though.' By the end of the evening, when he has sent his guests home clutching the ingredients of the starter that he never found time to make, he says, 'At least ten just for effort, clearly.'

Another contestant, relegated to last place, says before storming out, 'My food was better than any of yours [...] My presentation was amazing, far better than any of yours.'

And why is it that so many contestants are incapable of assessing their own ability? The answer may lie with the Dunning-Kruger effect (Dunning, 2011 and Dunning, 2017).

## The Dunning-Kruger effect

We're all familiar with the idea that you don't know what you don't know. In educational terms, this is known as the Meno Paradox. This was first formulated a couple of thousand years ago, when the Greek philosopher Plato recorded a dialogue between Socrates and Meno. Meno suggested that it's impossible to seek something you don't know, because you'll have no idea when you've found it. If you know what you're looking for, inquiry is unnecessary, and if you don't know what you are looking for, inquiry is impossible. Socrates' response involved asking an enslaved child questions about geometry. The boy answered several of these correctly, but he was equally confident of his incorrect answer. An early example of the Dunning-Kruger effect.

In most areas of knowledge, you start with what Gullander (1974, p20) calls 'unconscious incompetency'. Take the example of tying a shoelace. As a small child, you had no idea this was a skill that could be acquired, so you didn't realise you had anything to learn. You gradually became aware this was a skill your parents or others possessed, at which point you moved on to 'conscious incompetency'. You knew the skill existed, but you hadn't acquired it. Somebody showed you how to tie your shoes, enabling you to reach 'conscious competency'. At that point, you had the necessary skill but, in order to succeed, you still had to think carefully about the process every time you carried it out.

The final stage in the process was 'unconscious competency', the point at which you could tie your shoelaces without giving the matter any thought. This is the level most people have reached in the things they do regularly in their daily lives. But try learning a new way to tie your shoelaces (Fieggen, 2023), and you're right back to conscious incompetency again.

Dunning and Kruger carried out several experiments to investigate how well people are able to gauge their own competency. One of these involved undergraduates at a US university. The students completed a test of logical reasoning, and were then asked to rate their skills and performance relative to their classmates. Half of them then received a short training session on logical reasoning, while the other half of the group received a short training session on something unrelated. They were then all asked to rate their skills and performance once again. Those who had done very badly on the original test overestimated their results at first, but their estimates became significantly better after receiving training in logical reasoning. Those who had originally done badly and didn't receive relevant training remained unconsciously incompetent and continued to believe they had done well on the original test.

As well as investigating logical reasoning, Dunning and Kruger carried out other investigations. One of these focused on grammar and was carried out with students from Cornell University. The two scientists found that more than half the students thought they were above average at grammar (statistically, only half of them could actually have been above average) and that, overall, participants overestimated how many grammar questions they had answered correctly. The students who were least able to assess their own performance correctly were the ones with the lowest scores. The scientists noted that this group 'grossly overestimated their ability relative to their peers' (Kruger & Dunning, 1999).

Although individual students believed they could identify grammatically correct standard English, this may have been because they didn't actually know some of the formal rules of the language. They considered writing to be grammatically correct not because that was the case, but because they weren't aware of its flaws. At the other end of the scale were those who had unconscious competence. They knew all about grammar, they had all the necessary skills, and they took them for granted, assuming that everybody has a similar set of skills. So, the people at that end of the scale tended to underestimate how competent they were. They misjudged their own competence because they mistakenly over-estimated the competency of their peers. At both ends of the scale, people misjudge how competent they are in relation to others. Experiments by researchers in different countries have shown this inability to judge your own competence is widespread.

Investigations and experiments have repeatedly shown that people tend to inflate their ability in specific areas. One study (Svenson, 1981) asked drivers in the USA and Sweden whether they rated themselves more or less skilful than the median driver (if you lined every driver up in order of skill, the median driver would be the one in the middle). In the USA, 93% of respondents thought they were better than the median driver. In Sweden, 69% of drivers put themselves in that category. Overall, there was a strong tendency for people to believe they were safer and more skilled than the average driver.

This supported the findings of an earlier study (Peston and Harris, 1965) that compared 50 drivers who hadn't been involved in accidents with 50 drivers who were similar to them in many ways but had been hospitalised in car accidents. Thirty-four of the people in this second group had actually caused the accident that had put them in hospital. Overall, the group involved in accidents had been responsible for more traffic violations. It seemed clear which set of drivers was the most skilful. However, when people in the two groups were asked how skillful they were as drivers, both groups gave the same response. Both groups felt they were closer to 'expert' than 'very poor'.

Surely, though, educators – people who spend considerable amounts of time assessing the performance of others and do that, in part, because they have been subject to a great deal of assessment themselves – will not fall victim to the same effect? Turns out they do. Over 90% of faculty members believe they're above-average teachers, and two-thirds of them believe they're in the top 25%.

'But wait!' we hear the die-hard *Pedagodzilla* fans cry. 'We listen to every episode of your podcast, without fail. We know from the introductions that Markzilla is a man with a PhD, while Mikezilla is Impostor Syndrome Incarnate. If everyone thinks they're much better at things than they really are, how can anyone ever develop that syndrome?'

What the literature agrees on is that Impostor Syndrome occurs when people doubt their own skills and talents, fearing that they'll be exposed as frauds. They may not feel they deserve their success; they may not feel they're as intelligent as others believe them to be; they may feel they're deceiving others about their abilities. Initial research into the syndrome was carried out with women who had displayed academic achievement and had been formally recognised for their professional excellence. Despite external validation of their skills, they believed their success was due to luck, or to others over-estimating their skills. Since then, research has shown that this insecurity affects both men and women, and that up to 70% of the population may experience this anxiety at some point in their lives.

While most of the emphasis in work on the Dunning-Kruger effect is on people overestimating their abilities, at the other end of the scale are the people who are experts or who are capable of performing well above average. These people misjudge their own competence because they mistakenly over-estimate the competency of their peers. Once they have skills and knowledge, they overestimate how much others possess the same skills and knowledge. So, Impostor Syndrome in this group is likely to arise because they overestimate the abilities of those around them.

In experiments, when top performers are shown how others have responded to a test or quiz, they see that others have done less well, and they revise their estimates of their own performance. They can do that because they can distinguish between good performance and poor performance. Poor performers, on the other hand, remain unaffected by seeing the responses of others because they have no way of judging which responses are good or bad.

There are multiple episodes of *Come Dine with Me* where the Dunning-Kruger effect has been clearly apparent. Many contestants have been sure they were not only fantastic hosts but also 'incredible chefs' and have believed that winning was a foregone conclusion, only for things to unravel when their ability did not live up to their self-belief.

## The answer

So, **how can you possibly know if what you are serving up is any good?**

If you don't know what good looks like, then you have no way of knowing whether what you're doing is good, or of judging accurately whether you're performing better or worse than others. Up to the point at which someone's current knowledge and skills are challenged, they've usually been surrounded by people who don't have the experience and criticality to challenge their assumptions. If you're part of a community that agrees with you, but lacks the expertise to set your performance in a wider context, its members have no way of providing feedback that can increase your understanding of the objective standard at which you're operating.

The Dunning-Kruger effect makes for gripping television. Hours of footage are selected and edited to emphasise mismatches between individuals' beliefs and reality. Potential contestants who are aware of their own inadequacies are unlikely to apply to take part, and even less likely to be selected. Those who believe they are the best cook in the region on the basis of their neighbour's opinion are more likely to make for an entertaining set of episodes, especially if they're paired with someone so supremely confident they're an excellent chef that they decide to make their first-ever soufflé in front of a national audience.

Reality show producers must always be on the look-out for people who are at the point of maximum confidence combined with minimum competence. Appearing on *Come Dine with Me* forces such people to face something they've never confronted before – a real-world assessment. The resulting clash between self-belief and external reality may be traumatic for contestants, but riveting for viewers.

Of course, food tastes vary. As in so many areas of life, feedback is subjective. One of the problems for the show's participants is that there are no predefined and transparent criteria that can be used to assess their expertise and provide feedback. Trying to meet undefined criteria is a frustrating process that leaves them vulnerable to the Dunning-Kruger effect as they strive to produce something that is objectively good, when all they have to base their assessment on is their own subjective judgment, usually based on very limited experience. A clear assessment framework would provide a structure for commenting on what has gone well and what needs improving – but where's the fun in that?

*Come Dine with Me* contestants have the bare bones of a framework for assessment along the lines of – What did you think of the starter, the main, the dessert, the presentation, and the evening as a whole? What they don't have are any criteria for that assessment other than personal taste. There are no guidelines that are applied in all cases. Here's where the show differs from ones such as *Masterchef* or *Lego Masters*. Those shows have experienced judges, who usually state in advance some of the characteristics they're looking for. Part of the reality TV appeal of *Come Dine with Me* lies in the variable criteria applied subjectively by each participant.

---

*Until I visited Japan, I believed I had a minimal knowledge of Japanese culture.*

*I share this in some of the* Pedagodzilla *episodes, reflecting on* Ghost in the Shell, Godzilla *and Studio Ghibli movies. However, once in Japan, I walked into a warehouse full of manga and DVDs and didn't recognise anything in there. I'd expected the visit to confirm I had some knowledge and expertise. Instead, the experience showed me I really knew nothing. ~Markzilla*

---

Therefore, it's easy to reject feedback that doesn't align with the way you see your own abilities. It's difficult to have your viewpoint or judgment challenged, particularly if it relates to a piece of work or skill you're proud of. It's tempting to ignore feedback (research shows that many students never look at tutor feedback), to reject the expertise of its provider, or to plunge into anger or depression. It's difficult to be open to the fact that your worldview may have been correctly challenged by somebody who knows a bit more than you do. As the Muppets showed us in the previous chapter, learning is about transformation, and transformation is tough.

It's important for learners to develop the resilience to keep going as the world shifts around them and they are introduced to a whole new perspective on their abilities. The key to skill acquisition is to practise; to try and try again. When you're new to a skill and most likely to be deceived by the Dunning-Kruger effect, it's useful to bear in mind skill-acquisition logic – you're probably not as good as you think you are and you need to keep practising and developing. This is a useful way of thinking that prevents your level of incompetence from clouding your actual ability.

So, whether teaching or dining – **how do you know if what you are serving up is actually any good?** On your own, you can't know for sure but there are ways of checking your beliefs that can help you to identify when you are on the right path, and where you should be directing your attention. Definitely don't rely only on your own judgment or the judgment of those immediately around you.

## Tips for practice

A set of skills we introduced in the previous chapter and that we'll return to several times are the ones related to self regulation. These are the skills needed when learning to learn. They relate to metacognition (thinking about how you think), motivation, and learning strategies. Some of them, such as goal setting and time management, may seem to be innate skills that people assume don't need to be taught. As a result, some students never acquire them and struggle unnecessarily, not because they're unintelligent, but because they lack crucial skills that would make study much easier. In fact, the Dunning-Kruger effect is strong when it comes to self-regulation – people neither recognise their own expertise nor identify the gaps in their knowledge.

Zimmerman and Moylan (2009), who have done a lot of work in this area, identified a self-reflection phase to self-regulation. One aspect of this is self-evaluation: comparing your own performance with a standard. For students, that standard might be their own prior performance, the challenge of mastering all components of a skill, or social comparisons – how well they think they're doing in relation to their peers. The standard they choose to assess themselves against influences both their perceived outcomes and their future motivation. It may also leave them vulnerable to the Dunning-Kruger effect.

One strategy here is to foreground and discuss the process of self-evaluation. Which standards are students using to evaluate their own performance – and which standards matter to them? Although it's easy to assume everyone is aiming for a top grade, students know that not everyone can be top of the class. They're likely to have their own goals: gaining a pass grade, getting a better grade than a specific individual or group of individuals, or positioning themselves to coast along unnoticed in the middle of the pack. These private goals need not be shared publicly. However, encouraging learners to reflect on what their personal goals are provides opportunities to clarify those goals, revise them, and consider the standards on which they're based. It can also open up discussion about how we judge the skills and performance of others.

Participants on *Come Dine with Me* start with the disadvantage that they may never have hosted, or even attended, a dinner party in the past. Even if they have, the performance of most contestants suggests their experience is fairly limited. This means they have only the haziest idea of what good looks like and nobody provides them with criteria on which to base their judgment. You'd think by this point they'd have a better idea – after all, they've had the opportunity to watch all the previous episodes – but if they've watched previous series they show no signs of learning from them. The situation is different for students to some extent, because they have teachers who can assess their work using a framework and provide feedback within this framework. Surely this helps them to avoid the Dunning-Kruger effect? Possibly, but some approaches to assessment leave students vulnerable.

A lot of assessment is norm-referenced. That is, it works on the basis that half the learners in a cohort are above average, and the other half are below average. If you wanted to, you could line them all up in order of ability and identify the top 50%, or the bottom 10%. That's very handy if you're using assessment as a selection process. The local employer has 20 jobs this year? Take the first 20 in that ability line. There are 30 spaces at the grammar school? Take the first 30. There's one scholarship available? Take the person at the front. Of course, in reality things aren't quite that simple. For one thing, learners aren't evenly spaced. Assessment results tend to put most learners towards the middle of the line, with only a few doing very well or very badly. In statistical terms, the line isn't an evenly spaced ruler, it's actually a bell curve – imagine the outline of a bell with a steep hump in the middle and a wide rim. Most students make up the body of the bell and are likely to be fairly close in ability. Bell curves are handy because they represent a normal distribution of results, with two-thirds of the results clustering around the average, and the other third evenly divided between high and low. Normal distributions are found all over the place, in areas as diverse as biology and economics, and they're one of the basic building blocks of statistics.

Bell curves underpin a lot of assessment, particularly when it comes to formal exams. They're the reason why grade boundaries change from year to year. If an A is always awarded to the top 5% of students, then one year it might go to students with a score of over 98 and the next year to students with a score of over 90.

It's not a measure of how much a student knows about a subject; it's a measure of how much they know in comparison to the rest of the group. The bell curve is so baked into assessment that many teachers norm reference without thinking. They base their understanding of good, bad, and average on their experience of work that has been handed to them before. This can result in extremely opaque marking schemes.

If learners' experience of assessment is that it's always norm-referenced, then they're vulnerable to the Dunning-Kruger effect, because their only option is to judge their performance in relation to their limited knowledge of the performance of others around them. Criterion-referenced assessment would help them to avoid this. This type of assessment makes judgments based on predetermined criteria that are available at the time the assessment is set. The intention is to determine how well someone has mastered an area of knowledge or skill, rather than how well they've mastered it in relation to others. Think of driving tests or music exams. You don't pass these because you have the highest score in the group; you pass because you can demonstrate that you meet all the predefined criteria.

Putting this into practice means making use of criterion-referenced assessment, drawing attention to the criteria, making links with assessment, and encouraging self-reflection. It might involve giving students practice in breaking some of the skills they have already mastered down into separate elements or discussing criteria that future learners might be expected to meet. It can also involve going into detail about what adequate, good and excellent responses to a particular question might look like.

# Enjoy the academic credibility.
# I hope it makes you happy. And these References.

Dunning D. (2011), 'On being ignorant of one's own ignorance', *Advances in Experimental Social Psychology*, 44.

Dunning D., (2017) *Why incompetent people think they're amazing*, TedEd Available at: https://ed.ted.com/lessons/why-incompetent-people-think-they-re-amazing-david-dunning

Feiggen, I.W. (2023). 'Shoelace knots', *Ian's Shoelace Site*, Available at: https://www.fieggen.com/shoelace/knots.htm

Gullander, O.E. (1974). Conscious competency: the mark of a competent instructor. *Canadian Training Methods*, 7(1), 20-21.

Kruger, J., & Dunning, D. (1999). Unskilled and unaware of it: How difficulties in recognizing one's own incompetence lead to inflated self-assessments. *Journal of Personality and Social Psychology*, 77(6), 1121–1134.

Preston, C.E. & Harris, S. (1965). Psychology of drivers in traffic accidents. *Journal of Applied Psychology* 49, 284-288.

Svenson, O. (1981). Are we all less risky and more skillful than our fellow drivers?. *Acta Psychologica*, 47(2), 143-148.

Zimmerman, B. J., & Moylan, A. R. (2009). Self-regulation: where metacognition and motivation intersect. In D. J. Hacker, J. Dunlosky & A. C. Graesser (Eds), *Handbook of Metacognition in Education* (pp. 299-315). Routledge.

Scan the QR code to listen to
the podcast episode

**CHAPTER 4:**

# HOW DO ONTOLOGY AND EPISTEMOLOGY HELP YOU ELIMINATE JAR JAR BINKS WITH HEADCAN(N)ONS? PART 1

*Mark Childs, Olivia Rowlands, Rebecca Ferguson and Mike Collins*

*Mikezilla and Markzilla continue their journey through the Realm of Pedagogy. They ask each other, 'How will we ever be able to tell we're not making more bad decisions about what's out there?' Before they can take another step, Markzilla is hit by a pink light. Stunned, he falls to the ground, then slowly rises. 'I see it, I see it all!' he cries.*

*Mikezilla is unconvinced. 'Isn't the meaning of life the sort of stuff you get at the end of a quest?'*

*Markzilla shakes his head. 'We need these now, before we go any further. Behold! The Sword of Epistemology, the Magic Backpack of Ontology (see all the pockets!), and the Sorting Hat of Critical Realism. With these we shall know our way.' Revelation finished, he reverts to his normal self and starts swashing his new sword.*

This chapter and the one that follows began as a response to Scott Cowan, Information Services Librarian at the University of Windsor, who asked us to try to explain ontology and epistemology, as they're concepts that frequently confuse many of the people he works with. These are key concepts because they form the foundation of how people see the world, what counts as evidence, and what doesn't. The theories we talk about in the rest of the book differ from each other because they're grounded in the different world views of the people who developed those theories.

The explanation we've put together here has been road tested by people who didn't understand the concepts of ontology and epistemology, and then grasped them as a result of our explanation. However, with each iteration the explanation has grown longer, because there are so many nuances: around colonialism, around hierarchies, and ultimately, philosophically, because people don't entirely agree about what 'real' means. There are still gaps, but what we present here is one way to make sense of different views of what makes up the world.

Oh, and the chapter also brings in *Star Wars*, which crops up a couple of times in this book. But then it's a very big media juggernaut, which also seems to keep growing in the telling. The question we're working with is: **How do ontology and epistemology help you eliminate Jar Jar Binks with headcan(n)ons?**

## *Star Wars*

Of all the pop-culture narratives we discuss in this book, *Star Wars* is possibly the one that needs least introduction. For the unfamiliar, it is an extended battle between good and evil, set a long time ago in a galaxy far far away, with spaceships, lasers, princesses, aliens and nerf herders. The key elements any reader needs to know about *Star Wars* to make sense of this pedagogic metaphor are that, at the time of writing (2024), it has been going for 48 years and those 48 years can be split into three discrete periods.

The first period started in 1976 with the first three *Star Wars* movies. Although these stopped being made in 1983 (don't talk to us about the Ewok movies) there were masses of books, comics, TV cartoons and games which built on those films with sequels, prequels and stories set in between the films. That takes us up to 1999, which was the point at which George Lucas, the creator of *Star Wars*, returned to that narrative and began releasing the prequel trilogy.

That second period started with the prequel trilogy, plus an animated movie. It continued with more comics and books, and especially the TV series *The Clone Wars* (arguably the best thing to come out of that second period), which introduced a new helm to the *Star Wars* universe in the showrunner Dave Filoni. That period continued until 2012, when George Lucas sold Lucasfilm to Disney.

Since 2012, there has been a whole new trilogy of movies, a TV show called *The Mandalorian*, and there are other series in the works at the time of writing, as well as new books, comics, games and so on, all under the Disney umbrella.

During the first two phases, no one was really keeping track of continuity. Yes, there was continuity within the movies, but there was also a radio series version and then a books version, neither of which necessarily tied in with the other. The solution was to establish degrees of canonicity; a hierarchy by which, where there was a conflict, one version was held to be correct.

The films make up the highest echelon in the canon, although even this is complex due to Lucas's tendency to revise his first three films (Lyden, 2012). Next in the hierarchy is the information that's shared in licensed media, the comics, novels and games (Spelling, 2005; 48). Finally, at the bottom of the heap, there's the world created by the fans. Although there was some attempt to codify and keep track of this whole extended universe through publications such as the *Star Wars Encyclopedia* (Sansweet, 1998) and there was some trickle up through the hierarchy, in that George Lucas would sometimes reference the *Encyclopedia* when developing further films, Lucas wasn't beholden to the continuity established elsewhere. This sometimes led to radically different versions of events.

Also, not everything is canon to start with. So the *Star Wars Holiday Special*, for example, was disavowed instantly, even though it includes the main cast of the original *Star Wars*. Films set in the Star Wars universe like *Caravan of Courage: An Ewok Adventure* (script by George Lucas) even seem to have been largely forgotten. Just canon-fodder.

Why canon matters is because it supports effective world building. You need a consistent view of your imaginary world because the audience inhabits the narrative (Saler, 2012). Without consistency, instead of being drawn into the story, conflicting versions remind audiences they're watching a narrative because the internal reality is undermined.

For example, there are currently three different versions of how the plans for the Death Star were stolen and passed to the rebellion. The radio series adaptation gave us one; there's the Dark Forces trilogy, a series of video games, novellas and their audio adaptation in which Kyle Katarn steals them; and then, most recently, there was the film *Rogue One*, which offered yet another version. The dilemma for a member of the audience is – well, which one do I believe is the 'true' version?

The idea we mentioned earlier of resolving narrative conflicts by giving different versions of the narrative different statuses in a hierarchy doesn't really work if you're trying to create a single coherent world, so when Disney took over they took a different route. They decided they needed a definitive 'in canon' with everything fitting together so that they had one single consistent narrative, and with everything else non-canon. The question then becomes, who gets to define canon?

Disney created this one, internally-consistent, world in one fell swoop by ditching everything that wasn't part of the original six live action films, or the *Clone Wars* animated film and its TV series continuation. Everything else was consigned to a bin labelled 'Legends'. Disney also established a team, called the LucasFilm Story Group (Burton, 2014) which from that point on has made decisions about continuity. Every time a book is written, a comic is created, or another TV show is made, all of it now ties in to what has gone before, so it all forms part of a single continuity. There is one canon version. The question, 'Who gets to choose?', has the answer: 'Disney, because they paid $4 billion dollars for that right' (Krantz et al, 2012).

All long-term narratives have different ways of dealing with the issue of continuity (Childs, 2012), but not all these solutions meet the needs of audience members. In addition, not all audience members acknowledge the authority of those who decide the canon, which is where headcanon comes in. Headcanon is how individuals make their own choices about which bits of the narrative to include, and which bits not to include.

## Ontology and epistemology

- **Ontology** = What is, what isn't and how should we categorise everything?
- **Epistemology** = What do we count as evidence? How do we go about making those decisions?

Although they're not specifically pedagogical in nature, discussions about ontology and epistemology align with pedagogical theory because, as you'll see in the following chapters, the approach you favour pedagogically is likely to depend on your epistemological viewpoint. We are not aiming to engage readers fully with the philosophy behind the terms but simply to enable you to distinguish between them.

In brief, ontology is what does and doesn't exist and how you categorise it.

### What does and doesn't exist

We've all seen ontological debates. For example, there's an episode of the comedy series *Father Ted* (S 3 Ep 2 – *Chirpy Burpy Cheap Sheep*) in which Dougal is talking about the Beast of Craggy Island and Ted says 'Now we have to put it on the list'. On the wall is a list of things that are not real, and they add The Beast to that list, alongside the Loch Ness Monster and Darth Vader. That's ontology. It's a constant debate about what is and what isn't, what exists and what doesn't exist.

(LEGALLY DISTINCT FATHER TED ONTOLOGY GAG PARODY)

To keep everything simple (but not Dougal-level simple), we propose the use of a scale of what's real and not real, rather than Ted and Dougal's binary. This is adapted from a scale that Richard Dawkins used in *The God Delusion* (Dawkins, 2006) to define different degrees of belief in the existence of God. Dawkins says that there aren't simply two categories, atheist and believer, but that a person's position on the existence of God lies on a seven-point scale. At one end of that scale, you've got somebody who 100% believes in the existence of God. At the other end, you've got someone who is 100% certain that God doesn't exist. In between are strong believers, weak believers, those on the fence, those who are inclined to be sceptical and those who are extremely sceptical. The scale has its weaknesses – for example, it assumes everyone means the same thing by the word 'God' – but it's useful for us here because it provides a nuanced way of examining reality.

We can apply the same scale to everything. Whenever you're looking at the ontological nature of something, you could state that it 100% definitely exists at one end of the scale (1), or that it 100% doesn't exist at the other end of the scale (7). Rational scepticism would state that nothing can be a 1 on this scale because of the possibility, however remote, that we live in a simulation, or something similar, which we talk about more in our chapter on experiential learning and *The Matrix*. Or because we can never be absolutely sure we know what's going on.

We see the limitations to our knowledge of what is true time and time again. For example, for a couple of hundred years, scientific consensus was that Newtonian physics absolutely described the motion of objects. Two centuries later, we have Einsteinian physics, and Newton is not considered a true reflection of reality any more. All we can say is that a particular description of the Universe is the best one we have based on the evidence available to us at the moment. Our perspective is limited, so we can't say with certainty that anything is 100% definitely true. Nothing is a 1 on the scale, at best it's a 1.1 or thereabouts.

At the other end of the scale, we can't say for certain something doesn't exist, just because there's no acceptable evidence for it. You could even say *Star Wars* might have really happened somewhere, a long, long time ago in a galaxy far, far away. We can't say for absolute definite that it didn't. It's a big universe. Father Ted may have been wrong to add Darth Vader to his 'Not real' list. Just because you don't have evidence for something, that's not evidence of absence.

So the other end of the scale is nearly, but not quite, a seven. At that end of the scale, something almost certainly doesn't exist, but we can't know for sure. Ontologically, you're looking at a scale that, for anyone who isn't omniscient, goes from 1.1 to 6.9, rather than 1 to 7. Both Dawkins' original scale and our adaptation here represent a spectrum that can be quite fluid.

'Did the Universe begin with a Big Bang or not?' is an ontological question. Originally there were lots of competing theories about how the universe started. Scientists would probably have ranked some of the non-mythological theories around 3 (we're uncertain but inclined to believe this is right) or 4 (this theory may be right or wrong – the probabilities are equally balanced). But the Big Bang Theory predicted cosmic background radiation and once this radiation was found, instead of the theory being a 3 or a 4, it became a 2 (we can't know for certain but we strongly believe this is the case) or thereabouts, and now it's as close to 1 as you can get. So, when we're looking at anything in the world around us, looking at the shifting evidence for and against and weighing probabilities will mean things are always moving up and down that scale.

To reiterate, this scale is one we have adapted to make our explanation of ontology clearer.

## How we categorise things

The other aspect of ontology is concerned with how we categorise the world around us. For example, birds and reptiles were, until recently, considered separate classes of animal. That was because animals were classified based on their phenotype, their observable characteristics. Birds had feathers and looked one way; reptiles had scales and looked very different. Clearly they were different classes of animal. However, the field of genetics has developed and it's now possible to tell how closely animals are related by looking at their DNA. So animals are now classified according to their genotype. They are arranged in clades, groups of animals that share a common descent. Birds and reptiles are descended from a common ancestor so are members of the same clade. This means we have two competing ways of grouping lifeforms, but the one based on closest common ancestors is more consistent and objective than the one based on what creatures look like. Cladistics is therefore a preferable ontological framework.

Grouping elements of the world around us into classifications and categories is an ontological process. However, choices about what sorts of evidence we use to do this – in this case, whether we go by looks or by what the DNA shows us – are epistemological decisions, so the two concepts are interrelated.

Two factors can make ontology and epistemology difficult to discuss.

1. The words are uncommon, which makes them sound much more complicated than they actually are (we propose what-it-is-ism and how-do-we-find-out-ism as alternatives).
2. It's easy to cross from a discussion about one to a discussion of the other. To agree on what exists and what doesn't, those taking part in the discussion must agree on their epistemology. Conversely, it's important to adopt the appropriate epistemology for the area that is being discussed.

## How we find things out

Our way of finding things out should be based on how concrete or abstract those things are. In other words, we need to adapt our epistemological approach to the ontological nature of what we're investigating. Which brings us to positivism and interpretivism.

Positivism is an approach to finding things out that focuses on things you can measure, things that you can count, things that have a repeatable, observable relationship between cause and effect. It underpins all the natural sciences. Physics, biology, chemistry, and the disciplines derived directly from them are all sciences you can point a telescope at or put on a pair of scales and so on. A strictly positivist viewpoint would say that the only kind of knowledge that exists is that which you can measure. In the chapter on *Pokémon Go* and behaviourism, we'll see that behaviourism developed from a very positivist approach.

There are limitations to this type of approach. The decisions scientists make about which questions to ask, which subjects are important to investigate, and what should be measured are not purely objective, but are all influenced by culture and environment. Even though scientists have instruments taking measurements, it's impossible to be absolutely sure that those instruments are working correctly. When instruments don't provide the results that scientists expect, deciding why the results are different requires a degree of interpretation. Things are never quite as concrete and objective as positivists would like to make out.

For instance, something fires neutrinos through the Earth and you find out they're travelling faster than light (CERN, 2012)! Later, though, you figure out that a loose cable has thrown your timing off. Or you carry out a brain scan and see effects that suggest there's a causal relationship between showing someone pictures and changes in their brain. However, it turns out you also get a reaction if you plug a dead salmon into the scanner rather than a live human (Scicurious, 2012). You always need to account for random fluctuations that just happen to coincide with what you're doing.

Like any investigation, positivist investigations are prone to cultural bias. Vast numbers of people are excluded from carrying out research due to social inequities. These limitations reduce the pace and extent of the development of knowledge. They have also led to researchers wasting time going down dead ends because of pet theories held by handfuls of old white men.

To some extent, and given enough time, the process is self-correcting for cultural bias. If a theory doesn't work, you'll have lots of people doing experiments in all parts of the world, and coming up with theories based on what their various experiments show, not what they wanted them to show. Eventually, it will be agreed that one theory explains most of the measurements, and that's the one that generally gets adopted. You get a consensus that is largely irrespective of culture – although it tends to be the richer countries that decide which subjects are important, which questions are asked, and which evidence is acceptable.

At the boundaries there's contention, but in the main body of this positivist end of science there's relatively little. Physicists have now (largely) reached a consensus on more or less everything that happened from the first $10^{-35}$ seconds after the Big Bang until now (Cox et al, 2017), everything bigger than a quark, and anything smaller than the observable universe (Cox, 36). You may find local differences – Chinese scientists may use a different abbreviation for copper nanotubes than Americans (Duan, Zhang & Xu, 2014), for example, or Indian scientists may call for clinical trials of Vedic medicine (Pilapitiya and Siribaddana, 2013) but, on the whole, this main core of the positivist end of science is the same for everyone, no matter where or who they are. It has been contributed to, and tested by, people on every continent on the planet (Mac Sweeney, 2023; Hamacher, 2017).

However, although this is consensus knowledge, it is still not objective, which would require it to be truly independent of human experience. Using DNA to categorise a lifeform is more objective than using what it looks like, because if you examine the DNA most experts will agree what that reveals about the evolutionary history of the lifeform, whereas fewer people will agree which physical features should take precedence. But it is still not a 1.0 on our scale (definitely 100% true), it still requires human intervention and interpretation. It is, at best, inter-subjective (d'Espagnat, 1983) and the more the 'inter', the less the subjective. All observers agree, but what's actually going on in an objective, external-to-humans way we do not know.

As an aside, we've found the word positivism is a barrier to understanding the meaning of the word, because it sounds as if it's related to being positive. Positivists aren't necessarily optimists, (although they're often very excited about what you can do with just numbers), and they're not necessarily positive that they're correct. We propose 'measure-it-ism' as an alternative word, which makes it clearer what is involved.

When we encounter the limits of what measure-it-ism can do, there are two options. The first is to dismiss anything that can't be measured, on the grounds that it's impossible to know anything definite about it. That would leave educators largely in the dark, because with learning there's a lot that goes on that you can't measure. The other option is to take a good look at what we can't measure and develop the best explanation we can, for which we turn towards interpretivism.

With interpretivism, the aim is not to prove anything, but to make the best possible statement about what reality might be, based on the available evidence. To make these statements as good as possible, we typically look at the thing we're observing from many different perspectives, involving as many people and in as many contexts as we can. Collecting a range of people's accounts of their experiences is sometimes dismissed as anecdotal evidence by people who only value measurable data. But, in fact, if we're interested in people's attitudes and experiences, then this type of non-numeric data is exactly what we need to draw upon.

These accounts can also help to explain or contextualise numeric data. For example, a survey might assign a code to each country in the world and then ask respondents to select their location by country, treating this as numeric data. Another survey might prompt participants to expand on this information with a free-text response to be analysed qualitatively, which might reveal that some respondents had been in the country for less than a year, some were responding while on a short holiday, some had misinterpreted the question and given the country where they were born, and some had assumed the question was actually asking about the country which they considered home. On the whole, numeric data can be collected about very specific aspects of a large amount of things, while data that will be analysed qualitatively can provide a much more detailed picture of a smaller amount of things.

Note that we're talking about numeric and non-numeric data here rather than quantitative and qualitative data, as they're commonly referred to. That's because it's actually the analysis, rather than the data, that's quantitative or qualitative. You can count or classify anything – there are multiple examples of images, text and conversation being analysed in a quantitative way. Corpus linguistics, conversation analysis, and content analysis all take a quantitative approach to non-numeric data.

On the other hand, numeric data can be analysed for its context and built-in assumptions. Beckzilla's favourite example of this is the statement '1+1 = 2', which seems very straightforward if you make the assumptions that the sum isn't phrased in binary (1+1 = 10 in binary), that the numbers are Arabic rather than Roman (I+I = II in Roman numerals) and that the things you are counting are the same (1 apple + 1 orange = 1 small fruit salad). Data feminism stresses the importance of examining the context and power structures associated with data, asserting that 'data is not neutral or objective. It is the product of unequal social relations, and this context is essential for conducting accurate, ethical analysis' (d'Ignazio & Klein, 2020).

To avoid non-numeric data simply becoming a mass of beliefs and opinions, we need to be systematic in our data collection, careful not to exclude data that doesn't fit with our ideas, and avoid as far as possible any bias in how we collect the data. We also need to be as inter-subjective as possible about the analysis, drawing upon different viewpoints as we create categories, and looking for exceptions as well as similarities. Above all, we need to be reflexive throughout the research process, examining and making visible our beliefs, judgments and practices. The final result of qualitative research isn't a measurement, instead it's the interpretation of the data that makes the most sense in that particular context. Qualitative analysis can't show a generalisable one-to-one correspondence between cause and effect in the way that quantitative analysis can, but it can certainly assemble evidence that there's a connection between the two.

It may seem as if positivism always involves quantitative research and interpretivism always involves qualitative research. Although positivists may come up with theories about things they can't measure (both the position and speed of a particle) or that they can't yet observe (dark matter), their work is aimed at making these measurable, because positivist research is always quantitative.

Interpretivist researchers may use qualitative or quantitative approaches. They might carry out thematic analysis on a text, or they might count the number of times a particular word is used, or how long the pauses are. They might ask people to rank from 1 (love it) to 7 (hate it) how they feel about something. Although these are numbers and can therefore be counted, they are still (at their roots) a subjective decision about what something means, so are ultimately interpretivist. Interpretivist studies often explicitly employ a viewpoint that informs the design of the study and the interpretation of the data. For example, feminism or Marxism will suggest that an effect is due to the ways in which society is constructed, and that within that model you will see certain things happen as a result of other actions. These aren't predictive models like those in the natural sciences, but they are still valuable. Identifying the theoretical perspective that has influenced a piece of research makes it clear why it has been structured as it has and foregrounds some of the decisions that have been taken. In the natural sciences, these political and cultural influences are present but more rarely acknowledged. In both cases, the preferences of funders will determine which research areas and designs are prioritised. The impact of colonisation by a particular (for example northern, white, straight) perspective limits the questions we ask, the methods we use, and the interpretations we consider (Ramakrishnan, 2020). For any researcher, decolonising your discipline is not only fairer, it's more robust and helps you get close to that elusive 1 (I'm absolutely certain this is true).

Let's go to Part 2 in the next chapter for the answer to our question, **How do ontology and epistemology help you eliminate Jar Jar Binks with headcan(n)ons?**

## Mesa just sharing my references with yousa

Burton, B. (2014) Who decides '*Star Wars*' canon? Meet the Story Group, *CNET*, 8 January. Available at: https://www.cnet.com/news/who-decides-star-wars-canon-meet-the-story-group/

CERN (2012) OPERA experiment reports anomaly in flight time of neutrinos from CERN to Gran Sasso, *Press Release*, 8 June. Available at: https://press.cern/news/press-release/cern/opera-experiment-reports-anomaly-flight-time-neutrinos-cern-gran-sasso

Childs, M. (2012) Transmedia narratives: examples to definitions, *The London Transmedia Fest 2012*, Ravensbourne College, London, 26 to 27 October.

Cox, B., Ince, R., and Feachem, A. (2017) *The Infinite Monkey Cage – How To Build a Universe*, William Collins, UK: London

d'Espagnat, B. (1983) *In Search of Reality*, Springer-Verlag, USA: New York

Dawkins, R. (2006) *The God Delusion*, Bantam Books, USA: New York

d'Ignazio, C. and Klein, L.F. (2020) *Data Feminism*. MIT Press, Boston, USA.

Duan, Y., Zhang, J. & Xu, K. (2014) Structural and electronic properties of chiral single-wall copper nanotubes. *Science China Physics, Mechanics and Astronomy* 57, 644–651. Available at: https://doi.org/10.1007/s11433-013-5387-8

Hamacher, D. (2017) Stars that vary in brightness shine in the oral traditions of Aboriginal Australians, *The Conversation,* 8 November. Available at: https://theconversation.com/stars-that-vary-in-brightness-shine-in-the-oral-traditions-of-aboriginal-australians-85833

Krantz, M., Snider, M., Della Cava, M. and Alexander, B. (2012) Disney buys Lucasfilm for $4 billion, *USA Today*, 30 October. Available at: https://eu.usatoday.com/story/money/business/2012/10/30/disney-star-wars-lucasfilm/1669739/

Lyden, J.C. (2012) Whose film is it, anyway? Canonicity and authority in Star Wars fandom. *Journal of the American Academy of Religion*, 80(3), 775–786. https://doi.org/10.1093/jaarel/lfs037

Maani, N., and Galea, S. (2021) What science can and cannot do in a time of pandemic, *Scientific American*, 2 February 2. Available at: https://www.scientificamerican.com/article/what-science-can-and-cannot-do-in-a-time-of-pandemic

Mac Sweeney, N. (2023) The myth of the 'Dark Ages' ignores how classical traditions flourished around the world, *Smithsonian Magazine: History*, 18 May. Available at: https://www.smithsonianmag.com/history/the-myth-of-the-dark-ages-ignores-how-classical-traditions-flourished-around-the-world-180982190/

Pilapitiya, S. and Siribaddana, S. (2013) Issues in clinical trials in complementary and alternative medicine (CAM), *Current Opinion in Pharmacology*, 13:2, 311-312. Available at: https://doi.org/10.1016/j.coph.2013.02.007

Ramakrishnan, A. (2020) Science writers urged to tell stories that include Indigenous perspectives, *National Association of Science Writers*, 13 November. Available at: https://www.nasw.org/article/science-writers-urged-tell-stories-include-indigenous-perspectives

Saler, M. (2012) *As If: Modern Enchantment and the Literary Prehistory of Virtual Reality*. USA: New York: Oxford University Press.

Sansweet, S.J. (1998) *The Star Wars Encyclopedia*, USA: New York, Del Rey Books. Scicurious (2012) IgNobel prize in neuroscience: the dead salmon study, *Blog: The Scicurious Brain, Scientific American*, 25 September. Available at: https://blogs.scientificamerican.com/scicurious-brain/ignobel-prize-in-neuroscience-the-dead-salmon-study/

Spelling, I. (2005) New hopes, *Starlog*, 337, August, 46- 52. Available at: https://archive.org/details/starlog_magazine-337JPG/337.djvuconvert/page/n45/mode/2up

Scan the QR code to listen to
the podcast episode

**CHAPTER 5:**

# YEAH, BUT DO ONTOLOGY AND EPISTEMOLOGY HELP YOU ELIMINATE JAR JAR BINKS WITH HEADCAN(N)ONS? PART 2

*Mark Childs, Olivia Rowlands, Rebecca Ferguson and Mike Collins*

*'That's a very fancy sword,' says Mikezilla, sceptically, 'And I can see how the backpack would be useful, but I think we're still lost?'*

*'Ah well, that's the thing,' says Markzilla, momentarily pausing his sword swishing to stop the hat falling over his eyes. 'With these, we can work out what "lost" actually means.'*

## Answering the question

As mentioned at the start of the previous chapter, when discussing ontology and epistemology, there's always another nuance you can bring to the discussion. We had to stop critiquing what we were saying and adding another level when we found a generalisation that didn't apply, or a definition that needed disambiguation before this topic took over the book, which is why you'll still be able to identify a couple of holes here and there. At the point at which we'd stopped it had still grown to fill two chapters. Which is why this is part two.

If you've not read part one, then we strongly suggest you start there as the following won't make sense otherwise (unless you're already very familiar with ontology, epistemology and *Star Wars* fandom, in which case, skip both parts). Still with us? Right then, let's bring this back to education and answer our question.

Pedagogy, learning and related areas such as engagement, collaboration and affect are subjective experiences that translate badly from a classroom to a laboratory environment, so a purely positivist approach only helps to understand some aspects of them in some contexts. Classrooms aren't good settings for positivist experiments – there are far too many variables to take into account, and good ethical reasons to avoid wasting the time of students and teachers by restricting their behaviour to make your research easier.

Interpretivist investigations can try the same intervention in different contexts, or repeat a study in the same context. The more detail you have about the effects of an intervention, the more certain you can be that it has certain effects under certain conditions. These findings can be used to help guide practice.

A particular challenge when it comes to researching education is that learning can rarely be observed, so a positivist study has to select measurable proxies for learning. Typically, this involves a test before the study, to assess what learners know at that point, and a test after the study, to assess what learners know at that point.

However, this leads to multiple problems: individuals may have learned things that are not covered by the test, they may have taken information on board that will lead to learning in the future, or they may have a bad day and perform worse on the post-test than on the pre-test. A positivist stance can be harmful because it attempts to quantify things that are not quantifiable, and it attempts to classify when that classification is of no benefit to the learner. All these measurements use a positivist proxy to answer a question that is not positivist in nature: 'Are people learning?'

If a question can be answered by measuring something, that's usually the approach that will provide the most definite answer. For example, if we want to know about the ways a virus can be transmitted, then we take a positivist approach, carry out laboratory trials, make appropriate measurements and come up with definitive answers. A positivist answer (when applicable) is always going to be more robust than an interpretivist one. In terms of the scale we introduced in the previous chapter, a 2 is better than a 3.

But if we want to know the best way of encouraging people to change their behaviour to minimise transmission of a virus, then we need an interpretivist approach. We don't have a set of identical planets on which we can run a comparative experiment testing alternative approaches. Even if we did, that would be an ethically dubious experiment. Interpretivism is the way forward, even though we can't be sure that we have definitely got the right answer.

So, although you need to go to medical scientists to find out how a disease is transmitted, if you're telling people how to limit its transmission, it's best not to leave this to the medical scientists, because decision-making is a process that deals with people's feelings, which requires a different approach (Maani and Galea, 2021). If you want to get a message about conservation out to indigenous peoples, you need to mix the science about the environment with the knowledge of local people, as they are the experts on what the natural world means to them (Novera and Kark, 2022).

Mixing epistemologies in this way is called Critical Realism (capital C capital R). If pressed, some Critical Realists would say they're at the positivist end of the scale and are pretty sure that there's an observable reality out there (1 or 2). Some would be at the interpretivist end of the scale and believe it all depends (6 or 7). Others would be less certain, hovering in the middle of the scale. However, when it comes to selecting a research approach, they'd all begin by asking, 'What are the ontological properties of that which is being investigated?' They'd then apply the correct epistemological frame. For a fuller explanation of this approach, take a look at Tom Fryer's *Short Guide to Ontology and Epistemology and Why Everyone Should be a Critical Realist* (Fryer, 2022).

To recap, then:

1. Ontology is what does and doesn't exist and how it is categorised.
2. Epistemology is what you choose to count as evidence and how you go about finding things out.
3. Epistemology offers two potential approaches – positivism aspires to be objective, while interpretivism is consciously subjective.
4. Some forms of knowledge are open to measurement, in which case measure them. Some aren't, in which case, don't.

5. No knowledge is completely objective, but some is more objective than others. Where it's more open to interpretation, the more 'inter' your subjectivity, the more trustworthy your results will be.

## The answer

Now that we've looked at the extent to which something can be said to be real or not, let's mess up our whole picture of reality by introducing the concept of kayfabe. Kayfabe is a term used in professional wrestling, but the phrase reveals wrestling's roots in the carnival tradition (Childs, 2022).

Basically, kayfabe is a term for a world of pretence, where you put reality on one side for a while and treat a fictional world as if it were real. The idea of 'as if' is inherent in a lot of human experience, if not the majority, and is explored in Michael Saler's book of the same name (Saler, 2012).

We use kayfabe a lot in this book. When we talk about Yoda as a supply teacher, we know he's not really a supply teacher. In fact, we know he's not real, full stop. Within the first part of each chapter we discuss the reality of the pedagogical theory (or degree of reality of it) and the real history of the aspect of popular culture we are focusing on. But in 'The Answer' parts, we engage with the fictional world as if it were real, only rarely stepping out of the pretence. We don't explicitly acknowledge every time that we know those texts exist in that way for a whole set of cultural, business, production, narrative reasons. While we're in the as-if space, those things are put to one side.

The distinction is slightly blurred in the chapters that are about real events like the von Trapp family's escape from Austria, or the Apollo 13 mission, but even then we mainly talk about the slightly fictionalised account we've seen in the movies.

So, to get back to answering our question here: **How do ontology and epistemology help you annihilate Jar Jar Binks with headcan(n)ons?**

We're going to enter the kayfabe of pretending that the *Star Wars* universe is real. For the metaphor to work, we're going to pretend that the reality of that universe, the laws, the history, the lifeforms all have their reality determined, not by what has actually happened or what actually exists (what we would call 'objective reality' in our actual universe), but by the mysterious God-like (to any fictional characters within that universe) entity known as the LucasFilm Story Group. This is what is meant by canon within the *Star Wars* universe. If you live in the *Star Wars* universe, it's what's real.

Let's start with Jar Jar Binks, who's probably the most detested character in the *Star Wars* universe. He's a Gungan, an amphibious indigenous lifeform on a planet ruled by humans. Discussing Jar Jar means we need to depart from the single author voice, as Mikezilla and Markzilla have different takes on the character.

Mikezilla describes him as:

> *Possibly the most loathed character in all of creation, a slightly racist CGI-nightmare creature introduced in the prequel trilogy, who essentially added nothing to the story at all. It's just a horrible, wretched, irritating character who served no significant narrative purpose.* ~Mikezilla

Markzilla's view is:

> *The prequel trilogy is basically about Emperor Palpatine's rise to power. There's the Republic, the good guys. There are also the Separatists, who are challenging the good guys. But*

> *Palpatine is the head of both. He's a chancellor of the Republic and he's also secretly running the Separatists. Because the Separatists are a threat, this is used by Palpatine to accrue more and more power in order to defend the Republic. It's Jar Jar who moves the motion to elect Palpatine to be the head of the Senate. Jar Jar is the biggest stooge ever. He's the reason why the Empire ends up being created. It really all comes down to that one bad decision that Jar Jar Binks makes.*
> *~Markzilla*

Post-structuralism states that differences in interpretation like this occur all the time. From their perspective, no literary text has a single meaning – instead, every reader assigns it a new meaning. In his seminal text, *Mythologies* (1957), Roland Barthes proposes that speech, photographs, movies and other types of text all have a language in them that has already been worked on. The meaning presented in them may be presented as natural, but they're never simple representations of reality because they contain an element of myth, an implicit set of assumptions. He gives the example of a photograph on the cover of *Paris Match* magazine showing a black soldier saluting the French flag. The editor's intent is to convey that the French Empire is so great everyone accepts it, whereas the viewer may interpret the image as an example of the pervasiveness of indoctrination. Images and words have a different meaning for each reader, the meaning is not inherent in the text itself.

Any individual text, movie or photograph will be interpreted in different ways. However, a transmedia narrative such as *Star Wars* is made up of multiple texts, providing an additional option. People can decide for themselves which of these texts form part of the narrative. The texts they include constitute their personal headcanon. Headcanon is the individual's personal selection of which version 'counts'. Each viewer makes ontological decisions as to what does and doesn't exist within their *Star Wars* universe.

Here's Mikezilla's view, which eliminates Jar Jar Binks by removing his very existence from the *Star Wars* reality:

> *What I choose to count as evidence would be something very interpretivist. It might be what I felt spoke to me the most; which bits I find most compelling in the* Star Wars *universe. I might canvas my friends to see which bits are their favourites as well and build that into my wider narrative. Based on that, I would essentially eliminate the prequel trilogies and go back to a situation where we've just got the original three movies, probably some very heavy director's cuts of the most recent three movies, all the old video games and the the Young Jedi Knights books would be my personal headcanon, which would in turn murder Jar Jar Binks with a headcan[n]on. ~Mikezilla*

Here's Markzilla's interpretation, which reinstates Jar Jar by accepting the texts that contain Jar Jar Binks as part of his headcanon:

> *I like my narratives to be as full as possible, so I'll include any text that's going, as long as it fits. So the prequels, the cartoons, the audio plays, all of it will go in (although my jury is still out on fan fiction). Where I struggled with the sequel trilogy is that there's such a long gap between* Return of the Jedi *and* The Force Awakens *that the* Star Wars *universe feels as if it's been in suspended animation. The lack of movement of the key players for 30 years just feels empty compared to the* Legends *stuff with the Dark Empire, the Yuzhan Vong invasion and so on. So my headcanon is the Disney canon stuff up until 5ABY (the end of* Return of the Jedi*) and the* Legends *stuff from that point on. Jar Jar Lives! ~Markzilla*

Parts of the *Star Wars* fandom can be quite aggressive in their interactions with other parts. Particular headcanons become so important to some fans that they feel the need for other people to validate and accept their headcanon. They don't acknowledge the interpretivist nature of the selection process by which they constructed their personal narratives. Instead, they produce what they claim to be objective rationales for that selection, then become angry when others interpret the reality of the *Star Wars* universe in a different way.

However, the views of both Markzilla and Mikezilla are interpretivist, in that they are picking and choosing which bits they want to include in their version of the *Star Wars* universe.

A positivist approach would be to reject any personal selection, and only include elements that are confirmed as part of the official version by the LucasFilm Story Group. Within our metaphor, they are the final arbiters of what is, and what isn't, real within that world.

Our power as audience members, rather than helpless fictional peons within that universe, is that as it's our money, our bookshelves, and our hard drives, we can create our own narrative. The key thing is to acknowledge that this has no validity beyond our own heads, but that it also doesn't need to.

In summary, the answer to our question is that if we were to take a positivist approach to what is (after all) a fictional universe, we would accept the observational data presented by the Disney Corporation that everything it produces counts as objective reality for the consumers of the *Star Wars* franchise.

Both Mark and Mike take the ontological view that reality in the *Star Wars* universe depends on the elements that they find the most compelling. Although both of their epistemological approaches are interpretivist and subjective, Mark accepts Jar Jar's reality, but Mike's interpretation eliminates Jar Jar Binks by denying his reality.

## Tips for practice

Whether you're at the positivist end of the scale and are convinced there's an observable reality out there, or at the interpretivist end and believe that everything depends on the context, in practice, your choice of approach needs to depend on the ontological nature of the area you're looking at. If you can measure it, then positivism is the way to go. If you can't, then interpretivism is appropriate. The more your approach is based on valid and reliable measurements, the more possible it is to be sure you're near the right answer, but no answer is ever absolutely the truth. That's no reason to give up trying to be as objective as possible. Conversely, a subjective approach is the only way of answering some questions, even when we know the results won't generalise beyond a certain context. What's important is that, along with 'What do we know?', we're also asking 'How well do we know it?' If you want to use a 1 to 7 scale (or 1.1 to 6.9), feel free.

Another top tip is: don't get flummoxed by the terminology. There's always a temptation in academic discussions to batter each other with big, long words (see our chapter on cognitive load and the *Hitchhiker's Guide* for more examples). If it's useful to replace them with words that mean something to you, and which make things clearer for your reader, that's OK too. Just remember to define those words for your reader at the start.

## There's always a bigger reference

Barthes, R. (1957) *Mythologies* (English translation, 1972, Annette Lavers): Jonathan Cape, London.

Childs, M. (2022) On ludicity, bullshit and Loraine, Blog: *The Body Electric*, 19 September. Available at: https://markchilds.org/2022/09/19/on-ludicity-bullshit-and-lorraine/

Fryer, T. (2022) *A Short Guide to Ontology and Epistemology and Why Everyone Should be a Critical Realist*. Available at: https://tfryer.com/ontology-guide/

Maani, N., and Galea, S. (2021) What science can and cannot do in a time of pandemic, *Scientific American*, 2 February 2. Available at: https://www.scientificamerican.com/article/what-science-can-and-cannot-do-in-a-time-of-pandemic

Novera, J. and Kark, S. (2022) Backyard conservation in traditionally owned lands, *Trends in Ecology and Evolution*, 1, 3-7, DOI: https://doi.org/10.1016/j.tree.2022.08.006

Saler, M. (2012) *As If: Modern Enchantment and the Literary Prehistory of Virtual Reality*. USA: New York: Oxford University Press.

Scan the QR code to listen to the podcast episode

**CHAPTER 6:**

# MAPPING THE REALM OF PEDAGOGY

*Rebecca Ferguson, Mark Childs and Mike Collins*

*Armed with their knowledge of knowledge, and their understanding of understanding, Mikezilla and Markzilla can finally journey deep into the Realm of Pedagogy. But the landscape before them is confusing, full of thick woodlands, deep caves and scattered villages.*

*'Where do we go? What does it all mean? Shall we go back?' they ask. Just then, someone emerges from the land before them. It's Beckzilla.*

*'Are you lost?' she asks. 'Follow me, I can show you around.'*

*Mikezilla and Markzilla breathe a sigh of relief. 'Do you know where we're going?' Mikezilla asks.*

*'Indeed I do,' says Beckzilla. 'In fact, I have a map. Look here.'*

# Why do we need a map?

Throughout this book we talk about lots of theories of learning and teaching, some of which are closely related, others not so much. One of the issues Markzilla had when he was first studying pedagogic theory was that he encountered these theories as a series of separate ideas. The links between them may have been pointed out, but the hierarchy of broader theories and subsidiary approaches was never explained, and it wasn't clear which ideas were considered most important. This was why publications that came out in the early-2000s, such as the Mayes and de Freitas (2004) review of pedagogies and the book *Effective Teaching with Technology in Higher Education* (Bates & Poole, 2003) were such a help to him; they organised the various approaches into three overarching themes (different themes in each case), and located other approaches within these themes.

As an aside, two principles have guided us during our discussions in the world of *Pedagodzilla*:

- No model is true in all cases; some models are useful.

- Where there are two or more competing theories, you probably just need to take a step back and look for a single theory that encompasses the others.

So, when we're talking below about our map, this was designed to be a useful guide to what's out there. But, as with all maps, it's a representation of reality, but not the only way of understanding that reality. And it's not the actual reality. A map of the neighbourhood where you live might focus on the roads, or the underlying geology, or the underground network of pipes and cables, or the economic status of the inhabitants.

All the maps would (probably) be accurate, but not all of them would help you find the area you're looking for.

Our map is designed to help you navigate the theories we cover in this book. Like the other chapters, this one's not purely theoretical – we've used Dwarves and Elves to draw attention to significant differences between theories. You'll read more about the Dwarves, Elves and the lands where they live in the short introductions to each chapter.

Our map may not arrange pedagogic theories in quite the same way as other representations you've encountered. You may find the Dwarves and Elves distracting, or infuriating. If that's the case, use the representation that makes most sense to you. Some overviews of pedagogical theories blur the distinctions between categories, or alternate between them. Getting hung up about which category something falls into isn't something we do in this book. In fact, we spend a lot of time pointing out the links and overlaps between theories, and waving cheerily at metacognition (thinking about thinking), which pops up all over the place.

In addition, we don't see these theories as being in competition with each other. Sometimes one will be helpful, sometimes another. Where the arguments always break down within the literature (or certainly on social media) is when one approach is adopted to the near exclusion of another. But more of that later.

Our map looks like this (see over). The Zillas arrive in a harbour at the northwest of the Realm of Pedagogy and step ashore into Positivist – the Land of the Dwarves. The capital of this land is Behaviourism, which is situated near the caves and megaliths that make up the land's cognitive foundations. To the west lies the Quagmire of Neuromyths and Learning Styles, which all well-informed Dwarves and Elves will avoid at all costs. To the south is a narrow land bridge that leads to Constructivism

– the Land of the Elves. This land includes the twin towns of Problem-based Learning and Active Learning, as well as the town of Experiential Learning. A mist conceals the boundary to the *Matrix*-like town of the Cyber Elves, where reality is known to fluctuate. Moving further south, another land bridge leads to Social Constructivism, which neighbours the Situative land. The Pedagogue's Arms pub is located in this area, together with the Vale of Constructionism and the Communities of Practice. The map ends at this point – perhaps there is more to be discovered, or perhaps the virtual realms of the *World of Warcraft* are too complex and too well copyrighted to be included here.

In our model, the Realm of Pedagogy is divided into four lands. In the north is the Land of the Dwarves. These Dwarves like to delve deep into the earth – a metaphor for delving deep into the brain. The Land of the Dwarves is where we've located all the theories based on how the brain works and how memory functions. Some approaches you can find in this region are concerned with structuring subject matter to take advantage of our knowledge of memory and the brain, for example those that use schema and similar ideas. When we employ Barak Rosenshine's principles, or take cognitive load into account, we're focusing on ways of constructing the learning content that experiments have shown can help students learn as effectively and efficiently as possible.

The Land of the Dwarves is where people from the world of cognitive science like to hang out. On other maps, this region is often assigned the umbrella term of behaviourism. That's not really accurate, though, because behaviourism is a specific theory that was developed before we were able to investigate the brain in as much detail as is now possible. In fact, behaviourism was developed specifically because, at the time, it wasn't possible to observe the brain at work. Because we're aware of the difference between approaches based on cognitive science, we've named

6: MAPPING THE REALM OF PEDAGOGY

this region according to the worldview shared by the people who developed the pedagogies in this area, a positivist worldview that comes to conclusions based on measurements, systematic observations, and quantitative analysis. We've characterised the Positivist people as Dwarves, not because they're short in stature, but because they like efficiency and solid things they can count.

When we travel south, we're in the Land of the Elves. Elves try to understand the point of view of the learner. They generally carry out interpretive investigations involving qualitative analysis. This land contains the constructivist theories, including experiential learning and problem-based learning. It's where researchers hang out who like to spend time perfecting their stories about what goes on in people's minds. Practitioners in this region like to provide opportunities for students to construct their own knowledge, helping them to construct firm foundations and then enabling them to build on those. Most Elves have little interest in cognitive architecture, in fact, the Dwarves would argue that their stories have little basis in how the brain works, but the Elves do their singing and their magic and it all seems to work anyway.

The Realm of Pedagogy includes many different approaches to education that look at learning from a constructivist perspective. Those in the land of Constructivism focus on the development of individual learners, and are concerned with how those learners might build on their own experience, being guided to find solutions to authentic problems, and engaging actively with their learning.

Constructivism is neighboured by Social Constructivism. Here's where we find the theories about how people learn through interacting with each other. Collaborative Learning and Communities of Practice are located in this region. The residents of this land are interested in how people interpret their learning, but are also interested in using different perspectives to provide richness, challenge, extension and critique. Think of this as the land of the Wood Elves, because they're pretty gregarious and they like their wine. Good thing they have the Pedagogue's Arms close at hand to provide a site for conversation and debate.

The final land on our map is Situative, which is closely connected to social-constructivist ideas. So closely connected, in fact, that it's difficult to spot the boundary between the two lands. The Deep Elves live here. They focus on how people learn by interacting not just with other people, but with the environments around them, with the tools they use, as well as by co-creating things. So constructionism and all the narratives about learning together by developing things externally belong in this region. The Deep Elves make use of both positivist and interpretivist approaches because they recognise that not only does learning take place in the minds of those involved in the co-construction but also the objects created during that process leave a trail and can be used as data sources.

The behaviourist arguments of the Dwarves draw on the more empirical evidence of neuroscience and laboratory experiments and tend to be favoured by people with a more positivist approach (which – if you skipped it – we covered in the previous chapter). Those who have a more interpretivist approach to data collection and analysis give more credence to constructivist and situative narratives.

These are rough and ready divisions, designed to make our exploration of the different theories a bit easier to understand in relation to each other. You could easily argue that an approach contains elements from several lands. Some concepts, such as constructionism (Chapter 17) clearly bridge many approaches.

The rest of this book represents a journey across the Realm of Pedagogy as mapped here, crossing each land in turn. The first part is concerned with the Land of the Dwarves. Chapter 7 looks at behaviourism, Chapter 8 sets out Barak Rosenshine's ten principles of instruction and Chapter 9 deals with cognitive load. Moving on to the Land of the Elves and different constructivist approaches, Chapter 10 looks at active learning, Chapter 11 at problem-based learning, and Chapter 12 at experiential learning – with the added bonus of a brief exploration of the nature of reality. In Chapter 13, we pick apart the discussion between positivist and constructivist approaches. After that, we take a brief tour of social constructivism in Chapter 14, before moving on to situative learning in chapter 15, with communities of practice covered in Chapter 16. Chapter 17 shows how constructionism brings together many theories.

That's the map we'll be using. Just remember: no map is completely true, some maps are useful. Feel free to explore the lands we describe. Just be aware your mileage may vary.

> *I tried a few ways of wrapping my head around the different domains of pedagogy in the early days. One of the best I found was writing awful jokes, here's the least worst:*
>
> *A behaviourist, a constructivist, and a social constructivist walk in to a pub...let's call it the Pedagogue's Arms...*
>
> *The behaviourist, straight to the point, walks up to the bar and says to the bartender, 'Every time I say, "Bring me a beer," I want you to bring me a beer.' He repeats this instruction three times, just to drill it in. The bartender, a bit taken aback by the straightforwardness, obliges and throughout the night, diligently brings the beers. With each delivery, the behaviourist offers a tip, nodding to the concept of 'positive reinforcement.' It's a strange way to order, but hey, the bloke leaves satisfied.*
>
> *Next up, the constructivist ambles to the bar with a thoughtful look. He says, 'Consider the times you've felt thirst, found yourself in a bar, and had cash to spend. Reflect on*

*your experiences as a bartender. What solution comes to mind for my current parched state?' The bartender, intrigued by this philosophical approach, ponders his own experiences and decides on a proactive strategy, delivering a pint every hour on the dot. The constructivist enjoys his evening, thoroughly inebriated and grateful for the insightful service. He ends his night asleep outside a kebab shop.*

*Lastly, the social constructivist doesn't head for the bar. Instead, he settles at a table and gathers the other patrons around for a grand discussion on the most effective method to acquire beer. The bartender, busy with a barrel change, returns to find a full-on collaborative workshop in progress. They're deep into devising a prototype for an extendable beer pump, based on collective research and feedback. Alas, the night ends with the call for last orders, and the social constructivist, absorbed in the thrill of collaboration, forgets to actually drink. Badum-tish.*

*~Mikezilla*

# References: an unexpected journey into further reading

Bates, T. and Poole, G. (2003) *Effective Teaching with Technology in Higher Education*, San Francisco: Jossey-Bass/Wiley

Mayes, T. and de Freitas, S. (2004). *Review of E-Learning Theories, Frameworks and Models*. London: JISC. Available from: https://core.ac.uk/download/pdf/228143942.pdf

# PART 2

## THE PLATEAUX OF PARADIGMS

*In which our Zillas explore the big theories of how to teach – and in the process uncover cognitivism, constructivism and how they taste when blended together in a bean casserole.*

*Also why Dwarves and Elves don't always get along.*

## CHAPTER 7:

# HOW DOES BEHAVIOURISM HELP PLAYERS CATCH 'EM ALL IN POKÉMON GO?

*Rebecca Ferguson and Mike Collins*

*With the map thoroughly digested, the travellers, now numbering three, are now fully prepared to explore the Realm of Pedagogy. At least, there should be three. Markzilla is nowhere to be seen. Losing one of the group is not a very good start to the journey. 'I'm sure he'll catch up with us,' says Mikezilla, though knowing Markzilla, he's not very sure at all.*

*'Let's start with a visit to the capital of the first land in the Realm of Pedagogy,' says Beckzilla. 'It's the Land of the Dwarves and their capital city is called Behaviourism. It's the historic gateway to the lands beyond. Also, see this cool game on my phone – we can play it as we explore.'*

Behaviourism gets a lot of bad press, and not just because it's spelt different ways in different countries. 'Behaviorism is called a cult, absurd, nonsense, grim, unethical, and poison' (Abramson, 2013). Google, when prompted, suggests questions such as: 'What is the problem with behaviourism?'; 'What are the main criticisms of behaviourism?'; and, more bluntly, 'Why is behaviourist approach bad?'

Is it really a theory from the bad old days of rote learning and corporal punishment that should now be cast into the Quagmire of Neuromyths, along with learning styles? Or is it actually a way of learning that, under the alias of gamification, is used extensively and successfully in everyday life? In this chapter, the Zillas investigate by asking their own question: **How does behaviourism help players catch 'em all in *Pokémon Go*?**

## *Pokémon Go*

*Pokémon* was originally a Gameboy game released in 1996, a fantastic little adventure where you play a ten-year-old who meets a crazy old professor who sends you on a quest across all the islands in the Kanto region. While there you, as a ten-year-old, battle and collect a series of creatures with the aims of suppressing Team Rocket and becoming champion of the *Pokémon* League. It's a multimedia franchise that grew into trading cards (more than 42 billion of these have been sold), cartoons, many video games, films, television, film soundtracks, clothing, soft toys, bedsheets, bath towels, and toys. Pikachu is probably the Pokémon most readily associated with the game. A cute, friendly little electric hamster with red cheeks, it sits on the shoulder of its trainer. Any saleable item you could conceivably stick Pikachu on has had Pikachu added to it at some point.

Pokémon battle each other under players' guidance. If they lose a battle, they faint and then revive, smiling. There is no death in *Pokémon*, even though there are challenges, villains and battles. It's a game that encourages people to make connections with each other, trade with each other, befriend each other, and (with *Pokémon Go*) get outside and move around. Like many other games you play on your phone, you can play for free (after your original investment in the phone, in data, and perhaps in an external battery pack to support extended playing sessions) but there are also opportunities for micro payments within the game, which is what makes it vastly profitable. *Pokémon Go* made $1.21 billion in 2021, the second year in a row it had made over $1 billion, and it is just one part of the hugely successful brand.

Overall, *Pokémon* is one of the biggest video game franchises of all time. It's beaten by *Mario* and *Tetris* but, apart from that, it's everywhere and has been everywhere for more than a quarter of a century. *Pokémon Go*, produced by American software company Niantic, is the augmented reality version of *Pokémon*. Its appearance in 2016 widened access from game consoles such as the Gameboy and the Switch. You can play *Pokémon Go* on your phone, which means you can play it out in the wild. It was the real breakthrough point for augmented reality. Until the game's launch, augmented reality was a relatively niche interest that enabled people to overlay things on to day-to-day reality. Once the game launched, everybody was overlaying little Pokémon onto their day-to-day reality, staring through their phones at what was going on in the game world.

So, just what was going on in that game world? Interactions with an ever-expanding range of creatures (Pokémon), trainers (players), locations (pokéstops and gyms found worldwide) and tasks. As the developer, Niantic, says: 'You create your own story in this RPG [role-playing game]!' That's rather vague, but

Niantic has tried to explain the game on Apple's app store, which is one of the places it can be downloaded.

> '*Pokémon Go is an immersive open-world experience that enables you to live the Pokémon adventure in augmented reality. Find and evolve all Pokémon to complete your Pokédex, and battle other players in PVP [player versus player] in this multiplayer RPG.*'

It adds that you can 'join one of the three teams and customise your avatar. Choose your Buddy Pokémon from your Pokédex to travel at your side'.

On The Open University campus, where some of the Zillas work, you'd see large groups of people going for walks past the beautiful landscaping and artwork with their heads buried in their phones, occasionally stopping in weird clusters. You'd later find that was because a particular Pokémon was spawning, or there was a gym there where Pokémon could battle. People who were not usually seen in the open air would be spotted walking in clusters with their phones. There were three gyms around the library, which meant large numbers of people would head there at the same time and then stand around outside the doors rather than going in to use the resources. People were nipping out for a coffee and catching a Pokémon or two on the way. This activity died down during Covid lockdown but has gradually returned.

When *Pokémon Go* first came out, it was a major event and people signed up worldwide. The game was downloaded 260 million times in its first year. Collectively, players walked 8.7 million km while playing, getting much needed exercise (Schilling, 2016) and triggering security alerts (Whistlecroft, 2016). The initial flurry of activity was inevitably followed by news articles saying nobody was interested anymore, interest had died down, and lots of players had left. However, eight years later it's still huge. There are Pokémon gyms all over the place, in almost every country in the world. Many of these change hands several times a day.

This means the *Pokémon Go* franchise has to keep moving forward in order to cater for all these people engaging multiple times a day. Some people are playing the game whenever they're moving around. Some are playing it at their desks at work. To keep them engaged, there have always got to be new things. Originally, there were 151 Pokémon, but at this point there are over 800, plus a range of variant forms. You might have a shiny Pikachu, a lucky Pikachu, a poisoned Pikachu, a purified Pikachu, and a set of Pikachus wearing a range of cute little hats. You can just keep collecting.

There are two main aims for Pokémon players. You can aim to win the league because you are best at battling the Pokémon or you can aim to catch 'em all, which is the game's slogan, and part of the question the Zillas are answering here. As the leagues keep shifting, and the variant Pokémon forms keep increasing, both goals remain tantalisingly out of reach for players, but subgoals and challenges keep them engaged.

*Pokémon* has prompted a lot of serious research, including research into education. There's a professor of education in America – Joseph Tobin – who does a lot of ethnographic studies, investigating subjects such as how communities work. He found that what keeps people engaging with *Pokémon* – certainly something that keeps children engaging with *Pokémon* – is that there are very long lists of the different creatures, and the more you know about these the more successful you can be. They exist in an increasingly rich fictional universe and each type has different characteristics and personality. Jigglypuff, for instance, sings a little song, which sends its opponents to sleep, leaving it free to draw pictures on their faces. Cubone, on the other hand, is adorable – except it dresses in the skull of its dead mother. Children can learn these things and show off to their peer group about their knowledge.

Researchers at Stanford (Gomez et al, 2019) have carried out MRI scans of the brains of people who are very good at playing *Pokémon* and of others who haven't played the game at all. These scans showed that certain parts of the brain fired up when the experts recognised Pokémon. This was not the part of the brain that fires up when they recognised a word or a place, it was a specific 'Pokémon recognition area'. Looking inside players' heads revealed that the game had literally changed their brains. Which takes us on to behaviourism.

## Behaviourism

More than a hundred years ago, at the start of the 20th century, anyone who wanted to investigate learning didn't have the opportunity to look at what was going on in the brains of living learners. There were no MRI scans – those weren't developed until the 1970s – and so scientists had to rely on self accounts to find out what people were thinking. At the time, psychoanalysis was becoming increasingly influential. Its leading proponent, Sigmund Freud, argued that behaviour and cognition are largely determined and driven by the unconscious mind.

Behaviourists were sceptical about that view. In their opinion, we don't know what's going on in people's heads, so it's no good coming up with a theory about something we can't see; something we can't observe. They felt that the scientific approach should involve looking at things we can see; doing experiments with things that we can observe. They couldn't observe the brain at work, but they could observe behaviour, so that was what they chose to study. How do we know if somebody has learned something? They change their behaviour. This was a logical scientific approach that made learning measurable.

It also provided a definition of learning. When we talk about learning, we usually don't particularly define the term, even though one of the things academics love is defining terms! If you asked a behaviourist, 'What is learning?' they would answer, 'It is a long-term change in behaviour based on experience.'

That's a useful definition. It excludes some sorts of learning, because not all forms of learning *are* long-term changes in behaviour. You could know something in your head without expressing it in your behaviour in any way. Nevertheless, it's a useful definition and it has the advantage that it can be investigated scientifically.

While Freud was publishing case studies in Vienna, the Russian scientist Ivan Pavlov was famously working with dogs, in research published in 1897. He trained a series of dogs to expect their dinner when he rang a bell. He rang the bell, then he gave them meat. He rang the bell, they began to salivate because they were expecting food and he gave them meat. Eventually, he could ring the bell and they would salivate even though they received no meat.

Breaking that down a bit further, if you give a dog meat, it will salivate. That's an unconditioned response, as that is what the dog would do naturally. Pavlov's influential experiment developed this unconditioned response into a conditioned response. By the end of the experiment, he could ring a bell and the dogs would salivate. They weren't consciously thinking, 'A bell is ringing, we must salivate' – partly because that's almost certainly not how dogs think – but mainly because the salivation response is not under conscious control. They salivated involuntarily.

These conditioned responses and the discovery that you could induce reactions in this way proved to be of great interest and were part of the work that gained Pavlov a Nobel prize in

1904. Developing a conditioned response in this way came to be known as 'classical conditioning' and it fed into behaviourism.

Classical conditioning was demonstrated in humans by John Watson and Rosalie Rayner in what came to be known as the Little Albert experiment, published in 1920. The two scientists set out to use conditioning to produce a phobia. They selected a nine-month-old child, 'Albert', and gave him a series of baseline tests, exposing him to stimuli including a rat, a monkey, a dog, and a rabbit. Albert showed no signs of fear when he encountered any of these. When Albert was 11 months old, the scientists gave him a laboratory rat to play with. He did this happily at first, but then the scientists began to make a loud and frightening noise behind him whenever he touched the rat. After some time, Albert was presented with the rat but no noise. Nevertheless, Albert became very distressed when he saw the rat. In fact, in further experiences, Albert appeared to generalise the experience to other furry objects, from dogs and rabbits to a Santa Claus with a furry beard.

Although the design of the research was weak (there was only one subject, so no evidence that this reaction would be common to other children or adults) and ethically dubious (no effort was made to reduce the phobia that had been induced) there were no serious challenges to the idea that classical conditioning applied to humans.

Behaviourism developed ideas around conditioning further, moving into operant conditioning. This is a way of modifying behaviour using the effect of its consequences. If someone engages in behaviour you want to encourage, you make sure it produces an effect that reinforces that behaviour. If they engage in behaviour you want to discourage, you make sure it produces an effect that inhibits that behaviour. The classic example of this is the carrot/stick approach. If a donkey moves in the right direction you give it a carrot. If it moves in the wrong direction (and you're not too concerned about cruelty to animals), you hit it with a stick. After a while, it's conditioned to move in the direction you prefer.

In the USA Edward Thorndike, like Pavlov, was carrying out animal experiments, most famously with a series of puzzle boxes from which animals had to learn to escape. These experiments led him to propose a law of effect – that consequences are needed for learning. Behaviour followed by pleasant consequences is likely to occur again; behaviour that is followed by unpleasant consequences is less likely to be repeated.

*STIMULUS → BEHAVIOUR (PHWOAR...) → REINFORCEMENT (GROSS!) ↑*

To some extent, that response is baked into us, just like salivating when given meat is baked into dogs. We touch a fire, it burns us, we don't touch it again. We eat a cake, it tastes delicious, we eat some more. The law of effect suggests that these automatic reactions can be harnessed to help individuals to learn in other situations. Thorndike also proposed the law of exercise – learned behaviour fades without practice. Again, this is a principle that can be built into education to help people to retain knowledge.

The animal experiments carried out in the USA, Russia, and elsewhere made use of a relatively limited range of variables – food, pain, and freedom. Human learning offers a wider set of options, with actions leading to consequences that provide either a positive or a negative social response. On the other hand, reactions to these responses are not clear cut – what one person views as positive another may view as negative, and vice versa.

Overall, the behaviourists thought about learning in terms of observable behaviour rather than in terms of what was going on inside people's heads. They noted that external events and actions change the behaviour of individuals. In the classic nature/nurture debate, behaviourists come down heavily on the side of nurture. Yes, some elements of behaviour are innate, automatic reactions, but these reactions can be harnessed to change what individuals do. John Watson, one of the scientists involved in the Little Albert experiment, said in a lecture:

> *'Give me a dozen healthy infants, well-formed, and my own specified world to bring them up in and I'll guarantee to take any one at random and train him to become any type of specialist I might select – doctor, lawyer, artist, merchant-chief and, yes, even beggar-man and thief, regardless of his talents, penchants, tendencies, abilities, vocations, and race of his ancestors. I am going beyond my facts and I admit it, but so have the advocates of the contrary and they have been doing it for many thousands of years.'*
>
> (Watson, 1924)

The claim is impressive, but less so when compared with real-world experience – three of Watson's four children attempted suicide, and one of his grandchildren developed psychological issues that she attributed to being raised according to his theories.

The behaviourists were taking a systematic approach to understanding animals, they were taking a systematic approach to understanding humans, and they were trying to be objective about psychology. They were finding out that if we do X, then Y will happen. There are all sorts of good scientific reasons why you'd want to go down those routes. And the classic thing that you come to is operant conditioning. You either reinforce the behaviour that you want or you punish a behaviour that you don't want.

If you're training your dog and it's done something you want to encourage, you might give it a doggy treat. That would provide positive reinforcement. Or you might take off its lead, removing something it doesn't like. In both cases you're reinforcing the desired behaviour. On the other hand, your dog might do something you want to discourage. In that case, you might add something negative to its life by speaking to it sharply or even giving it a whack on the nose. Or you might take its food away, removing something pleasant from its life.

Constructivists might not see this as operant conditioning. They might argue that the dog is making connections between events and building schema that link the behaviour and the response. So the constructivists would infer something unobservable (the building of schema) is taking place, while behaviourists would focus on what they could actually observe and measure – changes in the dog's behaviour. And, because these classic experiments were carried out with cats, dogs, rats and pigeons, maybe it would be a mistake to assume that schemas were being constructed.

If you use positive and negative reinforcement to teach a pigeon to peck a lever, you're not assuming that the pigeon has some mind map behind its behaviour; you're simply aware that if you act in certain ways towards a pigeon then that pigeon will change its behaviour in a predictable fashion. Obviously, humans are also animals, and in many ways we behave in the same way as other animals, but that doesn't mean we can assume a pigeon is thinking in the same way as a human.

Nevertheless, teaching children and animals in similar ways is where behaviourism can work very well. It's a good strategy for prompting children to memorise foundational knowledge; not the things they need to build and interpret themselves, but the essential pieces of information, such as times tables or number bonds, that can give them a head start. You'd be very unlikely to set a seven-year-old child a piece of problem-based learning that required them to work out how to count in fours from first principles, but most seven-year-olds will be encouraged to memorise that times table. That process will be supported by positive and negative reinforcement – they'll receive praise, good marks and approval when they succeed, whereas they'll get bad marks, removal of privileges, or even punishments if they don't succeed.

A lot of early-years education is based on call and response – the teacher says something and pupils receive positive or negative reinforcement that encourages them to respond in the way the teacher expects. The phrase 'two times two' elicits the response 'four'; the phrase 'eight plus two' elicits the answer 'ten'. This is often referred to as 'rote learning', which is a strategy for memorising information by repeating it multiple times. But operant conditioning isn't simply rote learning, because it always involves either positive or negative reinforcement.

Again, constructivists would say there is more to it than that. The aim is not simply to get children to be able to parrot a set of phrases – they have to understand what they are saying, in what contexts this knowledge can be used, and how to apply it. In reality, it's helpful to do both – to memorise basic facts so you can do simple calculations without reaching for a calculator, but also to understand the meaning of those facts so you can use them outside the classroom.

Behaviourist techniques help people to acquire the building blocks that are used repeatedly in learning situations. Throughout our lives, our education builds on our previous education. The chapter you are reading requires both reader and writer to have learnt how to read and write the English language, to have grasped complex vocabulary, and to understand how books are structured. Since we were very young, if we live in an English-speaking country, we have been conditioned to do those things, and we have had the very powerful incentive of using language to make our thoughts and wishes understood. Throughout our lives, we have built up metacognitive toolkits that enable communication through the written word. For psychologists and linguists there's an issue about whether classical or operant conditioning is involved, but for our purposes we can note that, in most situations, understanding what is happening leads to positive reinforcement, and remaining confused leads to negative reinforcement.

When teaching pedagogy, or Western educational theory, a common approach is to summarise behaviourism, then cognitivism, and to go into more detail about constructivism and social constructivism. Behaviourism is often treated as something from the past, a theory of learning that has been superseded by other, better theories. It may be dismissed as the wrong way of approaching teaching. To some extent that is true, but any method of teaching can be the wrong method in certain circumstances.

Behaviourism has been very influential in many areas, including language learning. The drill, response, repeat pattern is used in many language classrooms around the world. This sort of approach is associated with the conjugation of verbs ('amo, amas, amat' or 'Je vais, tu vas, il va'); with standard responses

('Comment vous appelez-vous?' – 'Je m'appele Pedagodzilla'); and with listen-and-repeat sessions in language labs. There are several problems with this approach, the most obvious being that it doesn't prepare learners to use the language outside the classroom.

From a behaviourist point of view, a significant issue is the extent to which rote learning is confused with behaviourism and, particularly, with operant conditioning. As we said earlier, repetition alone is not enough for operant conditioning; positive or negative reinforcement is also required. For the conditioning to be effective, the reinforcement must be directly linked with the behaviour and not delayed until a test at the end of the week, an exam at the end of the year, or until the learner is in a situation where the language is needed. This confusion of repetition with operant conditioning is one of the things that has got behaviourism a bad name and, incidentally, goes some way towards explaining why so many people in the UK fail to learn a language even after years of being urged to 'écoutez et répétez – listen and repeat.'

However, despite decades of misapplication in the classroom, behaviourism was used by at least 54 million language learners a month in 2022. That's the number of monthly active users reported by *Duolingo* that year, and *Duolingo* makes heavy use of behaviourism, under the guise of gamification.

Gamification is the practice of taking something that isn't a game – in this case, language learning – and using strategies and mechanics from games in order to encourage engagement, motivation, and loyalty. The game elements that are used include point scoring, competition with others, timers, badges, and leaderboards. Done well, gamification can shift learners' emotional responses, making them happy to engage with learning, eager to progress, and able to progress successfully while in a flow state. On the other hand, gamification is often presented in the style of chocolate-covered broccoli, an attempt to disguise something considered unpleasant by adding a superficial layer of something more enjoyable. In those cases, its use may emphasise to learners that even their teachers regard these learning tasks as boring drudgery. For more on gamification, and why it's different from game-based learning, take a look at a *Pedagodzilla* journal paper on the subject (York at al, 2022).

A gamified app, such as *Duolingo*, can apply operant condition flawlessly. Has the learner completed the task correctly? They immediately receive positive feedback, a green bar, a large tick, the word 'correct', and the chance to move forward. Are they making good progress? Then they move forward on the golden trail to the treasure chest. Have they engaged with the tasks for several days in a row? Don't break that streak! Motivational messages – 'You're crushing this', 'Keep it up, slugger' – encourage engagement, as does the opportunity to move up a league and to join the week's leaderboard. Their streak grows, and they acquire new titles: Superstar Learner or even Galactic Legend. They fail to engage for a day, an undesirable behaviour, and immediately lose both their streak and the title associated with it. The app plays the part of a constantly attentive instructor, ready at any time of the night or day with immediate feedback or consequences designed to encourage the learner to engage in the desired behaviour of producing a stream of correct answers every day. Behaviourism at its finest.

## The answer

Once you've spotted behaviourism at work in *Duolingo*, you can see it being used across many apps. Not necessarily to encourage you to learn – the desired behaviour is typically to keep you spending time and/or money in order to make a tidy profit for the app owners. However, most games encourage players to undertake some learning, even if it's simply how to use the controls and score points. More complex games require a lot of knowledge to play successfully.

In his book, *What Video Games Have To Teach Us about Learning and Literacy*, James Paul Gee details how the game *Tomb Raider* teaches users a complex backstory, and how to play, and how to be subversive within the game – all without breaking the bounds of the game world. Gee's work shows how complex the pedagogy of video games can be – he identifies 36 learning principles that are used. One that is particularly relevant in the case of both *Duolingo* and *Pokémon Go* is the amplification of input principle: 'For a little input, learners get a lot of output.'

*Pokémon Go* cleverly uses operant conditioning to keep you playing, providing a great deal of output in the form of feedback and rewards. The more you play, the more you learn about Pokémon and the imagined world they inhabit. If you're going to catch a Pokémon, you need to know things about that Pokémon, such as where you might find it, which berries you might feed it, and how you might catch it. Some Pokémon are usually only found in the wild in certain parts of the world. Mr Mime appears in Europe, Volbeat in Asia, and Pansear in Africa. If you don't live or travel in those areas, you'll need to know how to make friends, trade, cheat, or access special events. Some Pokémon evolve from others, so you need to know and meet the preconditions for evolution. The game prompts players to learn all this information, and it does this using operant conditioning.

There are four possibilities with operant conditioning. Desirable behaviour is reinforced, either by adding a reward or by removing a negative feature. Undesirable behaviour is discouraged, either by adding a negative feature or by removing a reward. If a player learns enough to be in the right place with the right equipment to catch a Pokémon, they'll receive experience, points, virtual candy and stardust as rewards. If it's the first time they've caught that type of Pokémon, it will be added to their Pokédex (which records all the species and whether they have already been caught by that player), and that effectively removes the task of catching that type, thus removing a difficulty.

On the other hand, the player might display undesirable behaviour. They haven't learned enough about Pokémon, their strengths, weaknesses, attacks and defences. This has the negative consequence that when the player sends their Pokémon into battle they lose. Not only that, they have to give up things of value within the game, revives and potions, in order to restore that Pokémon's energy.

These positive and negative consequences are relatively minor, not enough to discourage a player or to stop them playing the game. Together, though, they support a plan of action that involves learning more and more about Pokémon in order to maximise positive reinforcement and minimise negative reinforcement. Learning is rewarded – if not immediately, then fairly quickly. Failure to learn leads to a string of negative consequences, but also repeated chances to learn and to develop skills.

## Tips for practice

Immediate feedback is a crucial aspect of operant conditioning. The algorithms behind apps are on the lookout 24/7 for input and will respond at any time of the day or night. Human teachers can't provide feedback at the same rate but providing it as soon as possible remains important. Students are often asked to carry out complex activities but may not receive a response for days, weeks, or even months. Completing a task successfully doesn't immediately lead to reward, and completing a task unsuccessfully doesn't immediately produce a negative reaction. Building in opportunities for fast, responsive feedback can help to build good learning behaviours.

Behaviourist approaches can be used to encourage a variety of good learning practices. If you don't want students to cram for an exam at the end of term, but to keep returning to material throughout the term, then provide immediate positive feedback when they do this. If you want children to sit down with a book when they come into the classroom, rather than milling around chatting, then set that initial expectation and provide positive reinforcement. You can do this openly – no need to conceal the pedagogy. Explain what you want to happen, explain what the rewards and sanctions will be, and apply them immediately and consistently. We'll see these principles in action in the next chapter when we look at whether Yoda an effective supply teacher was.

Looking beyond behaviourism, consider *Pokémon Go* more broadly. A quick scan of *Bulbapedia*, the online encyclopaedia and fan site for the game, gives an indication of how much there is to know about the game, its characters, its species, its items and its moves. Listed in a text book, this information would almost certainly feel dry and uninteresting. If players were set to learning all this information, and examined at regular interviews, with a test pass enabling them to level up, and a test fail leaving them to go over the same ground, how many would persevere? How many would fail and drop out? A big part of the game's success in keeping people interested is that new knowledge and skills can immediately be put to use, are directly relevant to what players are trying to achieve, and have clear value to the players. These elements are important in all disciplines and can be built into any subject area.

# References: Gotta Catch 'Em All

Abramson, C.I. (2013) Problems of teaching the behaviorist perspective in the cognitive revolution. *Behavioral Sciences*, 3:1, 55-71.

Bulbapedia, the *Pokémon* version of Wikipedia. Available at: https://bulbapedia.bulbagarden.net/wiki/Main_Page

Davis, B. (2017) Six A/B tests used by *Duolingo* to tap into habit-forming behaviour. Econsultancy 27 October. Available at: https://econsultancy.com/six-a-b-tests-used-by-*Duolingo*-to-tap-into-habit-forming-behaviour/

Gee, J. P. (2007) *What Video Games Have To Teach Us about Learning and Literacy*, Palgrave Macmillan.

Gomez, J., Barnett, M. and Grill-Spector, K. (2019) Extensive childhood experience with *Pokémon* suggests eccentricity drives organization of visual cortex. *Nature Human Behaviour*, 3:6, 611-624.

*OpenLearn* on behaviourism: https://www.open.edu/openlearncreate/mod/page/view.php?id=146085. (OpenLearn is really good, and we're not just saying that because we work at The Open University, which runs OpenLearn. Free learning is good in general.)

Schilling, D. (2016) *Pokémon Go* can boost health by making gamers exercise, says GP, *Topic: Pokémon Go, The Guardian*. Available at: https://www.theguardian.com/technology/2016/aug/10/pokemon-go-health-players-exercise-obesity-walking

Tobin, J., Buckingham, D., Sefton-Green, J., Allison, A. and Iwabuchi, K. (2004). *Pikachu's Global Adventure: The Rise and Fall of Pokémon*. Duke University Press.

Watson, J. B. (1924) *Behaviorism* (1st ed.). People's Institute.

Whistlecroft, C. (2016) *Pokémon Go* causes an actual security alert at a Leicestershire police station – this is madness! *Blog: Video Games, Digital Spy*. Available at: https://www.digitalspy.com/videogames/pokemon/a801552/pokemon-go-causes-security-alert-leicestershire-police-station/

York, J., deHaan, J., Childs, M., and Collins, M. (2022) How is gamification like being trapped in the Matrix? And what is the 'real-world' of game-based learning *Digital Culture and Education*, 14:3, 35-54. Available at: https://www.digitalcultureandeducation.com/volume-143-papers/how-is-gamification-like-being-trapped-in-the-matrix-and-what-is-the-real-world-of-game-based-learning?

*I've learned my lesson, can I come out now?*

Scan the QR code to listen to the podcast episode

**CHAPTER 8:**

# WAS YODA AN EFFECTIVE SUPPLY TEACHER (AND WOULD HE HAVE BEEN BETTER IF HE'D USED BARAK ROSENSHINE'S TEN PRINCIPLES OF INSTRUCTION)?

*Mark Childs, Mike Collins and Rebecca Ferguson*

*As Mikezilla and Beckzilla emerge from the city, Markzilla finally catches up with them. Mikezilla turns to him and says, gleefully: 'I've learned so much about Behaviourism! Look, here's a guide book I bought in the gift shop when I left. It explains so many of the city's cognitive structures. It's by Barak Rosenshine, it's really neat.'*

*Markzilla flicks through the book, scanning the bullet points. 'Yeah, there's some good stuff in here. But ... hmm, some doubts I have. Tell you about them, I shall.'*

This chapter is another one that uses the example of *Star Wars*, mainly because we liked the idea of Yoda as supply teacher, as he is forced to come out of retirement against his will to step up to teach Luke Skywalker when Luke's previous teacher is no longer able to do the job. We're also looking at a set of principles that has become widespread as key basic guidelines for teachers who want to teach effectively and efficiently. We discuss why we're not exactly on board with the idea that the principles cover all the basics, but they're a good place to start. We're interested in finding out: **Was Yoda an effective supply teacher (and would he have been better if he'd used Barak Rosenshine's ten principles of instruction)?**

It's a slight change to our usual format, in that we don't have a section on the pop-cultural thing we're using as an example, but just jump straight into applying the ten principles to Yoda's teaching style. We talked about *Star Wars* at length in Chapter 4, and it's a safe bet everyone knows who Yoda is, anyway. We've provided a brief recap of the key points, though, in case you skipped Chapter 4 and/or have been living on Tattooine for the last 46 years.

## The ten principles

Barak Rosenshine was an emeritus professor of educational psychology in the College of Education at the University of Illinois at Urbana-Champaign when he published his ten principles in *American Educator* back in 2012. Since then, he's extended the list to 17 principles.

A key part of Rosenshine's approach is declared in his subtitle for the article, *Research-Based Strategies That All Teachers Should Know*. Rosenshine calls these 'classroom practices of master teachers', which he unpacks with the care heavily associated with the positivist end of the scale as far as evidence goes, although the article itself doesn't cite any research data.

1. Begin a lesson with a short review of previous learning.
2. Present new material in small steps with students practising after each step.
3. Ask a large number of questions and check the responses of all students.
4. Provide models and worked examples to help students learn to solve problems, using frameworks to hang ideas on.
5. Guide student practice.
6. Check students' understanding
7. Obtain a high success rate.
8. Provide scaffolds for difficult tasks.
9. Require and monitor independent practice.
10. Engage students in weekly and monthly review.

The links to cognitive science are apparent in that some of these principles draw on behaviourist ideas about giving immediate feedback, while others are concerned with how memory is laid down in the brain – review at certain points can help reinforce learning. Memory is key for learning. The more information we have available for immediate recall, the lower the cognitive load (covered in the next chapter) when we are learning new information and the more links that are available on which to build further connections.

Memory is built effectively through reiteration, so including these approaches is vital. Most people will have found it's the material that's reiterated, and employed, that stays in the mind. With Mikezilla it's *Warhammer 40000* stats, with Markzilla it's (classic) *Doctor Who*. Things that haven't been thought about for a decade or more spring instantly to mind because, for a period, they were recalled on a regular basis. If we want students to recall massive amounts of useless trivia, this is exactly the approach we should take in the classroom.

That's the strength of these approaches. However, Rosenshine's principles surface the problem with an approach based on how the brain most efficiently acquires information. If it's used exhaustively, or exclusively, it can have a detrimental effect on learning. Unless the principles are applied imaginatively, they're demotivating because they're really, *really*, boring.

When we looked at the various approaches to learning in the previous section, we pointed to the issues associated with taking only one approach to learning and teaching (we'll look at the issues with purely constructivist approaches in the final chapter in this section). There's nothing in the ten principles about going off and doing things, making things, creating things, or talking to other students. These aren't a core part of Rosenshine's strategies, because they aren't evidenced in a positivist way by our knowledge of how memory is laid down in the brain.

A core part of learning is acquiring skills, which usually requires enacting them. The main skill you develop by reading a book is how to read – learning isn't a simple process of transferring information from one mind to another. But it is in part that process. Acquiring knowledge from others creates a strong basis on which to build skills, but it is only a basis. Memorising reams of information and formulae in the way that a lot of education requires of learners is like flint-knapping, a skill that's time consuming and no longer necessary, since every piece of information we could ever need is literally at our fingertips if we have a phone and an unrestricted Internet connection to hand. Learners need to acquire essential knowledge that they can draw on as they build their skills, but additional knowledge is almost certainly stored within easy reach – what learners need are the skills to access that information, assess it and, where appropriate, employ it.

With those caveats in mind, we'll explore the principles in more depth.

## Principle 1: begin a lesson with a short review of previous learning.

Daily review can strengthen previous learning and improve recall, and it's essential if the day's learning builds on the previous day's knowledge. If a student hasn't got the foundational material straight in their mind, the step that builds on that material isn't going to be understood. In addition, if learners must make an effort to recall what they have learned in the past at the same time as they are taking new knowledge on board, then this creates extra work and adds to their cognitive load. Where this departs from a constructivist approach to building on previous knowledge is that Rosenshine refers to knowledge as a set of principles to be understood, rather than as a set of principles that will be learned and understood in different ways by different students.

An issue with this is that, particularly when teaching at secondary level, if you see students only once a week, then the chances are they will have forgotten a lot of what was talked about in the previous session, because when you're 12 a week is a very long time. Applying this principle can mean spending a lot of time revisiting what's gone before without making any progress. The importance of this as a tip is the implication it contains – getting through the material is not as important as laying the right foundations. Without reiteration, establishing and re-establishing the information the students need to know, they will not learn new things effectively. You may get through the syllabus, but the amount learned by the students will be much less than it could be.

## Principle 2: present new material in small steps with students practising after each step.

Don't overwhelm students, introduce new ideas a few at a time, asking more questions and adding activities as part of that process. The idea is that you only can learn so much, and what you learn depends on your starting point. Video games are very good at this, introducing new skills incrementally, and giving players opportunities to practise those skills before moving on. It's the same in class. Rather than presenting a large amount of information at once in a video or lecture, or as a large amount of text, it's more effective to provide a small amount, discuss or think about it, produce some output that requires it to be processed in some way, then continue.

## Principle 3: ask a large number of questions and check the responses of all students.

Questioning helps students make use of new information and connect materials prior to learning more. It also determines how well the material has been learnt before moving on. However, it's difficult, particularly with larger classes, to ensure everyone has a chance to respond to questions. One option is to use response software (originally through clickers and now through mobile phones) to check the understanding of an entire class by using multiple-choice questions and seeing how many get the answers right.

A low-tech way of doing this is to ask students to write the answers on paper or small whiteboards and hold the answers up for the teacher to scan quickly. Alternatively, by asking students to come up with a response in small groups, you can create opportunities for students to teach each other if one student has an answer and others don't or some have the wrong answer and others the right one. Lack of consensus within a group helps to identify misunderstandings that can be raised with the class as a whole.

One reason for checking everybody's learning and understanding while going through a lesson is that you can repeat part of the learning if necessary. This is a fantastic principle but incredibly hard to implement if the class includes learners with a wide range of abilities.

Rosenshine suggests using group activities to address this challenge, since these enable the students who have understood the most to consolidate their knowledge by supporting students who require further explanation. Another option is for each student to write down what they think the answer may be and pass their response along in a circular group activity. This becomes a community learning process in which students talk to each other about their responses, giving them a safe space in which to self-assess without calling out to an entire class, which can be hugely intimidating.

The most limited of the suggestions by Rosenshine is probably choral responses, when students shout the answers to the question together as a group. It sounds Dickensian but there's some evidence it works for learning in particular situations, such as language learning in schools (Heward et al, 1989). However, it would probably meet with resistance if physics undergraduates were asked to learn the names of bosons and leptons in this way.

An issue with all these techniques is that employing them too frequently or too slowly, for example by testing the knowledge of each student separately, will frustrate students who are ready to move on. They're likely to be banging their heads against the desk in frustration because they are so bored by the time you've finished checking the learning of the entire class.

## Principle 4: provide models and worked examples to help students learn to solve problems, using frameworks to hang ideas on.

One of the problems with learning any new area is that starting with the details doesn't work. Learners need a map of what the whole subject area looks like, so they know where specific areas fit.

An issue with some distance-learning practices is that learners can be let loose on a subject, reading around various elements, without an overview of the domain and how it's structured. Without a deeper knowledge of the subject discipline, it's often difficult to make sense of the material. It makes sense to present material in a linear way (Verheij et al, 1996) to facilitate this initial surface processing. Once that is done, and deeper processing is possible, then you can let learners loose on the whole domain. Without a decent taxonomy of the overall set of ideas, it's more difficult for learners to work out where they are at any point. They need a map, or they get lost, so the fourth principle is very helpful.

## Principle 5: guide student practice.

Successful teachers spend more time guiding students' practice of new material. Students need to internalise material by rephrasing, summarising and elaborating on it to rehearse and make connections. This links back to the second principle, presenting new materials in small steps. This all makes sense, but Rosenshine limits his examples to guided practice plus repetition of guided practice, without learners doing the same practice independently. The principle doesn't address teaching students to develop their own practice through open exploration and reflection, skills that are essential once students have finished their courses.

## Principle 6: check students' understanding.

The longer a misunderstanding persists, the bigger an issue this presents for learning. With younger children, a lot of what a teacher does involves addressing erroneous ideas the children have acquired. People build up, particularly around science, mental models that aren't accurate, but are based on perceptions of the world around them. Sadly, a lot of these erroneous ideas persist to the point where teachers retain and perpetuate them, if they're not addressed during teacher education (Ferrero et al, 2020).

A good example of this is one Beckzilla uses: projectile motion. If you throw a ball into the air, why does it stop moving upwards and fall to Earth? Children, and many adults, typically believe it is because somehow the initial impetus is used up. This feels like common sense, because the harder you throw the ball, the further it travels before beginning its descent. The only visible force that acts on it is the action of the thrower. However, the real answer is that the ball is acted on by gravity and friction. The idea that the initial impetus is used up is a common misunderstanding that arises because children are employing an intuitive interpretation of their direct observation rather than a scientific framework (Hynd et al, 1997). Checking on misunderstandings and then addressing these directly is essential for progress; to pre-empt the next section of this chapter, students must unlearn what they have learned.

## Principle 7: obtain a high success rate (this is a cracker of a principle!)

For learners, this relates to operant conditioning (see the chapter on behaviourism and *Pokémon Go*). If learners receive immediate feedback telling them they've responded correctly, they feel good, carry on trying, and maybe try harder because their behaviour is being rewarded. They'll be more engaged and more motivated because they're succeeding. The principle is the same in games. If you're winning a game, you want to play more. If you die ten times in a row, you're going to give up. The success rate Rosenshine cites in his principles is 80%. This was the best tip

Markzilla remembers from his teacher training in Cardiff. One of his lecturers gave the example from his own experience of teaching the lowest ability group at maths and getting them to a point where they were succeeding more than the group placed above them academically, simply by making the tests easy enough for them to score 80% (Fontana, 1995).

Of course, in a classroom with a wide range of abilities, many students will be getting low grades while some are scoring above 90%. In effect, you're aiming for the majority to succeed four times out of five, or 80% of the time.

From a practical point of view, this approach fails when learners are assessed by an external examination system. At that point the score achieved by lower ability learners drops and they become hugely disillusioned. It's a difficult set of competing pressures; the core principle of 80% motivates students to carry on learning, but it can lull them into a false sense of security, believing they're doing better than they really are.

The difference here is between criterion-referenced assessment, where learners work to meet specified goals, and norm-referenced assessment, which compares their progress to the norm for a much larger group (see Chapter 3 for more on this). The students may make fantastic progress from a criterion-referenced perspective, but if they are starting from a low baseline, they may be unable to attain the norm for their age group. Not only that, but if all the previously low-achieving students in the country do well, then the norm is raised. However much progress learners make, norm-referenced assessment will show that half are above average in demonstrating they've achieved the standards the institution has set in the form the institution wants them demonstrated, and half are below average.

As an aside we should draw your attention to the slight wordiness of the last sentence in that paragraph. Whatever assessment you choose, it's worth remembering it's not actually demonstrating learning, it's demonstrating the learning the institution has selected as important, in the form it's chosen to assess it in, using the tools (and overcoming the barriers) the institution has put in place. The best you can say is that it's the most effective proxy for identifying the actual learning, but always bear in mind it's not the same thing.

## Principle 8: provide scaffolds for difficult tasks.

The teacher shares a temporary scaffold to help students achieve something challenging. For example, a teacher might show students how to read and make notes on an article by drawing a central box and writing the article title within it, skim-reading the article, writing each main idea in a box below the central box, adding two to four important details under each idea, then summarising.

After the teacher has taken students through the framework on several occasions, they should be able to do this themselves, so there is no more need for the teacher to scaffold the task.

## Principle 9: require and monitor independent practice.

Students need extensive successful practice for skills and knowledge to become automatic. During this phase, not only should a teacher scaffold the work, but they should also check constantly that the student is handling the work.

## Finally, Principle 10: engage students in weekly and monthly review.

Rehearsal is the key to getting things locked into memory so they are remembered and can be used at appropriate times. This is explored further in the chapter that follows (*Hitchhiker's Guide* and cognitive load).

The essential elements of this principle are that, by forming and repeating connections between memories and associations, memories are recalled more effectively and are moved from working memory to long-term memory. Working memory only has limited capacity and does not store information for long, whereas long-term memory can hold a lot of information indefinitely. When information is shifted to long-term memory, this frees working memory to process new information and make more connections.

Although there are ten principles overall, the essential elements are *modelling, scaffolding, reviewing,* and *rehearsing*. All these elements contribute to an effective way of acquiring knowledge effectively.

Having broken down the ten principles, we'll frame them in the context of the ultimate supply teacher, Yoda, in order to answer the question: **Was Yoda an effective supply teacher (and would he have been better if Barak Rosenshine's ten principles of instruction he'd used, hmmm)?**

## *Star Wars* and Yoda

We covered the long and multi-faceted narrative of *Star Wars* in Chapters 4 and 5 (Jar Jar Binks and ontology). Here, we're focusing on the first two films to be released: *Star Wars* (1977), later retitled Star Wars: *Episode IV A New Hope*, and *Star Wars: Episode V The Empire Strikes Back* (1980). As the prequels and then interquels made the numbering system increasingly difficult to follow, both have since been re-retitled to remove the episode numbers.

*Star Wars: A New Hope* focuses on the story of Luke Skywalker, who is caught up in a quest to deliver plans for a Death Star to the good guys (the Rebel Alliance), while being chased by the bad guys (the Empire). He comes across an elderly Jedi knight called Obi-Wan Kenobi who teaches him the ways of the mystical Force. He also learns his father was killed by the villainous Darth Vader. On the quest Obi-Wan is then killed by Darth Vader.

In *The Empire Strikes Back*, Luke continues his schooling under a new Jedi Master called Yoda (a metre-tall green individual of an unnamed species). And, plot twist, when he quits his schooling to face Darth Vader, he finds out that Darth Vader is his father. That's possibly the biggest spoiler in film history but, as we mentioned in the podcast episode, if you haven't watched the movies by now, you're probably never going to watch them.

It's also worth noting that, as it's Luke's father who kills his teacher, *A New Hope* contains possibly the worst-ever meeting of a parent-teacher association.

It's because Yoda has to take over from Obi-Wan after Obi-Wan is killed that we're referring to him as a supply teacher, though it's worth mentioning that as: 'There is no death, there is the Force,' Obi-Wan turns up occasionally as a ghost to dispense more words of wisdom. He also comes up with an explanation for why, when he told Luke that Darth Vader killed Luke's father, he somehow mixed up the words 'killed' and 'is'.

## The answer

The following tables (see overleaf) examines how many of Rosenshine's principles Yoda applies as a supply teacher (rather than just getting out the telly on wheels and the VHS player, then putting on a film for everybody to watch[1]. ).

---

1. Non-Boomers should fill in their own supply-teacher example at this point. Perhaps dusting off a tablet that hasn't seen a software update since before COVID, or a treasure hunt for an HDMI cable.

| Rosenshine's principles | Yoda's teaching strategies |
|---|---|
| Does Yoda begin each lesson with a short review of previous learning? | No, he basically leaves Luke to find his own way with a bit of extra guidance here and there. |
| Does Yoda present new material in small steps with student practice afterwards? | No, in fact he gives quite a long monologue at one point.[1] |
| Does Yoda ask a large number of questions and check responses of all students? | No, in fact he doesn't check understanding at any point, even though he only has one student. |
| Does Yoda provide models? | Both the Jedi – including Yoda – and their opponents, the Sith, use a cognitive apprenticeship model for learning. The master models particular behaviour, which the student then has to adopt. |

*Table 8.1 Yoda's applied principles*

---

1. 'Size matters not. Look at me. Judge me by my size, do you? Hmm? Hmm. And well you should not. For my ally is the Force, and a powerful ally it is. Life creates it, makes it grow. Its energy surrounds us and binds us. Luminous beings are we, not this crude matter. You must feel the Force around you; here, between you, me, the tree, the rock, everywhere, yes. Even between the land and the ship.'

| Rosenshine's principles | Yoda's teaching strategies |
|---|---|
| Does Yoda guide student practice? | Not really. There's a scene where Luke gets a feeling that there's something inside a tree. He goes inside it and then finds he's fighting Darth Vader, but when he strikes off Darth Vader's helmet, he sees his own face. He learns from this, but there's no guidance from Yoda, who is sitting outside, drawing things with a stick. In the NPR radio version, Luke thinks about the significance and concludes, 'My enemy's face is my own', but Yoda doesn't lead him to that conclusion. Or even ask what on Earth (or, rather, Dagobah) that even means. |
| Does Yoda check student understanding? | He asks some questions. But he doesn't allow Luke to ask questions, so he doesn't allow Luke the opportunity to identify the guidance he needs. |
| Does Yoda obtain a high success rate? | Well, yes, in that Luke does become a Jedi by the end of the first act of *Return of the Jedi*. That's a 100% success rate. |

*Table 8.1 Yoda's applied principles (continued)*

| Rosenshine's principles | Yoda's teaching strategies |
|---|---|
| Does Yoda provide scaffolds for difficult tasks? | No. The training he provides is experiential learning but without any scaffolding. Unless you count the advice, 'Try not. Do or do not. There is no try.' |
| Does Yoda monitor independent practice? | Luke is required to be an independent learner, but without any real framework that helps him to find his own way. |
| Does Yoda engage students in weekly and monthly review? | No, in fact his one student drops out before completing his training. |

*Table 8.1 Yoda's applied principles (continued)*

From the table we can see that Yoda would fail any teaching assessment, he's not prime material for a teacher training course and, if he lived in the UK, he certainly wouldn't be in line for Fellowship of the Higher Education Academy.

In his defence, the entire structure of the training regime had been destroyed (and the student base murdered) 22 years previously, as shown in the prequel *Return of the Sith*.

Also, much of the curriculum is based on the concept of the Force, which is a vague ephemeral thing that is never properly defined: your own model of what it is might not necessarily be somebody else's because it's dependent upon a personal connection. Overall, Yoda definitely does not apply the ten principles.

Possibly the worst example of scaffolding teaching is when Luke is trying to lift his X-Wing out of the swamp with his mind. When he gives up, instead of breaking down the task into a sequence of more straightforward elements, Yoda simply lifts the X-Wing himself, mainly, it seems, to put Luke in his place.

When Luke reacts, 'I don't believe it,' Yoda puts the pedagogical boot in further by responding, 'That is why you fail.' A great scene, but a very demotivating teaching approach. From a behaviourist perspective, Yoda is much more in favour of acting to discourage failure than of acting to encourage success.

On the other hand, the teacher who Yoda replaced, Obi-Wan Kenobi, does a much better job of teaching before he dies. He continues to outshine Yoda as a teacher even after his death, which must rankle. Obi-Wan adopts an effective apprenticeship model in which he presents activities and then encourages Luke to copy them.

For example, when Luke is struggling to let go of his conscious thoughts, Obi-Wan suggests he should wear a helmet with the blast visor down and attempt the action again in a controlled safe environment, as opposed to chucking him into the middle of a swamp full of monsters and asking him to pull an X-Wing out of it. Obi-Wan applies some of Rosenshine's principles and includes experiential elements, encouraging his student to undertake practice and then guiding that practice.

The approach Yoda should really have taken was to suggest to Luke that he should try moving a small rock, then a larger one, then a boulder, moving him up to X-Wing-sized rocks before setting him off on the actual X-Wing.

After that, he could have presented the mental model, which is that size matters not, the difference is in the mind, therefore all your concepts about mass and weight are your own impositions. Ultimately, by the beginning of the Dark Empire trilogy, Luke is moving Star Destroyers with his mind, so he does learn eventually.

But the initial approach, 'Try this massive leap in ability, then gloat when your student can't do it,' is bound to destroy a learner's confidence. Something we'll return to in Chapter 13 (BeanDad and constructivism).

In short, to answer our question – no, Yoda was not an effective supply teacher and, at some point, someone at the Jedi Academy should have pointed him in the direction of the ten principles – or whatever the equivalent would have been a long time ago in a galaxy far, far away.

## Tips for practice

In summary, for guidance, Rosenshine's tips are an entirely practical set of principles. As far as they go, they work well at creating effective and efficient learning opportunities. But there's a lot more to learning than acquiring knowledge efficiently and effectively.

It's also worth pointing out that one of the reasons why Obi-Wan Kenobi is such a good teacher is that he colossally failed at teaching 20 years earlier (one of his padawans was Anakin Skywalker, who went completely off the deep end). Reflecting on our mistakes, and becoming better because of them, is also something we can draw on when planning our own teaching.

## Don't barrack, just rise and shine (and reference)

Ferrero, M., Konstantinidis, E., and Vadillo, M.A. (2020) An attempt to correct erroneous ideas among teacher education students: the effectiveness of refutation texts. *Frontiers in Psychology*, 9 October 2020. Available at: https://doi.org/10.3389/fpsyg.2020.577738

Fontana, D. (1995) *Psychology for Teachers*. London: Macmillan.

Heward, W., Courson, F. & Narayan, J. (1989) Using choral responding to increase active student response. *Teaching Exceptional Children*, Spring 1989, pp. 72-75. Available at: https://journals.sagepub.com/doi/pdf/10.1177/004005998902100321

Hynd, C., Alvermann, D. & Qian, G. (1997) Preservice elementary school teachers' conceptual change about projectile motion: Refutation text, demonstration, affective factors, and relevance. *Science Education*, 81(1), pp. 1-27.

Rosenshine, B. (2012) Principles of instruction: Research-based strategies that all teachers should know. *American Educator*, Spring 2012. Available at: https://www.aft.org/sites/default/files/periodicals/Rosenshine.pdf

Verheij, J., Stoutjesdijk, E., & Beishuizen, J. (1996) Search and study strategies in hypertext, *Computers in Human Behavior*, Volume 12, Issue 1, 1996, pp. 1-15, ISSN 0747-5632, Available at: https://doi.org/10.1016/0747-5632(95)00015-1

Scan the QR code to listen to the podcast episode

## CHAPTER 9:

# HOW DOES THE HITCHHIKER'S GUIDE TO THE GALAXY HELP ARTHUR DENT TAKE A COGNITIVE LOAD OFF?

*Mark Childs, Mike Collins and Mark Williams*

As the three Zillas are leaving the capital city of Behaviourism, clutching their Rosenshine guidebook, they see a pathway to the mines beneath the city.

'That must be where you can see the foundations of Behaviourism,' says Mike, in awe. 'The cognitive architecture the Dwarves keep banging on about.'

'It's dark, though,' Markzilla observed. 'They've delved too greedily and too deep.'

'Never fear, I bought more than one guide in the city.' Mikezilla stuffs Rosenshine's text in his backpack and holds up a small device. 'Markzilla of the Williams clan has produced a guide to cognitive load that will show us the way.'

We've noted in previous chapters that understanding how the brain functions is key to getting your teaching right. That includes the reward system that can motivate learners, and the ways in which thoughts are processed and memories stored. It's those latter brain functions we're looking at here, and the idea of cognitive load and how it can limit and support learning. We're also digging into *The Hitchhiker's Guide to the Galaxy*, which is another of those narratives that seems to crop up in multiple formats and in multiple versions. We'll be mainly looking at (listening to?) the radio series, as that's how it all started, and asking a question that relates to the central character: **How does *The Hitchhiker's Guide to the Galaxy* help Arthur Dent take a cognitive load off?**

## *The Hitchhiker's Guide to the Galaxy*

For those of you not familiar with it, we should first explain what *The Hitchhiker's Guide to the Galaxy* is. It was originally a radio series, released as six episodes in 1978, which were then adapted into books, and then a towel, and then a play, a text-based computer game, then a TV series, and then an LP [vinyl] and some comic books. Then follow-up novels. Then it was adapted again into a film. And the novels were adapted into more radio series. There's even a huge coffee-table book with photographs of people re-enacting scenes from the radio series.

The episodes that made up that first radio series are about a guy who survives the explosion of the Earth because he escapes with the help of his friend, who turns out to be from Betelgeuse (and not from Guildford after all). That's Arthur Dent and Ford Prefect, respectively. Ford and Arthur then travel around the galaxy trying to find the ultimate question to which the ultimate answer is 42. They're helped on their way by a useful little Guide, which pre-empted Wikipedia-on-your-iPad by about 30 years. The Guide interjects useful pieces of information into the narrative, which is useful for exposition, but also adds lots of short stories and philosophical observations along the way.

## Cognitive load

Next up, let's break down what cognitive load is. The theory was popularised back in 1988 by John Sweller. It's got deep roots in neuroscience and cognitive science, so you find it cropping up all over the place in other bits of pedagogic theory and modelling. The critical bits are that it's about the division between working memory and long-term memory and the concept that working memory is finite and that you must account for this. When you're trying to teach people, filling their working memory means that they'll struggle to acquire new concepts.

To back-pedal slightly, working memory contains a small amount of things you hold in your mind for a short time – typically, 5-9 pieces or chunks of information. For example, you might be able to remember the digits in a friend's phone number while you open your contacts app, but most people would struggle to remember the digits in two or three phone numbers in that way. Long-term memory, on the other hand, can hold an enormous amount of information for a lifetime. One of the challenges when you're learning is to shift new information and knowledge from working memory to long-term memory.

An excellent book on CLT (to minimise your cognitive load, we should explain that's short for Cognitive Load Theory), if you're interested in finding out more, is one put together by Jan Plass, Roxana Moreno and Roland Brünken (2010). It really digs into the empirical evidence for much of this. And regarding empirical evidence, there's a lot of it based on cognitive science and evolutionary theory. CLT generates principles that can be tested by experiment and that are reproducible across a wide number of disciplines and learning environments, which is why it's the touchstone for a lot of the positivists, like Barack Rosenshine, who you encountered in the previous chapter.

Cognitive load can be divided into three types.

- **Intrinsic load** is due to how difficult the materials are for the learner
- **Extraneous load** is additional complexity due to the way the materials are designed
- **Germane load** is the amount of mental effort required by the learner to learn the thing you're teaching.

Cognitive load isn't a fixed amount – we vary in the amount we can handle – but there's a capacity limitation. We can reduce the amount of cognitive load of learning by using schema, which is how the learning is structured.

Like the causes of cognitive load, schema can be divided into three elements; there's the direct initial instruction – which can be dismissed as spoon feeding – but the theory says spoon feeding is good, at least at first. There's the expertise principle, which says that if you already know a lot, it's easier to add new information, and there's the small step-size of knowledge change principle, so you break the learning down into manageable chunks. As the Swahili proverb says, 'haba na haba hujaza kibaba[1]'. The ways in which learners gather and process information make a difference too.

So, there's a lot going on, and lots of teaching strategies that can avoid hitting that capacity limit. And it gets more complicated when we look at how we deal with more than one student at a time, because what works for one student won't work for another. A good example of this is something that Slava Kalyuga (2014) calls

---

1. Little by little fills the pot. We upped the intrinsic load there for all non-Swahili speakers.

the expertise reversal principle. Basically, what works for a newbie (lots of additional explanatory stuff) just adds to the extraneous cognitive load for someone who already knows it. Of course, you can overcome this problem with online multimedia by making it individually adaptive. In a classroom, you can adapt the learning to suit individuals, but the larger the class the more difficult it is to do this.

Students also differ in their ability to process visual information due to their spatial ability, so showing visualisations to some students will hit their cognitive load limit, whereas the same visualisations might not overload others. To complicate things, cognitive load acts in combination with perceptual load (Naert et al, 2018) which is the amount of information you can pay attention to at once. Metacognitive skills can help reduce the germane cognitive load but the downside, and we'll see this in Chapter 13, is that 'thinking about your thinking' competes with just 'thinking' for capacity in the working memory.

Three more effects worth thinking about, if we haven't reached your capacity limit already, are the modality effect, the redundancy effect and automation. The modality effect is that, if you present information in more than one mode, it's easier to learn it. The redundancy effect is that extraneous information interferes with learning (you may have found that as you tracked down to the footnote to understand the Swahili proverb).

But the tool that is most valuable in reducing cognitive load is automation. Automation is the unconscious processing of knowledge. Although it involves thinking, because that thinking isn't conscious it doesn't add to your cognitive load. The more lower level schemata you have in your head, the easier it is to process higher level schemata. So, for example, unconsciously knowing the plural of 'schema' so you don't have to think about it, means that you have more capacity to think about what you're writing, rather than needing to concentrate on how to pluralise the words you're using (Sweller, 2010). We'll see this as a core part of the criticisms of problem-based learning in Chapter 11.

Automation is helped by repetition, and much of the construction of learning taking CLT into account ultimately boils down to that division between working memory and long-term memory (or learnt memory), because you can't squeeze too much into the processing or working memory. An effective schema keeps the demand on the working memory to a minimum while building up the unconscious memory. If you bash too many concepts together in too brief a period, while you're still trying to process what one thing means, you've got another thing in collision with it. There's then no way to bring those two separate ideas together to form the actual overlying overriding concept. As a result, you just get lost.

## In which we criticise much of academic writing

When we recorded the podcast on which this chapter is based, Markzilla of the Williams clan started by quoting a piece of *The Hitchhiker's Guide to the Galaxy: Earth Edition*, which goes like this:

> *Sesquipedalian Obscurantism: One who is inordinately infatuated with polysyllabic obfuscation, preferring never to employ a less complicated syntactic arrangement of descriptive words when there exists a single expressive unit that amalgamates the multiplicity of morphemes comprising the simpler phrase. Among the manifold objectives of multisyllabic, holophrastic verbalism are those of: rendering the author's meaning indisputably precise yet simultaneously incomprehensible; demonstrating through superior orthography and lexical awareness that the writer is manifestly more erudite than the reader; disempowering intellectual challenge to the proponent's argument by using logomachinations to divert discussion to the establishment of*

*the opponent's comprehension of the vocabulary as opposed to addressing the factual import of the treatise which, upon analysis, may well prove amphigorous. The obscurantist sesquipedalian is likely to compound the reader's difficulties by indulging in glossosynthesis, thus enabling the author to dismiss all opposing views as ultracrepidarious. In other words, a sesquipedalian is one who would call a spade a manuo-pedal excavationary implement.*

Saavik2 (2001)

Despite the excellent oratory skills exhibited by Markzilla W, it was pretty difficult to figure out what the passage was trying to say, though basically it just means that cognitive overload is used deliberately by some people, particularly academics, to ward off any criticism by sounding impressive, a technique that is particularly useful when the actual argument is thin. For some excellent examples of this, take a look at *Fashionable Nonsense* by Alan Sokal and Jean Bricmont (1998), incidentally published by the same people who published *The Hitchhiker's Guide to the Galaxy*. If you find any examples of sesquipedalian obscurantism in this book, please contact the authors and we'll find a way to clarify what we've written.

It's worth saying, though, that overwhelming people with terminology isn't always intentional. Sometimes it's done because the person doing it already has in their learnt memory knowledge of what those words or phrases mean. They draw on that information when communicating and they forget that other people don't have the same store of knowledge to draw on. We see the same thing with non-academics inventing words or, worse, changing the meaning of existing words, which is counter-productive because it adds to the cognitive load of everyone you're trying to communicate with. Again, by providing a schema, ideally explaining the words or phrases for people who may be unfamiliar with them, you can help reduce cognitive load. Or, and this applies to learning in general, check understanding or knowledge, and give people a chance to reflect on new knowledge before moving on to the next bit. The danger here, though, is that you run into the potential for appearing patronising and hitting the expertise reversal principle.

Finally, and something that brings in a whole range of other elements, such as fun, playfulness and so on, is the potential to make learning feel like less effort (or, in CLT terms, to reduce germane load) by making it fun, making the environment more comfortable, or creating rapport with the learners. If they're thinking about how they're going to pay their bills, or are occupied by how much their back aches because of the chair they're sitting on, or are feeling annoyed because you've just patronised them, that's all going to impact on their ability to process information. Which is why it can sometimes feel that you're caught in one of two feedback loops – either the students are comfortable because they're understanding things, which improves their capacity to understand new things, or you're making them feel stupid, which ultimately does actually make them more stupid.

> *Cognitive load is one of those nifty concepts that changed how I understood my own previous experiences of learning, and how I've looked at it since. One of the weird quirks I've noticed working in and around education is that cognitive load is often ignored in staff-to-staff learning, where we inflict brain-filling infodumps on one another that we would never consider trying to cram into student heads. Then we wonder why everyone forgets processes or what 'GDPR' stands for. ~Mikezilla*

To practise what we preach, we've tried to reduce your cognitive load with the following diagram summing up the key points.

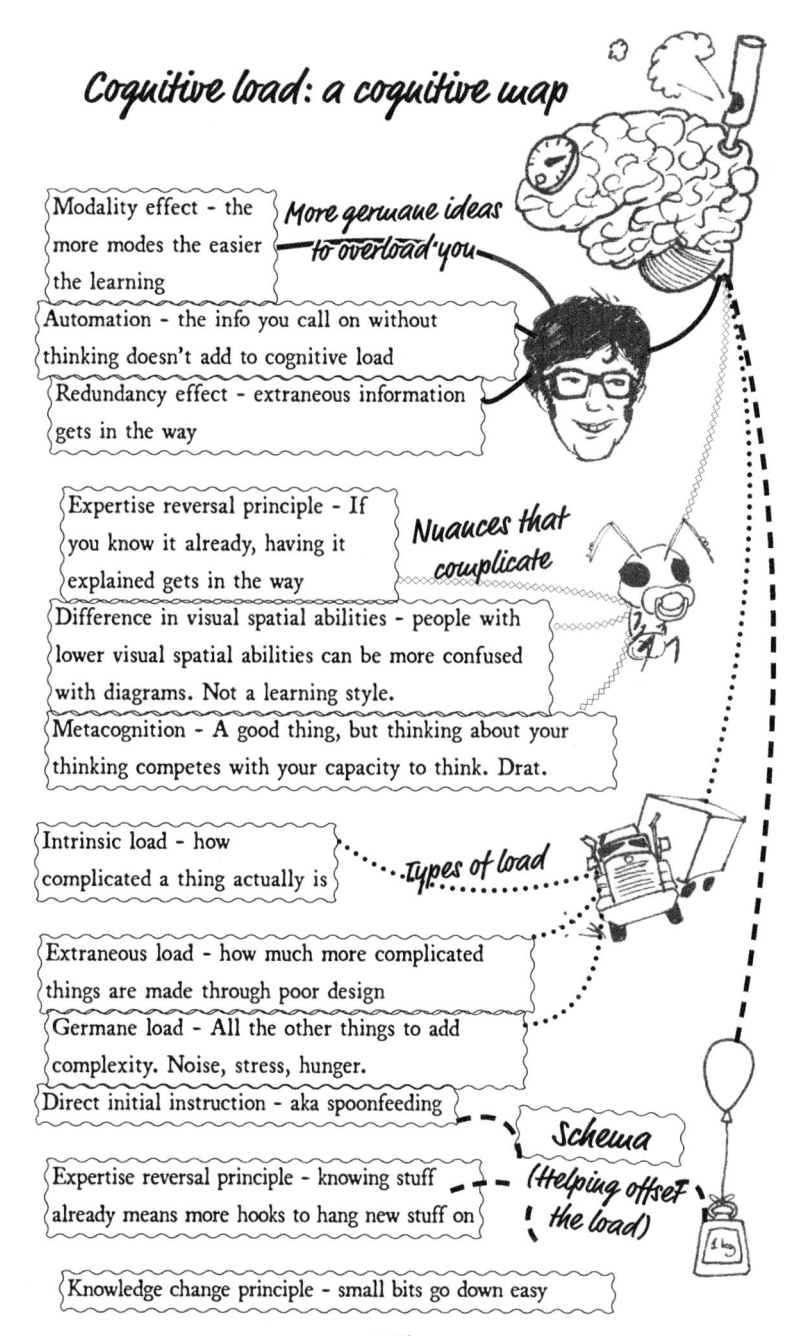

9: COGNITIVE LOAD AND *THE HITCHHIKER'S GUIDE TO THE GALAXY*

## Cognitive load: a cognitive map

*More germane ideas to overload you*

- Modality effect - the more modes the easier the learning
- Automation - the info you call on without thinking doesn't add to cognitive load
- Redundancy effect - extraneous information gets in the way

*Nuances that complicate*

- Expertise reversal principle - If you know it already, having it explained gets in the way
- Difference in visual spatial abilities - people with lower visual spatial abilities can be more confused with diagrams. Not a learning style.
- Metacognition - A good thing, but thinking about your thinking competes with your capacity to think. Drat.

*Types of load*

- Intrinsic load - how complicated a thing actually is
- Extraneous load - how much more complicated things are made through poor design
- Germane load - All the other things to add complexity. Noise, stress, hunger.
- Direct initial instruction - aka spoonfeeding

*Schema (Helping offset the load)*

- Expertise reversal principle - knowing stuff already means more hooks to hang new stuff on
- Knowledge change principle - small bits go down easy

135

## The answer

So, how does *The Hitchhiker's Guide to the Galaxy* help Arthur Dent take a cognitive load off? Arthur is first introduced to the Guide when he's transported to the flagship of the Vogon constructor fleet, moments before it destroys the Earth (ostensibly to make way for a hyperspace bypass). When he arrives, he's at first unable to process anything. One moment he was holding onto a rock while an alien spacecraft floated overhead, the next he's on that spacecraft, in the sleeping quarters of the Dentrassi – a race of beings the Vogons hire to cook and mix drinks for them.

That's a lot to take in at once, Arthur is so overwhelmed by culture shock, he's not even in a position to start panicking. It's a completely alien environment, which is the point at which Ford Prefect gives him the book *The Hitchhiker's Guide to the Galaxy* and Arthur reads the following passage:

> *Here is what to do if you want to get a lift from a Vogon... forget it. They are one of the most unpleasant races in the galaxy – not actually evil, but bad tempered, bureaucratic, officious and callous. They wouldn't even lift a finger to save their grandmothers from the Ravenous Bugblatter Beast of Traal without orders signed in triplicate, sent in, sent back, queried, lost, found, subjected to public enquiry, lost again, and finally buried in soft peat for three months and recycled as firelighters. The best way to get a drink out of a Vogon is to stick your finger down his throat... and the best way to annoy him is to feed his grandmother to the Ravenous Bugblatter Beast of Traal. On no account allow a Vogon to read poetry at you.*

(Adams, 1979, 45)

Bit by bit, as he encounters new things on his journey, the book explains them for Arthur. So when he gets a Babel fish in his ear, the book tells him a little story about what the fish is for. When he sees the Dentrassi and tastes the food, he gets background information on what the Dentrassi are. Each new encounter is unpacked and contextualised. Obviously, this isn't just for Arthur Dent. This is a device for listeners, so they can understand more about this world as they're hearing it, as it's being told to them for the first time by actors such as Peter Jones or William Franklin or Rula Lenska.

Why do this? Well, anyone who's engaged with any fantasy or science fiction will know that a massive amount of different information is thrown at the reader, or the listener, or the viewer at once. Anyone who's written in these genres will know that finding a way to introduce that information gradually to the audience is a really difficult thing because, on the one hand, you could confuse people by not explaining it (intrinsic load) but, on the other hand, they could get bogged down by masses and masses of explanation (extraneous load).

This is why not only does *The Hitchhiker's Guide to the Galaxy* (the book in the radio show) do a great job of reducing the cognitive load on Arthur Dent, but also *The Hitchhiker's Guide* (the show itself) does a great job of reducing the cognitive load on the audience. It takes crucial bits of information, boils them down and presents them very simply. Nice easy language that's used to break complicated concepts into easy-to-understand gobbets has made *The Hitchhiker's Guide to the Galaxy* one of the most successful books of all time.

Of course, there are limits. In the quote on the previous page there's a reference to the Ravenous Bugblatter Beast of Traal (an animal that's so amazingly stupid it thinks that if you can't see it, it can't see you). In the entry on Vogons this isn't explained, but within the context you have enough information for it to make sense (it's something you could feed a grandmother to) and when you encounter it again on the entry on towels (you can wrap a towel around your head to hide from these creatures), you can add an additional layer of information to your schema on them. At no point do you need to be working out what a Bugblatter Beast is while you're also trying to learn something else.

As you can see, it's passing on information in bite-sized chunks, at the time that they're most useful, that enables Arthur to assimilate as he goes along, allowing him to continue to manoeuvre around the universe with more success and less anxiety. Though still with a great deal of anxiety.

The use of clear language in *The Hitchhiker's Guide* helps Arthur connect new information to the information he's already learned. This does two things. It strengthens his retention of the knowledge by connecting to his existing schemata (stuff he's already learned or stored in long-term memory). And, because he's not having to keep extra stuff in his working memory as it's referencing the long-term memory, it frees up space in his working memory to learn new things.

This is one of the reasons why just-in-time learning works effectively – you already have the context for the information (your need for it) and the information you receive is just enough to meet that need. These days, the internet on your phone does the same job – you need the information, you Google[2] it, and then read the Wikipedia entry, watch the YouTube video or import the manual to your book reader. If you were travelling round the galaxy, you'd probably be checking Tripadvisor all the time. In fact, that's what gave Douglas Adams the idea for *The Hitchhiker's Guide to the Galaxy*. He was lying drunk in a field in Innsbruck with his *Hitch-hiker's Guide to Europe* next to him, looking up at the stars and thinking, 'I wonder if there's a *Hitchhiker's Guide to the Galaxy?*' Confusingly for proof-readers,

---

[2] Alternative websites are available for all those mentioned in this paragraph.

he dropped the hyphen in the process of creating that guide (Roberts, 2014, 29-30).

The difference between a guide and a teacher is that, when you're using a guide, the process is very learner centred because you as the learner are choosing the bits of information you need at that particular time whereas, when you're teaching, you have a scheme (not a schema).

So **how does *The Hitchhiker's Guide to the Galaxy* help Arthur Dent take a cognitive load off?** By providing just the information he needs, providing a schema for that knowledge, and giving him no more than he needs, the Guide reduces the need for him to either develop his own schema or draw on information that's not in his working memory. In doing so, it frees his mind to focus on adjusting to his new situation, so he can get on and go straight to the panicking part.

## Tips for your own practice

First of all, be aware that there is a limit to the cognitive load of your students. You can't exceed it. You can try, but there's no point, because they won't be learning anything. Provide a schema for what you're doing, because that enables the information to be structured as you go along. Use small steps. Reiterate these to make sure the schema is going into long-term memory. Check understanding before you move on.

Once the information is automatic and your students can call on it unconsciously, you can build on it. But your students can't consciously hold the basic schema and build on it at the same time. We won't go into detail here about balancing cognitive and metacognitive elements – but we will dig into it more in our chapter on BeanDad (Chapter 13).

Finally, cut down on the extraneous load elements. If you're online and learners are struggling with the interface, that's going to get in the way of their learning. If learners are offline and they're uncomfortable or have competing demands on their attention, do what you can to create a more comfortable environment, or to reduce the amount of content. You have limited cognitive load capacity if you have an aching pain in all the diodes down your left side. Unless you have a brain the size of a planet, that is.

## Life, the universe and references

Adams, D. (1979) *The Hitchhiker's Guide to the Galaxy*, Pan Books, UK: London

Kalyuga, S. (2014) The expertise reversal principle in multimedia learning. In R. Mayer (Ed.), *The Cambridge Handbook of Multimedia Learning* (Cambridge Handbooks in Psychology, pp. 576-597). Cambridge: Cambridge University Press. DOI: 10.1017/CBO9781139547369.028

Naert, L., Bonato, M., and Fias, W. (2018) Asymmetric spatial processing under cognitive load. *Frontiers in Psychology*, 9. DOI: 10.3389/fpsyg.2018.00583

Plass, J. L., Moreno, R., and Brünken, R. (2010) Introduction. In J. Plass, R. Moreno, & R. Brünken (Eds.), Cognitive Load Theory (pp. 1-6). Cambridge: Cambridge University Press. DOI: 10.1017/CBO9780511844744.002

Roberts, J. (2014) *The Frood: The Authorised and Very Official History of Douglas Adams and The Hitchhiker's Guide to the Galaxy*. Penguin Random House, UK: London.

Saavik2 (2001) 'Sesquipedalian Obscurantism', *h2g2 Hitch-Hiker's Guide to the Galaxy: Earth Edition.* Available at https://h2g2.com/edited_entry/A640207

Sokal, A. and Bricmont, J. (1998) *Fashionable Nonsense*, Pan Books, US: New York

Sweller, J. (1988). Cognitive load during problem solving: effects on learning, *Cognitive Science*, 12:2, April, 257–285.

Sweller, J. (2010) Cognitive load theory: recent theoretical advances. In J. Plass, R. Moreno, & R. Brünken (Eds.), *Cognitive Load Theory* (pp. 29-47). Cambridge: Cambridge University Press. DOI: 10.1017/CBO9780511844744.004

Scan the QR code to listen to the podcast episode

## CHAPTER 10:

# HOW DOES JULIE ANDREWS ESCAPE THE NAZIS WITH ACTIVE LEARNING?

*Rebecca Ferguson, Olivia Rowland, Mark Childs and Mike Collins*

*A new land in the Realm of Pedagogy welcomes the Zillas. Leaving behind the Dwarves and their delving, our three travellers enter the fair realm of the Elves, who call their land Constructivism.*

*The Elves very much enjoy singing, which Markzilla, who dislikes all musicals except* The Rocky Horror Picture Show, *and Mikezilla who prefers a very cheesy adaptation of* The Ugly Duckling, *meet with scepticism.*

*So when Olivzillia comes dancing and singing out of the town of Active Learning, and yodels that she will explain the region through the medium of* The Sound of Music – *well, there is hesitation.*

*But their journey so far has made them brave, and Markzilla thinks he has discovered how a spoonful of popular culture helps the medicine of learning about pedagogy go down. 'Wrong musical!' trills Olivzillia, 'You need to start at the very beginning.[1]'*

---

[1] A very good place to start.

Behaviourism and the ten principles of instruction, which we covered in chapters seven and eight, both focus on learning as something that goes on in an individual's brain. That's important but there's more to learning than that, as you'll see as the book goes on.

Learning takes place in specific contexts, with other people, and it's not confined to our brains. In this chapter, we'll look at how physical action and mental action can combine to build our skills and knowledge.

To explore those topics, we're asking: **How does Julie Andrews escape the Nazis with active learning?**

## *The Sound of Music*

*The Sound of Music* is probably best known as a film starring Julie Andrews. Although more than half a century old, it remains hugely popular in the UK, where it's usually shown on at least one television channel on Christmas Day. At other times of year, thousands of enthusiasts dress up to attend live 'Sing-a-long-a *Sound of Music*' events.

Although the events in the film seem unlikely, it was based on an autobiography, which was made into two films in Germany, the first of which was adapted into a Broadway musical before it took its current form. On its release in 1965 it was the highest-grossing film of the year, winning five Oscars, including best picture and best director.

The film is set in Austria in the late 1930s. Its basic plot is about a nun, Maria, who has not yet taken her vows. While preparing to do so, she's sent as governess to the seven children of a widowed naval officer, Captain von Trapp.

Long story short: the children all learn to sing together and then make use of their talents in very clever ways. To make a short story slightly longer, Maria is beautiful and rebellious, while the captain is stern, serious and sad about his late wife. He doesn't allow his children to have fun or to sing. Instead, they spend their days marching around the grounds of their country estate. When Maria turns up, she's horrified by this regime. She defies their father's strict instructions and teaches them to sing. When the captain hears them, his heart melts and his heart starts to melt towards Maria as well. They fall in love and marry.

Their marriage takes place at the time of the *Anschluss*, the annexation of Austria by Nazi Germany. Although this was welcomed by some Austrians, within a few days 70,000 people had been arrested, imprisoned or sent to concentration camps. Those who opposed the annexation lost their jobs or faced death. During his honeymoon, Captain von Trapp fails to respond to a telegram from Admiral von Schreiber of the navy of the Third Reich, requiring him to accept a commission to serve. On his return, soldiers arrive with orders to escort him immediately to the German port of Bremershaven, making it clear that he's being offered no choice. However, the captain is a patriotic Austrian who opposes the Nazis. So the family has to flee the country, and they use a singing performance as their cover.

To get more personal, *The Sound of Music* is a wonderful movie, a glorious movie, and a delightful movie. The film's early reviews reflect that. The *New York Post* refers to its 'strangely gentle charm that is wonderfully endearing', and *The New York World Telegram and Sun* calls it, 'the loveliest musical imaginable'. It's also an archetypal movie, spawning a host of parodies. Google provides more than ten million links to these, including the Covid-19 song (Serban, 2020), and the von Trapped family's lockdown songs (Kwai, 2021).

There are some differences between Maria's autobiography and the film. Many of these simply require a suspension of disbelief. People in Austria at the time didn't have North

American accents, but the actors do, resulting in exchanges along the lines of (although not exactly like): 'Heil Hitler', 'Hey, you too, Chad, you heil Hitler too. Nice one, bro.'

Compared to the essential suspension of disbelief with any musical (in real life people rarely suddenly interrupt their regular activity to break into a choreographed song and dance number) we'd suggest this is a minor issue.

## Active learning

Something that does happen in real life is the other component of the question in this chapter: active learning. Active learning is a broad umbrella, which we introduce here and then go on to explore in more detail in other chapters.

> *Learning through active participation will always involve learners being cognitively active – engaging their minds in their learning. It might also involve an actual physical action (such as making a poster, building a model or doing an experiment), but will always involve cognitive action. Just reading or listening to a lecture is insufficient; understanding is actively constructed by the learner through thinking about the new material, processing information and making connections with previous learning or established ideas*
>
> (TESS-India, 2022).

This is an approach to learning that involves being 'minds on', as well as hands on.

The idea of *understanding being actively constructed by the learner* is at the core of the set of approaches covered in the remainder of this book. It's what theorists mean when they talk about constructivism. In true constructivist style, rather than go into detail about constructivism as an overarching concept, we'll present various examples of constructivism (active learning being one) and let you piece together an understanding of it from this and consecutive chapters.

This is to give you, the reader, the experience of learning from a constructivist approach and not because we only realised when the book was about to go to print that we hadn't provided a detailed explanation of the term.

During the pandemic, as universities moved swiftly towards an online delivery method without the necessary resources or support, it was very easy to fall into 'Death by PowerPoint', simply converting all forms of teaching into presentations, videos and screencasts. This approach makes education a very passive experience for learners, an experience sometimes referred to as 'passive learning'. The majority of the work is done by the person who gives the lecture, writes the book, or produces the video, rather than by the learner.

Content-focused learning asks learners to read or watch or listen – absorbing another person's brainful of information into their own brain. It isn't the only way to learn, and it's not necessarily the best way for everything to be taught. For one thing, assimilating information without engaging in any other form of activity makes it difficult to acquire a skill. It's hard to teach people to communicate, or to present, or to solve problems, or to drive a car, simply by placing information in front of their eyes. You don't develop a wide variety of skills by reading a book, you mainly acquire the skills associated with reading a book. If you need to practise and apply particular skills or particular knowledge, then you need to move beyond simply reading books and watching videos – a point we frequently make.

This active engagement happens all the time when you engage in informal learning. You have a practical problem –

you might need to change a tyre, or put up a shelf, or fix a bit of equipment. You search for information online, you watch a video, and then you try it for yourself. If you still can't do it, you search for more information, or you review what you've already looked at, or you find a forum and ask questions, or you check to see if any of your family and friends can help you out. You assess your understanding by checking whether you can actually do what you wanted to do. Assimilating information is part of an active process but it's rarely the entire process.

Active learning is an alternative to passive learning. It cognitively engages learners, using a variety of tools to provide different ways of approaching learning, whether this takes place in a classroom or at a distance. These active options can be bolted on later, but it's best to take them into account when starting to plan teaching and design learning.

### Active learning in practice

Active learning is about prompting students to engage with materials, with each other, and with educators. They can do this in different scenarios in which they try skills out for themselves, or they can apply those skills in familiar situations. It's also about making sure that students build their own understanding, forming connections between what they already know and what other people know – building their own knowledge, not just taking in information.

Rather than simply reading, watching and listening, learners engage in a wide range of activities: finding, demonstrating, practising, developing, interpreting, investigating, designing, and creating. If the learning outcomes of a course are written in terms of active learning, then many of the relevant verbs may already be at hand. For example, the learning outcomes on a podcasting course might read something like:

*By the end of this course you will be able to:*

- *explain the mechanics of how sound waves work;*
- *source and critically review resources;*
- *create a short podcast;*
- *evaluate user experience and reactions.*

Working backwards from these intended outcomes for the learner, the course will need to inspire creativity, scaffold some of these processes, and provide opportunities for explaining, sourcing, reviewing and evaluating. Instead of students being expected to sit back and simply absorb information from their tutor or another expert, they can be guided to engage in a variety of learning activities.

Some of the learning comes from the tutor, some from existing resources, some from talking to peers, some from feedback, and some simply from making mistakes and realising that one approach works better than another. There are many different opportunities to learn, as long as active learning is implemented with care.

## Issues with active learning

People who are used to thinking of learning as attending a lecture, and online learning as watching a video, may think that selecting an arrow or moving a cursor is active learning because it involves moving a finger on a keyboard or trackpad.

For example, a piece of online training might be classified as 'interactive' because it requires users to select multiple tabs, or to click on various parts of an image to reveal information. This doesn't make learning more active, it simply makes the act of accessing and assimilating information more difficult. The important thing is to ensure that learners engage in a variety of ways rather than simply consuming information.

Another wrong assumption about active learning, which is covered in more detail in Chapter 13, is that it should come with minimal instruction, and that learners should be left to work things out themselves from first principles.

Evidence from multiple studies has shown that simply leaving students to get on by themselves does not work nearly as well as guiding the learning process (Kirschner et al, 2006). Part of the skill of the educator is keeping students engaging actively with the learning process while also being able to build on what's already known.

However, learning is built on a basis of knowledge and understanding. Active learning and passive learning are often intertwined. There's no need for every aspect of learning to be active. For example, if students are asked to create a short podcast, they'll need to find tools and write scripts but eventually they'll need to read an article on how to open and configure the relevant software, or watch a video tutorial in which someone explains the use of mixers, or find some other source of expertise. Assimilating information provides a foundation for active learning.

Bloom's Taxonomy classifies elements of the cognitive domain of learning. The original taxonomy has six major classes: knowledge, comprehension, application, analysis, synthesis, and evaluation. Bloom and his colleagues noted that these could be ordered in different ways. They preferred this arrangement because 'the objectives in one class are likely to make use of and be built on the behaviours found in the preceding classes in this list' (Bloom et al, 1956, p18). Knowledge is present in the taxonomy, but it alone is not enough – learners need to work with that knowledge in different ways. A revision of the taxonomy (Anderson et al, 2001) identified six cognitive processes: remember, understand, apply, analyse, evaluate and create – all of them active ways of engaging with different types of knowledge, and all going beyond simply reading or viewing.

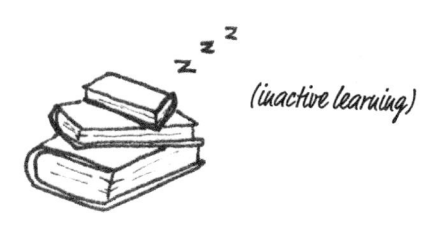

*(inactive learning)*

### Applying active learning

Active learning is an umbrella term. It brings together concepts covered in many of the chapters in this book: constructivism, social constructivism, experiential learning, reflective learning, and learning through doing. It's also a classification that uses everyday language. 'Active learning' sounds like something everyone can understand, whereas constructivism and constructionism sound complex and confusing.

One of the greatest advantages of active learning is that it aids retention. Students are much more likely to be able to remember something if they have done it themselves, worked out how to do it themselves (with support where necessary), made a few mistakes along the way, and asked a few people some questions about how they did it. When they start putting skills and information into their own contexts, those skills and information become more personal and easier to remember (Michael, 2006).

The approach also redefines what education is for. It's not simply about producing school-leavers and graduates who know a bunch of stuff and can memorise more stuff. It's about enabling people to go out, make changes, do things for themselves, and have an impact on the world around them because they've acquired skills rather than just a list of things that they remember.

It's also a transformative experience. When you learn to do something for yourself and you bounce ideas around and you listen to other people's perspectives, these activities change your own perspective. You're not just reading a book, you're talking to other people about the subject and their perspectives on it and presumably potentially learning an awful lot about their perspectives and why they have those perspectives.

## The answer

In *The Sound of Music* the active learning begins when Maria teaches the children some of the fundamentals of music. A major difference between the film and real life is that in real life the family were already accomplished singers, but in the film the children had never been allowed to sing and didn't know how to do it.

Maria uses the song 'Do-re-mi' to teach them how to sing. This is very active learning because they learn to sing and they learn about the underlying structure of songs and music by actually singing. They learn about individual notes and the relationship of those notes to each other in a scale, they hear them and sing them back, they practise them, and they add words.

Do-re-mi or, more technically, tonic sol-fa, is a way of understanding the notes of a scale and the intervals between those notes. Maria describes its elements as 'the tools you use to build a song'. She begins by introducing the note names but when the children look puzzled she quickly adjusts her teaching style to make the learning more active, adding a mnemonic rhyme.

The children try the new skill out, do some more practice, then use the notes that they just learned about to create a new song, with words. The basic concepts are broken down into small elements, and Maria's way of teaching pulls the children in, immediately involving them with the process of singing and with learning through singing.

Once they've learnt that song, which includes the rudiments of Western music, they continue to learn to sing, and their singing skills develop. A lot of the songs they learn then become part of the plot. They sing a folk song for their father. They sing at a family puppet show, and they sing at a music festival at the end, which is a critical part of the story. At that point, they've gone from not being able to sing at all, to singing in front of a huge audience.

Singing at the music festival in Salzburg earns the captain a brief reprieve from being marched off to join the German navy. The plan of the Nazi officers who sit in the front row is that he will be led off to war as soon as the event ends. After leading the audience in a stirring rendition of the patriotic song 'Edelweiss', the family sings a song of farewell.

While they're expected to be backstage, waiting for the results to be announced (they win, of course), they escape through a back door, drive away and escape over the mountains to Switzerland, which the film's script writer has conveniently moved a lot closer to Salzburg in order to increase the dramatic effect. So learning to sing together gets them to the music festival and the music festival is what enables them to escape the Nazis.

Of course, none of this was planned when Maria first taught the children to sing. One of the positive aspects of active learning is that if you learn to apply a set of skills, you can reapply those in different scenarios. You have more flexibility than if you simply learn a set of facts. This means there is an emergent property to the educational process. By learning and applying skills you open up new possibilities, and put yourself in a position to learn new things. Whereas, if you have a very tightly designed approach in which the curriculum specifies certain facts that must be assimilated, you have more limited opportunities. In that case, the learning situation has a very clear-cut resolution, which means opportunities to be creative, to take advantage of emergency situations and therefore to be responsive to changes in your immediate environment are a lot more limited.

Active learning can also build confidence. If you develop a new skill, particularly one you never suspected that you were capable of, you can gain an immense amount of confidence. This means you are more capable of going on and doing more things.

The children in the film start off almost cowed, militaristic and marching around in little starched uniforms. Active learning gives them the confidence to rebel against and successfully challenge their father's perspective. They get the confidence to wear clothes made of curtains in public, when Maria makes them outfits to play in. They gain the confidence to sing in front of the family and then in front of large groups of people. In the end, they are able to perform beautifully at a huge national music festival even though the entire front row is full of Nazis intent on taking their father away.

Overall, Julie Andrews (Maria) escapes the Nazis because she uses active learning to give those around her the skills, the flexibility and the confidence to manufacture and take advantage of an escape opportunity.

# Tips for practice

When planning for active learning, relegate content to the bottom of the list. Always start by asking, 'What are the students going to be able to do by the end of this course?' not, 'What am I going to teach them?' Starting with the content, starting with the stuff, is exactly the wrong place. The important thing to ask is, 'What skills are the students going to take away from the course in order to act on the world around them, to create things for themselves, and to have some sort of impact?'

Think about what students need to be able to do when they have completed the course, the activities they need to engage with in order to be able to do those things, and the ways in which you'll check that they can do those things. Only at that point do you need to start thinking in detail about course content. Focus on other things before focusing on what you intend to upload or what you'll ask students to read.

Fifteen years ago, many people saw content as king and looked for the best things to view, the best things to read or the best videos to watch. The focus is now much more on what the students are going to do, with the content being seen chiefly as a resource to enable them to do it.

Look for opportunities to introduce active learning. If you find yourself giving students reams and reams of text to read or multiple videos to watch, look for opportunities to add an active element. This will change how students approach their learning. If classes consist of, 'Read this thing, then read this other thing', students will either bypass that work or consume the content in a very passive manner. If it's, 'Read this thing and then use that information to create another thing', they will have opportunities to engage in a very different way.

Active learning can be made really meaningful, so encourage learners to apply the skills and information within their own contexts. That's one of the things that Maria does really well in *The Sound of Music*. She helps the children to learn songs that have meaning for them and their family. If she'd been working with cockneys in the East End of London, the song might have been completely different – 'Dough, some dosh, go treat yourself; Ray, a bloke from down the pub…'

When focusing on skills, it's important to build those up gradually. That's another thing Maria does well, she starts really simply and makes sure the children have got the basics before moving on to the next step.

Always keep an eye on workload and cognitive load (as we saw in the previous chapter). You don't want students to feel overwhelmed, so avoid piling up the active components. Think realistically about how much time each of those will take. Not how much time they will take you, as an expert, but how much time they will take a novice. Active learning can be very resource and time intensive for both educators and students and so it needs adequate curriculum time. Although it's a great way to build up confidence, learners can also lose confidence quickly if they can't do something and can't work out how to do it.

If you have the opportunity to take part in a singalong of *The Sound of Music*, or of another musical that you love, then these provide opportunities to engage in active learning. Unlike other shows, you're not passively sitting there, you're engaged, you're part of the experience. And that feels much more participative, fun, engaging, all those sorts of things. Part of engaging with an activity and performing a skill is that you get to see how other people do it and why they might do it differently from you, and there's learning there as well. It's a shared experience, just as life is a shared experience.

## These are a few of my favourite references

Anderson, L. W., Krathwohl, D. R., Airasian, P. W., Cruikshank, K. A., Mayer, R. E., Pintrich, P. R., Raths, J., Wittrock, M. C. (2001) *A Taxonomy for Learning, Teaching, and Assessing: Revision of Bloom's Taxonomy of Educational Objectives (abridged edition)*. New York: Longman.

Bloom, B.S.; Engelhart, M.D; Furst, E.J.,Hill, Walker H. and Krathwohl, D.R. (1956) *Taxonomy of Educational Objectives – the Classification of Educational Goals, Handbook I, Cognitive Domain*. London: Longman Group.

Kirschner, P.; Sweller, J. and Clark, R.E. (2006) Why minimal guidance during instruction does not work: an analysis of the failure of constructivist, discovery, problem-based, experiential, and inquiry-based teaching. *Educational Psychologist*, 41:2, 75-86.

Kwai, I. (2021) Von Trapped: the family is stuck inside, so why not sing parodies? *The New York Times* 19 February. Available at: https://www.nytimes.com/2021/02/19/world/europe/virus-YouTube-Marsh-family.html

Michael, J. (2006) Where's the evidence that active learning works? *Advances in Physiology Education*, 30, 159-167. Available at: https://doi.org/10.1152/advan.00053.2006

Serban, S. (2020) *Do Re Mi – Sound of Music Covid 19 song (March 2020)*. Available at: https://www.youtube.com/watch?v=MMBh-eo3tvE&ab_channel=Shirley%C8%98erban

TESS-India (2022) Learning through active participation, *TESS-India: Enhancing Teacher Education through OER MOOC*. The Open University. Available at: https://www.open.edu/openlearncreate/mod/oucontent/view.php?id=87872&section=1

Scan the QR code to listen to
the podcast episode

## CHAPTER 11:

# HOW DOES PROBLEM-BASED LEARNING HELP BUFFY THE VAMPIRE SLAYER ... ER, SLAY VAMPIRES?

*Rebecca Ferguson, Mark Childs and Mike Collins*

*'Well, actually,'* says Markzilla, *backtracking fast, 'I like lots of musicals.' He begins to reel off a list of obscure performances that includes both spaceships and songs.*

*'I bet you liked the musical episode of* Buffy the Vampire Slayer?*' interjects Beckzilla.*

*'Errm, no, I've never seen it. But I can compare any number of meerkats!'*

*The others look at him in astonishment and dismay. 'That's a shame!' says Beckzilla. 'I was planning to show you around the town that neighbours Active Learning, Problem-Based Learning. It would have helped if you'd known something of the challenges involved in vampire slaying.'*

*She stops again to look thoughtfully at her motley crew. 'Though maybe we're asking the wrong question...'*

Active learning is a broad category – most types of learning require a bit more activity than sitting at a desk and reading a book, watching a video, or listening to a podcast (however good!) Outside a formal education setting, learning and doing are closely intertwined and there may not be an opportunity to sign up for a course when a problem arises. In this chapter, we'll take a look at an active approach that can be applied both inside and outside the classroom and, as we do so, we'll answer the question: **How does problem-based learning help *Buffy the Vampire Slayer*, er, slay vampires?**

## *Buffy the Vampire Slayer*

*Buffy the Vampire Slayer* is a US TV show that ran for seven series. In it, actress Sarah Michelle Gellar plays Buffy Summers, a student at Sunnydale High. Sunnydale is an all-American high school that just happens to sit on top of the Hellmouth. This is not only a source of demons, vampires and other terrifying monsters but it also attracts monsters. Luckily for her classmates and fellow citizens, Buffy is not simply any student – she has been selected to be the Slayer.

The role of Slayer comes with enhanced abilities, strength and self-healing powers but also with the demand to take on a stream of evil beings single-handed, because there is only one Slayer in every generation and the role is traditionally concealed from others. So Buffy spends her nights slaying vampires, and her days trying to be an everyday teenager with friends, family and relationships. Mikezilla describes the show as, 'Wonderful and funny and witty and silly and great. And it's... oh, it's gorgeous.' (Can you tell that Sarah Michelle Gellar was his teenage heartthrob?) Buffy is supported by the school librarian Giles, whose role as a Watcher involves training and guiding the Slayer.

Show creator, Joss Whedon, 'wanted a scene where the petite blonde went into the dark alley with the Big Bad, and then she kicked its ass' (Fudge, 2009). This underpinning idea means the series continually inverts or thoroughly subverts expectations. The first time Beckzilla watched Buffy, she just happened to have the television on, saw a young blonde girl walking into a graveyard and thought, 'This is just so stereotypical.' A minute later, when Buffy took on the monsters and won, Beckzilla was, like[1], 'Wow, what happened there? This is a show I have to watch.'

Alongside that inversion of expectations, the show has a major underlying metaphor, certainly for the first three series: high school is hell. The episodes explore in detail how that would play out if it were literally true. Mikezilla remembers that, in the first episodes he watched, some of the worst and hardest-to-watch moments weren't when a vampire was threatening to eat somebody or characters were engaged in mortal combat. Instead, it was when nasty people were being unpleasant and snide. It was those true-to-life experiences that made him shudder.

An example from S1 Ep 11 *Out of Sight, Out of Mind* is villain-of-the-week Marcie, a girl who is invisible but also extremely vindictive. She beats one pupil with a baseball bat, pushes another downstairs, tries to suffocate a teacher and mutilate a classmate. While trying to locate and defeat her, Buffy finds out that Marcie became invisible because she has been ignored all her life. Whenever she approached other people, they ignored her or turned away. They haven't heard her or paid attention to her, either inside or outside the classroom. That's an experience that so many people have had, of feeling on the outside, feeling ignored, and perhaps wanting to punish the people who are pushing you away. The show takes that situation one step further. What would happen if you were literally invisible? What would happen if you were given the opportunity to punish those people? There are

---
[1] Well, it is, like, Buffy.

so many things that the show takes one step or even ten steps further.

Markzilla hasn't ever watched Buffy (a major impediment to any geek credentials he's purporting to have) but he's still able to place it in its wider context as the start of a big wave of postmodern 90s TV which included a monster of the week, as well as grand, overarching plots that joined everything together across seasons. To take one example, in a huge story arc, Buffy Series 5 leads up to her heroic death, followed by her unwilling resurrection at the start of Series 6 and the fallout from those events.

This could easily have become an example of 'jumping the shark', when a show has reached a high point, runs out of ideas and so introduces over-the-top gimmicks to maintain interest (TV Tropes, 2022). Instead, the scriptwriters brazenly acknowledged and mocked that possibility in S6 Ep 8 *Tabula Rasa* by taking the shark motif and developing it further, introducing a demon with shark features who provides kittens to vampires for their poker games then demands repayment at a high rate (a literal loan shark).

Series 6 also included a musical episode, S6 Ep 7 *Once More with Feeling*, consistently rated as one of the best in the show. In the songs they sing, each character is forced to expose their inner thoughts. This means they reveal things they wouldn't have chosen to tell other people as well as things they had been hiding from other characters for a long time. Open expression of characters' inner monologues makes this a revealing episode, which not only provides a catalyst for future story arcs but is incidentally revealing about how musicals work as a genre. However, in this case, the premise is not, 'Isn't this a beautiful, lovely world where we're all singing to each other all the time?' Instead, the characters' perspective on the lyrics is, 'This is a hellish experience, and we have to stop it as soon as possible.'

Aside from such standout episodes, the show's typical structure is a monster-of-the-week format. In each episode – in addition to the big series-wide arcs – there is a new inciting incident; something weird and wonderful. It might be a strange happening in Sunnydale. It might be the appearance of a new, mysterious character. It might be people disappearing or turning up in bits on the lawn. In response to this inciting incident, Buffy and her friends, Xander and Willow, together with Giles, all work together from their base in the school library or, later, the Magic Box shop. Secondary plots typically provide them with an insight or revelation that enables them to understand how to defeat the monster.

In the early series, when Buffy is at high school or college, this format intersects at multiple points with education and learning. This happens in several ways. Most obviously, a crucial part of Buffy's context in seasons 1–3 is that she's a high school student. As a result, in the background of most episodes, there's some attempt at formal learning going on: lessons, books, homework and tests. These elements occasionally drive storylines. Something will happen in class, or on a field trip, and the plot takes that a bit further. However, formal learning is rarely central.

More important to the teenage characters is the learning that goes on informally during their years at high school. Learning about sex and drugs and rock'n'roll, and how relationships work, and how to negotiate with family and friends. Over the different seasons, viewers watch the characters grow in experience as they develop into adults. This form of learning is common to all the teenage characters, with the effects of adolescence always exacerbated by life on the Hellmouth.

Aside from that formal and informal learning, which will be familiar experiences for most viewers, there's learning that's specific to Buffy and her friends. A premise of the 'Buffyverse' is that there's one Slayer in every generation. More accurately, there's one Slayer at a time. In global terms, Slayers are disposable. As soon as one Slayer dies, another teenage girl somewhere in the world is assigned the role and acquires the powers. So while on the micro scale her own death is a tragedy for each individual Slayer; on the macro scale nothing has changed because there's still a Slayer. The role makes these young women into high-profile targets, so there's a high turnover rate. As a result, the Slayer is usually inexperienced and may, like Buffy at first, initially have no idea what's going on. One day she's a normal teenage girl. The next day she has superhuman powers and superhuman skills and lots of demons start turning up, which is difficult to handle.

Overseeing Slayer activity is the Watchers' Council. This organisation keeps records of Slayers: what they do, which enemies they face, how those enemies are defeated, and how each Slayer is killed. One Watcher from the Council is assigned to each Slayer. Sometimes, like Giles, they're supportive and work with the Slayer. In other cases, the Watcher is unnecessarily controlling, or may even have turned rogue. For the Slayers, an important benefit of Watchers is that they have access to a vast repository of knowledge about monsters and how to defeat them. So the Watchers represent one sort of approach to education, which relies on books, records, and adult experts. The Watchers we see in Buffy are mainly British, and conform to familiar US stereotypes of the British – they have knowledge that comes from books but not necessarily from direct experience, they tend to be very formal, and sometimes their 'dark academic' veneer conceals a villain.

The Watchers' Council does offer value. Members have knowledge and experience that can be used to save the Slayer and even the world. However, they're determined to maintain their control. Their support and teaching are not designed to produce a fully independent Slayer. Their stance is that they are the wise ones who will share knowledge with the Slayer but will also retain control of that knowledge.

In S3 Ep 12 *Helpless*, when Buffy turns 18, the Watchers' Council forces an absolutely pointless test on her as a rite of passage. This very nearly kills her. The obvious parallel in normal high-school life is the pressure of examination, and the imposition of meaningless assessment, which can severely damage the health of the students who are engaged in that process.

A final type of learning is the one Buffy must engage with as she is faced with a different demon every week; a different set of challenges in every episode. In other forms of learning, she has a model to work with. That may be a formal model, as in high school, or learning from her Watcher. It can be an informal model of learning with and from her peers, because they're all going through similar experiences. However, in taking on the demons, it's largely up to Buffy to find a model of learning that's flexible enough and effective enough to keep her alive. Which is where problem-based learning comes in.

## Problem-based learning

Problem-based learning is an approach that was developed in medical schools during the 1960s. It was a response to the observation that medical students would work hard for many years to learn all the facts presented to them. However, when they went out into the world and interacted with patients, they weren't necessarily able to apply what they'd learned. It seemed that a more practice-based approach to learning was needed, which is where problem-based learning came in.

Problem-based learning can be considered as a series of steps that take the learner from, 'Here is the situation and it presents a problem,' to, 'Let's work together as learners, consult with our lecturer, and come up with a solution.' The approach focuses on authentic situations and issues. It's concerned with the application of knowledge learners already have, and the need for them to work out what knowledge they still need to acquire. It also requires teamwork.

Problem-based learning is typically a group task rather than a puzzle set for individuals to solve. Again, this is authentic. People are rarely in an artificial situation where they have to work alone for extended periods without any access to help, support, or reference materials. We are typically members of a team, living with family, spending time with friends or working alongside colleagues. Outside formal learning settings, most people are in a group, or have access to a group, when faced with problems they must solve.

The educator's role in problem-based learning is not as a 'Sage on the Stage' who shares information for novices to absorb, but as a 'Guide on the Side', facilitating the experience and supporting learners through the process. The role includes offering prompts and asking questions in order to progress the learning. This is a classroom-based approach and so, even when the problem is relatively open-ended, the educator will usually know a way of reaching a solution, which sorts of solution are valid, and which are inappropriate.

## Problem-based learning in practice

Maastricht University in the Netherlands uses problem-based learning across its faculties. Lecturers aim to design experiences that are collaborative, constructive, contextual and self-directed. The intention is to prompt students to activate prior knowledge, relate any new information to that knowledge, structure new ideas and critically evaluate their findings and solutions.

Markzilla worked in the Faculty of Engineering and Computing at Coventry University as they introduced problem-based learning for new students. When first-year students joined the faculty, they were set a problem. They had to work together to solve this during their first six weeks of study. In one case, the challenge was to design a MIDI controller – a piece of hardware or software, such as an electronic keyboard, that's capable of sending musical instrument digital interface (MIDI) data to a device. In order to solve the problem, each group of students had to produce a working controller (Tovey and Davies, 2011).

In the first week, a group might decide on the specifications and design their controller. In the following weeks they would build and refine it. They'd then develop a marketing campaign, and end by writing a report on the project, reflecting on what they'd done and how successful they'd been at each stage. Problem-based learning worked well for these students because they found it hugely motivating. While designing their controllers, many of them investigated ideas and concepts they wouldn't otherwise have encountered until their third year of university study, because that information was what they needed to make a really effective MIDI controller. Not all of them got that far, sometimes their solution to the problem was not as effective as ones devised by other groups. Nevertheless, at the end of six weeks, each group had come up with a way of solving the problem.

When the approach was first tried at Coventry, some lecturers were sceptical about it. However, once they started to receive feedback, Markzilla reports that the staff began to feel, 'Oh my God, this is the best thing ever,' and were keen to extend their use of the approach.

### Issues with problem-based learning

Despite positive experiences at Coventry and Maastricht, there are several criticisms of problem-based learning. It makes very heavy use of resources, teachers' time and lab space. For that reason, Coventry identified that it wasn't a practical approach to employ for the students' entire three years of study.

Due to these demands, planning is needed across the institution in order to support problem-based learning effectively. As the problems set for students are relatively open ended, the approach can be difficult to plan for. Educators need to be confident they'll be able to deal with a wide range of questions and different scenarios. Perhaps more significantly from the perspective of student learning, a problem-based approach reduces the breadth of curriculum that can be covered, because students need to spend a lot of time on exploration, breaking things apart, and working things out.

Another issue is that working in groups to solve problems can give students too much to think about at the same time. The cognitive load may prove too great for learning to be effective. Cognitive load theory is based on research into how well humans can handle information, and recognises that we have limited capacity for processing it. Because of this, it's very difficult to do certain things at the same time – for example, reading a book while watching a documentary, or trying to understand a complex PowerPoint slide while a presenter is talking. In the case of problem-based learning, students have to deal with forming a team, collaborating with each other, and dealing with a new situation, as well as with all the different aspects of the problem. If they have to take on all these aspects of the task at once, they may be overwhelmed. For more on cognitive load, read Chapter 9; for more on the issue of balancing cognitive load and problem-based learning, read Chapter 13.

In summary, though, the issues can be summarised by this quote: 'Teaching that only partially guides students, and expects them to discover information on their own, is not effective or efficient. Decades of research clearly demonstrate that when teaching new information or skills, step-by-step instruction with full explanations works best' (Clark et al, 2012). Over-enthusiastic proponents of problem-based learning can fall into this trap, encouraging students to work things out from first principles that can be taught much more easily through lectures, seminars and tutorials.

Neither approach will be the best in all situations. Students need support to learn and remember the facts and to get an idea of the overall lay of the land. Once they understand what the landscape for a particular discipline is, and have relevant information and tools to work with, then they can use problem-based learning to strengthen their understanding, particularly on work-related courses where they will later be required to apply their knowledge in practical settings.

Problem-based learning has its downsides: it's demanding in terms of time, resourcing, and student engagement, and is typically less effective than direct instruction when acquiring new information. On the other hand, when done well and applied appropriately it can be highly motivating, it can make connections between study and practice, and help to make the learning experience more authentic.

## Applying problem-based learning

Problem-based learning can be applied in a variety of ways but it has a set of basic steps (Schmidt, 1983) that are sometimes referred to as the 'Seven Jump' method. These steps are:

1. examine a case and clarify terms;
2. identify the problem;
3. analyse the problem;
4. draft an explanatory model;
5. establish learning goals;
6. work individually to collect additional information;
7. apply and discuss additional information.

To demonstrate how these steps can be put into practice, we've applied them to the problem set to engineering students in Coventry. Students and lecturers begin by examining the case and clarifying terms (1). Lecturers introduce the broad area of study and some of the important terminology, such as what a MIDI controller is. After this overview, the students are presented with the problem: Design a MIDI controller (2).

Each group of students then needs to analyse that problem in depth, identifying the different aspects that will need to be covered (3). Drafting an explanatory model and establishing learning goals involve deciding how the group will go about the task and how they will divide the different sub-processes, deciding who will find out about certain things and who will work on various elements of the controller (4&5).

From the educators' point of view, the learning goals that the students are likely to set themselves need to be considered when deciding what problem to set. In this case, MIDI controllers were chosen because the design problem required students to understand and employ a lot of the theory that they would return to throughout their university studies. Designing a MIDI controller is also a good introduction to a course of study because it's an enjoyable practical activity and students can use their controller to play music once they've designed and constructed it.

Although the educators set up the problem in a way that implied certain learning goals, the students had to identify for themselves what they needed to learn in order to solve the problem. It was up to them to shape their learning by deciding they needed to learn about arrays, MIDI files, soldering, or a range of other subjects. At this point, educators were able to act as guides on the side, checking that the learning goals identified by students aligned with what they were expected to learn.

In some cases, students were prompted towards important learning goals. For example, students who had never heard of arrays were unaware they needed to learn about them and so needed a prompt. Ideally, though, key ideas like these are introduced right at the beginning – either before the problem-based learning begins, or when educators and students are discussing the first step.

The next step (6) involves members of the group working individually to collect additional information. At this point the task is cooperative, with group members working in parallel rather than duplicating effort. In the final step (7), they pool what they've learned and apply it to the problem, so they're able to produce a solution in terms of a working MIDI controller.

So, the seven steps of problem-based learning can be applied in a classroom environment. Let's take this forward and use this knowledge to answer our question: **How does problem-based learning help *Buffy the Vampire Slayer*, er, slay vampires?**

## The answer

To do this we can work through the seven steps again, but we'll move the setting from Coventry to Sunnydale, and from a university to a high school perched above the Hellmouth.

At the start of the TV series (S1 Ep1 *Welcome to the Hellmouth* / S1 Ep 2 *The Harvest*), Buffy's new friends, Willow and Xander, are finding out for the first time about vampires and demons. This subject area is completely new to them. In terms of examining the case and clarifying the terms, they're very reliant on Buffy and Giles. Giles knows a lot more about the supernatural elements than Buffy, who's new to the role of Slayer and not too thrilled about it.

However, Buffy knows more about the specific situation that's facing them. She encountered two very powerful vampires in the Sunnydale graveyard and these vampires got away before she could slay them by putting a stake through their hearts. Having encountered this difficult situation, she went back to school in order to discuss it with Giles. Asking for advice from her Watcher is standard practice for a Slayer.

As well as talking to her Watcher, she also talks to Willow and Xander. One of the things that makes Buffy different from all previous Slayers, and more successful than all previous Slayers, is that she works with friends[2]. This means she learns things collaboratively and can draw on the skills and experience of others. No other Slayer back to the Stone Age has ever done this. So this is a really novel situation. The Slayer and her Watcher explain to two perfectly normal (at that point) people, Willow and Xander, what vampires are and what's going on. That Sunnydale is actually the Hellmouth. That there are demons living under the school, all sorts of really scary, freaky things, all sorts of new knowledge. So between them they examine the case, clarifying the terms and trying to work out what is going on (1).

Then Buffy goes on to identify the problem (2). In this case, the specific problem they're faced with is that people are being killed in the graveyard. She analyses the problem, splitting it down into its separate elements (3). One element is the vampires. One element is that these vampires have superhuman strength. And one element is that the vampires are hiding out in a lair. Nobody in Buffy's team knows where the vampires' lair is, so they can't stake them.

The explanatory model (4) is straightforward. 'If we find them, we can stake them.'

This leads to two learning goals (5): we need to learn the location of the lair, and we need to learn how to go about staking these super-strong vampires who escaped so easily in the past. This is where the strength of Buffy's approach comes in, because there are four people trying to achieve those learning goals,

---

2. They call themselves the Scooby Gang, or Scoobies. It's adorkable.

whereas any past Slayer would only have had support from her Watcher. The Scooby Gang can work individually or in small teams to collect additional information (6).

Giles investigates these particular vampires, trying to learn the best approach to slaying them. He searches through books and old documents and diaries in the library (as most pupils avoid the school library, Giles has managed to incorporate a large amount of ancient and arcane texts within the collection). Willow, who is a technical whizz, searches the internet, trying to locate the vampires' lair. She finds a map of the sewers and identifies a likely point. Meanwhile, Xander and Buffy explore both on the ground and under the ground. They descend into the sewers and start looking for the vampires. As the pair of episodes comes to an end, Buffy and Xander apply and discuss the additional information that has been gathered (7). This enables them to find the lair and deal with the vampires, taking them on successfully despite their superhuman strength.

However, as this is the start of a series, this turns out to be a beginning rather than an ending. Buffy finds the situation is much more complicated than she originally thought. The problem she has solved is the first of many because the vampires she has encountered are part of a wider group who are trying to open the Hellmouth so that demons will invade the Earth. So the Scoobies have worked together to solve one particular problem but their solution has opened up a whole other can of worms, which they will have to deal with as the series continues. Their problems are just beginning.

### Going beyond the answer

As Buffy looks forward to another 142 episodes in which her problems continue to pile up, it becomes clear that the question, **How does problem-based learning help *Buffy the Vampire Slayer*, er, slay vampires?** was not the right question. Although it sees her through some tricky situations, problem-based learning is only a small part of Buffy's learning strategy because it is, in essence, a classroom-based pedagogy.

When a problem is set, although it's not necessary for educators to know the solution, they'll have a broad idea of what the solution is. They'll know roughly which knowledge they expect students to apply, and the sorts of learning goal they'll achieve. The problem will also be time-bound. Even if the teacher allocates it a week, a month, or a semester of study time, there's a definite point by which it will have to be solved. In addition, there's always a presumption that there's a workable solution. Different groups will come up with different responses but they're aware that the challenge isn't impossible.

The approach works neatly in the early episodes described above partly because, seen from this perspective, series creator Joss Whedon has designed the plot as a learning experience. He has learning goals in mind for both Scooby Gang and viewers. Along with Xander and Willow, we are introduced to the basics of life and terminology in the Buffyverse, including Slayers, Watchers, vampires and the Hellmouth. Buffy, who already knows most of this, learns she cannot escape her destiny as the Slayer. Giles, who is an expert on the terminology and different types of monster, learns he has an unusual Slayer to watch over and begins to adjust to the idea of working in a larger team. The monsters learn there's a new Slayer in town and she's not easy to defeat. The viewers finally learn to understand Buffyspeak and can follow her cryptic, verb-heavy sentences.

The initial problem of specific vampires killing humans in the graveyard is solved within the confines of two episodes, and the scene is set for the next challenge. However, by Series 5, Buffy will be faced with seemingly insurmountable problems, not least of which is a god from a hell dimension. With the situation at that point declining rapidly from bad to apocalyptic, it becomes increasingly obvious that there's no good solution and no chance of reaching a happy ending before time runs out. At that point, the effectiveness of problem-based learning has clearly run its course and Buffy can no longer rely on existing knowledge to give her the answers she so desperately needs.

Problem-based learning helps Buffy to pull in and draw on her collaborative networks, developing the metacognitive skills and strategies required to slay the vampire of the week. However, if any of the Scooby Gang are going to reach the end of the series safely, she needs another learning strategy – computational thinking – in her toolkit, an approach we'll look at in detail in a later volume in the series, promise. Until then, you'll just have to listen to the podcast.

## Tips for practice

If your students have no immediate need to avert an impending apocalypse, but they'd find it helpful to be able to apply what they've learned in order to extend and deepen their knowledge, then problem-based learning is a pedagogic approach that could help.

As with any pedagogy or technology used for teaching and learning, there are some basic questions to be answered:

- What are the advantages of this approach, and how can I ensure learners benefit from those advantages?
- What are the disadvantages of this approach, and how can I ensure these don't outweigh the advantages for learners?
- Is this the best approach to use in this situation?

In order for problem-based learning to work well, students need strategies that enable them to work together confidently in groups. They also require a certain level of subject knowledge – there's little merit in making them work everything out from first principles. Educators need time and resources to use the approach, and they need to be both confident they can take on the role of guide on the side, and flexible enough to let learners take the lead.

Problem-based learning is a useful tool in an educator's toolbox, but learners need some grounding in a subject before they're ready to address problems related to it. Rather than starting with problem-based learning, it's better to lay the groundwork first, later introducing a problem that helps students to make connections between the different things they've learned. This can encourage learners to reach further, increase their learning autonomy, and develop additional skills. Mixing problem-based learning with a more traditional approach helps to scaffold it and also makes it less of a shock to the system for those who haven't encountered the approach in the past.

If problem-based learning is a major change in practice, it's important to acknowledge that's the case, especially if the intention is to use it across the institution. One way of preparing to introduce it is to set up a group whose members have time to think through how the approach will work, sketch out how this will change the curriculum, identify learning outcomes and clarify why problem-based learning is likely to be the most effective way of helping learners to achieve those learning outcomes.

It's also important to consider how assessment will be aligned with the problem-based approach. Assessment is one of the major factors that influence learner behaviour. If learners realise that although they are encouraged to work in groups they will be assessed individually, they will not be motivated to engage with the group. In that case, they're likely to focus their efforts on gaining a good mark rather than on being an effective group member. There are many different ways of assessing group work, so select one that suits the situation, one that your learners feel is fair to them as individuals as well as group members.

Educators will need training to act as facilitators, because this is a challenging role to take on. At the same time, bear in mind that learners come to you with a model of how education works. They'll be used to the idea that teachers tell them things and they learn those things. So students also need to be introduced to the approach and, because it requires more of them than simply sitting quietly and listening, they need to be convinced that this is an effective way of working. They'll need strategies for working together as a group. Task division, deadline setting, progress monitoring, accountability, and reflection are all techniques that can be taught and that help to avoid the problems that arise when learners are asked to work in groups but have no clear idea how to do this.

By laying your pedagogy bare, you involve students in the process of implementing a new approach. They can provide feedback and help to evaluate the implementation, identifying what worked well for them and what will need to be improved in future. This helps them to understand that there are different ways of teaching and learning, and that some of these only work in particular contexts. It also makes the process more interesting for everyone involved.

## There's no problem that cannot be solved by chocolate. Or references.

Clark, R.E., Kirschner, P.A. and Sweller, J. (2012) Putting students on the path to learning: the case for fully guided instruction. *American Educator*, 36:1, 6-11.

Fudge, K. (2009) The high school education of Buffy Summers. In R. Helfrich (ed.), *Buffy Meets the Academy: Essays on the Episodes and Scripts as Texts*, McFarland, London, 203-210

Schmidt, H. G. (1983) Problem-based learning: rationale and description. *Medical Education*, 17, 11-16.

Tovey, M. and Davies, John (2011) The design approach and activity led learning in DS 69: *Proceedings of the 13th International Conference on Engineering and Product Design Education* (187-192). University of Strathclyde, Scotland: Design Society.

TV Tropes (2022) Jumping the Shark, *TV Tropes* Available at: https://tvtropes.org/pmwiki/pmwiki.php/Main/JumpingTheShark

Scan the QR code to listen to the podcast episode

**CHAPTER 12:**

# DOES NEO REALLY EXPERIENCE EXPERIENTIAL LEARNING IN THE MATRIX?

*Mark Childs and Mike Collins*

*The Zillas have explored the twin towns of Active Learning and Problem-Based Learning in the Land of Constructivism. While Beckzilla explores further possibilities there, the others spot another town on the horizon, the signs beckoning them towards Experiential Learning ('You've seen it all, now do it all!'). 'Ooh, something shiny!' shouts Markzilla, and soon he and Mike are off track and headed towards a blindingly modern-looking house called Virtual Experience.*

*They're suddenly surrounded by a crowd of Cyber-Elves. Donning their wraparound shades to blend in, they continue towards the house. The road is a bit rougher and more populated by Elves than they anticipated, because they not only have to explore Experiential Learning but they also have to understand it while pondering the existential nature of reality. Have they made a huge mistake? If they have (and can admit it), will they reflect and learn from it?*

Constructivism is a broad category, which includes many pedagogies. Learners can build new knowledge on existing foundations in multiple different situations. Educators often try to support this knowledge building by making learning opportunities as 'authentic' as possible. Interpretations of authenticity vary, but they typically include activities in 'real-world' situations that are relevant to the learners. In this chapter, we'll tackle two concepts head on. The first is experiential learning, a constructivist approach that we'll examine with the help of *The Matrix* movie and its central character, Neo. The second is the concept of authenticity and reality in a virtual environment. Can we have an authentic, real-world experience in a world that has no physical existence? We need to consider both experiential learning and the nature of reality in order to answer our question: **Does Neo really experience experiential learning in *The Matrix*?**

## *The Matrix*

*The Matrix* franchise is a series of films, a couple of really good comic book collections and also a series of animated shorts; the imaginatively named Animatrix. Within *The Matrix* (the franchise) is the Matrix that *The Matrix* franchise is named after[1]; a computer-generated world that all humans are wired into, although the vast majority of them don't realise that's the case. Most humans think the Matrix is reality. The story follows one character, Neo (played by Keanu Reeves), who discovers the truth. Like Neo, the audience only discovers this deception part-way through the movie. We initially think that what's portrayed on the screen is a real world and then, suddenly, our perspective shifts and we realise that what was going on before that moment

---

1*Editor throws up hands in defeat*

was virtual. It's only after the point of the revelation that we see actual reality. And this reality is much bleaker than the simulation that most humans in the movie perceive, because robots have taken over the world and they're using humans as batteries.

Once humans realise that they're in a computer program, they can manipulate reality, and essentially attain superhuman powers. We see Neo make that shift. However, there are also independent artificial intelligences – agents – within the Matrix who try to stop the reality-aware humans.

Morpheus and Trinity are key characters. Morpheus is Neo's mentor throughout the learning process. Trinity, who has already been inducted into the nature of reality, teaches Neo about some of the steps involved. Rounding out the main cast of the first film are the crew of the airship Nebuchadnezzar, who battle the robots in the real world but also help Morpheus enter the computer-generated world.

In this chapter, we focus mainly on the first movie, partly because it's the best one, but also because it's the only one in the trilogy in which Neo does any learning or, rather, any well-structured learning. We note here that the movie franchise as of 2024 is now a tetralogy, although when we recorded the podcast, the fourth movie hadn't been released.

## Experiential learning

Experiential learning is another facet of the approaches we saw in the previous two chapters, in that being active, or solving problems, provides us with experiences that we can draw upon for our learning. This approach considers learning to be 'the process whereby knowledge is created through the transformation of experience' (Kolb, 1984). The additional element that experiential learning brings to the mix is its emphasis on *reflection* as an essential component. This provides a framework that makes the learning more highly focussed and a lot more structured. The approach stresses that 'learning is best conceived as a process, not in terms of outcomes' (Kolb, 1984). Concepts come from our experience and are modified by that experience – they're not fixed and immutable. The role of a teacher isn't simply to introduce new ideas; it's also to modify or dispose of old ideas (which links this approach to the transformative learning covered in Chapter 2).

The experiential learning model was popularised in the 1970s and 1980s by David Kolb and his co-authors, but its roots go even further back. As with most pedagogy models, it's not necessarily the work of a lone individual, but it has come to be associated with the person who described it and identified its different elements. One particular inspiration was Kurt Lewin and his field theory of social psychology, which has its basis in the idea of feedback in engineering. The idea of reflection as a learning tool has a lot of parallels with control engineering (Abdulwahed et al, 2008). There's also the storytelling cycle by Heidi Dahlsveen which involves audience feedback and revising your story. If you rewrite this as a loop, it looks identical to the learning cycle (Childs et al, 2015). So there are lots of models that only need very slight tweaks to become the experiential learning cycle.

The central elements of Kolb's experiential learning model are:

- concrete experience
- reflective observation
- abstract conceptualisation
- active experimentation (Kolb, 1984, Fig 2.4).

Although Kolb's visualisation of these elements followed Lewin by arranging them in a circle (thus giving rise to the idea of a cycle), he also drew on the model of learning and cognitive development proposed by influential psychologist Jean Piaget, which made connections across that circle. Kolb sees the learning process as having two dimensions: the first running from concrete experience to abstract conceptualisation, and the other from active experimentation to reflective observation (Kolb, 1984, 31).

## To break those elements down a little bit

Concrete experience, that's straightforward, it's your hands-on experience of doing something; trying, doing things, getting your hands dirty. This is followed by reflective observation; which at a basic level is pretty straightforward, it's simply looking back at what has just happened, either to yourself or to someone else. Kolb views this as a process of integrating ideas, combining experience with memories to create meaning.

To take an example from when we recorded the *Pedagodzilla* episode on *The Matrix* and experiential learning – Mikezilla couldn't get his microphone to work in a way that Markzilla could hear what he was saying. After spending a while struggling with various settings and checking the equipment, Markzilla realised his headphones were turned way down. Turning up the volume meant everything worked perfectly.

So that was the concrete experience. We discussed it, drew on our memories of past recording experiences and decided that focusing on the sound transmission technology but paying no attention to the sound reception technology (and its operator) was a really, really stupid thing to do. That was the reflective observation stage.

The **abstract conceptualisation** stage involves looking at what you've done and deciding what general principles can be taken from it. What does this tell us about what works and what doesn't? In many cases, this requires going to the literature, asking colleagues, looking for parallels elsewhere and building that information into the decision-making process.

A confounding variable in this particular example was that this was the Zillas' first use of Lavalier microphones, so the assumption was that the problem would lie with them. However, subsequent reflection led to the general principle that we should always start by assuming Markzilla is the problem, before we shift our attention to the technology.

This took us on to **active experimentation**, or incorporating the general principle we've just identified when planning the next activity. The Zillas built a new step into the recording process – if something fails, begin by checking Markzilla hasn't made an obvious mistake. If, for example, his microphone is back-to-front, then this concrete experience leads to further reflective observation, such as, 'He really is an idiot, isn't he?' The experiential learning cycle goes round and round, with our understanding gradually improving.

When Mikezilla accidentally spent ten minutes recording an episode in which everyone spoke about *The Lord of the Rings* while using monster voices, more reflection and abstract conceptualisation were needed, and it was time to add a new step to the recording process.

The experiential learning model describes the process we go through when we learn from what we do. We try something out. If it goes right, we do it again. If it goes wrong, we think about why that has happened (ideally drawing on what other people have experienced) and do something different next time. The model simply formalises these stages. If at first you don't succeed, try, try, try again but, if you want to learn from your experience, incorporate some reflection and rethinking into that process. As the quote misattributed to Einstein says: 'The definition of insanity is doing the same thing over and over again and expecting a different result.'

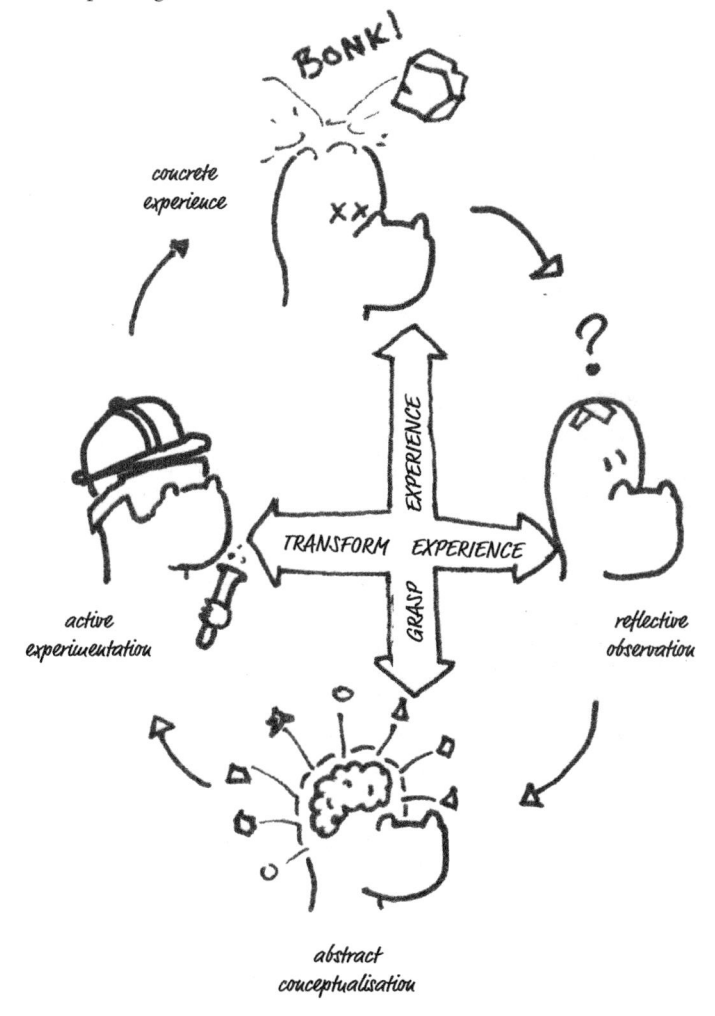

*concrete experience*

*active experimentation*

TRANSFORM EXPERIENCE

GRASP EXPERIENCE

*reflective observation*

*abstract conceptualisation*

*(highly accurate experiential learning diagram)*

## The answer(s)

The question of whether Neo uses experiential learning in *The Matrix* ought to be prefaced by more existential questions. Does what happens in a virtual space count as experience? Is it authentic? Is there a spoon? But we won't do it in that order, because the existential questions are more difficult.

Breaking down the learning moments for Neo, we see there's a scene in which he's sitting in the Nebuchadnezzar wired into a teaching machine by one of the crew members, Tank (who, incidentally, isn't fitted with the technology that enables him to enter the Matrix). Tank has a set of cassettes with different skills recorded on them, from which he chooses combat training ('Ju-jitsu, I'm going to learn ju-jitsu?'). The programs are directly loaded into Neo's brain. It's a good example of something that is clearly not experiential learning. Neo just sits there and receives the training with no active participation on his part. The experiential part of learning these skills occurs later when he has the chance to exhibit them to Morpheus in a virtual dojo that is a pared down version of the Matrix.

As a training space, this mini-Matrix is different from the construct the machines have created because it can be slowed down and paused for demonstration purposes. Morpheus could just have told Neo this, but placing Neo within the context of the situation Morpheus is preparing him for provides the concrete (or is it?) experience that makes the reflection more meaningful.

When Neo enters the virtual dojo, his brain and body contain the muscle memory skills he's acquired from Tank's download, but he also has to learn from Morpheus about the malleability of reality in order to make full use of his potential.

Here is the Warchowskis' script for part of this scene.

12: EXPERIENTIAL LEARNING AND *THE MATRIX*

> *Morpheus attacks him and it is like nothing we have seen. His feet and fists are everywhere taking Neo apart. For every blow Neo blocks, five more hit their marks until – Neo falls. Panting, on his hands and knees, blood spits from his mouth, speckling the white floor of the Dojo.*
> MORPHEUS: *How did I beat you?*
> NEO: *You – You're too fast.*
> MORPHEUS: *Do you think my being faster, stronger has anything to do with my muscles in this place?*
> *Neo is frustrated, still unable to catch his breath.*
> MORPHEUS: *Do you believe that's air you are breathing now?*
> *Neo squints at him.*
> MORPHEUS: *If you can free your mind, the body will follow.*
> *Neo stands, nodding.*
> MORPHEUS: *Again.*
>
> (Warchowski and Warchowski, 1996)

Morpheus takes Neo through an entire cycle of experiential learning in that short sequence:

- There's a concrete experience: 'Morpheus attacks him and it is like nothing we have seen. His feet and fists are everywhere taking Neo apart. For every blow Neo blocks, five more hit their marks until – Neo falls.'
- There's a reflective observation: 'How did I beat you?' 'You – You're too fast.'
- There's abstract conceptualisation: 'Do you think my being faster, stronger has anything to do with my muscles in this place?'
- Finally, there's the last part of this first loop. When Neo fights again, he attempts to apply active experimentation

(by freeing his mind, his body will follow), which results in a new set of concrete experiences as the cycle enters its second loop.

The most important part of the cycle as far as Neo's learning is concerned is the abstract conceptualisation – his actual muscles and speed have no effect on his performance within the space. As he learns that he can manipulate the reality within the space with his mind, he becomes better at fighting and, with each cycle, he develops not his muscle memory skills for combat but his skills at this manipulation.

Neo uses this cycle several times in the film in non-formal learning situations. The final point is when he's shot by several agents who have cornered him in a corridor. On that occasion, he realises that even bullets aren't subject to the normal rules of physics in a virtual space.

The evidence for the experiential learning cycle being employed by Morpheus in the training situations is pretty conclusive. What's more conjectural, because it is employed within a simulation, is whether these count as 'actual experiences', or whether they should simply be considered 'experiences'.

When this was being discussed in the podcast, Mike and Mark had different perspectives.

## The answer: Mikezilla's perspective

*'I play a lot of video games. I'd like to play more. I'm one of those people who on their deathbed will be saying, 'Man, I wish I'd played more video games.' I use the experiential learning model a lot in the games I play, but I'm learning how to do that in a virtual world. In that regard, my experience is perfectly legitimate. I think Neo's experience, all the relevance*

*of his experience, is couched in this virtual world in the first film. It's a perfectly legitimate piece of experiential learning because he's learning how to interact in a virtual environment. Therefore, it matches and is appropriate. Everything you learn, experience-wise, is appropriate to a particular scenario. For example, I don't think* Euro Truck Simulator, *which is the inexplicably popular computer game in which you drive a truck, would actually give you what you needed as a learning experience to drive a truck.' -Mikezilla*

## The answer: Markzilla's perspective

'*Though the stuff you learn in a virtual world won't necessarily be applicable to the physical world, that's true of moving from any one scenario to any other scenario. Some of it can translate into the physical world. A good example of an experiential learning project in a virtual world was the SWIFT (Second World Immersive Future Teaching) project at Leicester University (Childs and Kuksa, 2014, 153-154). Paul Rudman was the researcher on the project, David Burden at Daden Ltd built it, and they and others set up a genetics lab in the virtual world Second Life$^{TM}$. The problem they were addressing was that whenever the students were in the physical lab they could carry out the steps for genetic sequencing, but they didn't match that conceptually with what they'd learnt about the science of what was actually going on with the genes.*

'*And so, what Paul and David and the others set up was a space where the learner's avatar enters the lab and there are certain basic safety things the learner has to remember to do, otherwise they receive error warnings and alerts. The project didn't replicate the physical nature of turning the machines*

> *on and flicking particular buttons on and off, but what it did do was take the learner step by step through the operation of the equipment. As the student was doing a step, a little animation appeared above the equipment to show what was happening conceptually.*
>
> *'And that is experiential learning. It's not exactly applicable to the physical world because the student hasn't learnt how to operate the apparatus, but they have learnt the order of the steps that have to take place, as well as what's happening conceptually at that step. All of that applies in the physical world when the student's in the physical lab.*
>
> *'This also exemplifies the difference between simple simulation and replication. It doesn't replicate the physical world; it's a simulation in that it takes some elements of the physical world and maps them to the virtual environment, but also adds things which you couldn't do physically to enhance the learning.' ~Markzilla*

## The answer: the literature perspective

Due to the nature of the technology we have today, there are evident differences between the physical world and virtual worlds. No-one could mistake one for another. It's quite possible to drive a truck for a living and find the truck simulator so different from this experience you can play it in order to relax (Fesshole, 2022). However, if we're talking about whether there is an *intrinsic* difference between virtual and physical learning due to their essential nature, rather than the practical differences we see today, the literature is pretty consistent.

If you look at the neurological evidence, when you're playing immersive games such as *Minecraft*, the memories are stored in the same way as the memories from physical activities (Stark et al, 2021). The more you feel immersed, the better the recall (Bailey et al, 2012). In the case of something as technically sophisticated as the Matrix, the virtual reality is indistinguishable from the physical reality. The only way you could know which one you're in is that physical reality is noticeably shittier. Philosophically, you could argue, and in *Reality+*, David Chalmers does this extensively, that if they're indistinguishable, one is just as valid as the other, particularly if you take into account the possibility that we're all living in a simulation anyway or, at least, we can't prove beyond doubt that there is an external world (Chalmers, 2022). Conan the Cimmerian put it far more succinctly while pirating with Bêlit on the Black Coast in Robert E. Howard's Queen of the Black Coast 'If life is illusion, then I am no less an illusion, and being thus, the illusion is real to me' (Howard, 1934; 539).

This position is at odds with arguments such as Robert Nozick's thought experiment of an experience machine. This imaginary device can provide users with whichever desirable or pleasurable experiences they choose, and they cannot distinguish those experiences from the ones they would have apart from the machine. Nozick concludes that 'the connection to actuality is important whether or not we desire it – that is why we desire it – and the experience machine is inadequate because it doesn't give us that' (Bramble, 2016). But when the illusion is indistinguishable to us from actuality then, as Chalmers (and Conan) would argue, it is actually as actual as actuality is actual.

One crew member of the Nebuchadnezzar, Cypher, betrays the others under the promise that he'll be inserted back into the Matrix and not know it's a simulation.

*The real world. Ha, what a joke. You know what real is? I'll tell you what real is. Real is just another four-letter word. ... You know, I know that this steak doesn't exist. I know when I put it in my mouth, the Matrix is telling my*

> *brain that it is juicy and delicious. After nine years, do*
> *you know what I've realized? Ignorance is bliss*
> (Warchowski and Warchowski, 1996).

Philosophically, Cypher is the most pragmatic of the crew (although also a scheming double-crosser). He acknowledges that the so-called 'real' world is no more nor less illusory than the virtual one, so why not pick the one with better food?

It appears that neurologically, philosophically and therefore, we'd argue, pedagogically, simulation learning is no different from experiential learning. So our conclusion is that, yes, Neo does really experience experiential learning in *The Matrix*.

## Tips for practice

As we said near the start, the essential element that makes experiential learning distinctive is the reflection stage. But, the iteration of the cycle is also very important.

The two things that make experiential learning distinctive are the reflection stage and the iteration. And the movement between abstractions and practicality.

The three things that… oh, you see where this is going.

Experiential learning is, as we noted earlier, tied up with how we automatically go about solving problems. This helps the learning process, but also makes it more difficult for students to see what they're doing as learning. As educators, what can help is to:

1. Break the separate stages down for students during the learning process and make each stage explicit.
2. Scaffold each stage. We reflect all the time, but it's difficult to do this well. Provide students with questions to ask

themselves about their experiences. Take them through the process of abstract conceptualisation, pointing out how drawing on literature and generalising from their experiences helps. Give them some examples of the learning cycle (if you use *The Matrix*, we've already done the work for you).

3. Encourage both reflection in action and reflection on action. Reflection in action involves recording experiences as they're happening, maybe writing a short comment on social media, capturing something as a recording or making a note on your phone. Reflection on action is a more considered look back once the activity is complete. Learners might use blog posts to record these thoughts.

4. All the stages in a cycle can be built on when creating a plan to kick off a new cycle, but this new cycle can also be a fresh start. Encourage students to feel liberated by the process. This frees them from the tension associated with pressure to get it right the first time. In fact, the more they screw up the first time round, the more learning is available to draw upon the next time round. At least, that's how we justify to ourselves the fact that we screw up all the time. We're just fast-tracking the learning process.

5. Finally, Mikezilla gets to ring his metacognition bell, because foregrounding the cycle so it's explicit, supporting students in thinking about their thinking, is a very useful tool for them to have in their metacognitive toolkit. Possibly the most versatile of them all. Metacognition – the WD40 of learning – whichever reality you're in.

# How about some more (references)? Hell, yes.

Abdulwahed, M. Nagy. Z. and Blanchard, R. (2008) Beyond the engineering pedagogy: engineering the pedagogy, modelling Kolb's learning cycle. In: *Proceedings of The Nineteenth Annual Conference of The Australian Association For Engineering Education (AAEE 2008)*, to Industry and Beyond. Yeppoon, Australia, 7-10 December, M2A3

Bailey, J., Bailenson, J.N., Won, A.S., Flora, J., & Armel, K.C (2012) Presence and memory: Immersive virtual reality effects on cued recall, *Proceedings of the International Society for Presence Research Annual Conference*. 24-26 October, Philadelphia, Pennsylvania, USA.

Bramble, B. (2016) The Experience Machine, *Philosophy Compass*, 11:3, 136–145. Available at: https://doi.org/10.1111/phc3.12303

Chalmers, D. (2022) *Reality+*, Norton Publishing, USA: New York

Chappell, L., Lorig, C. and Williams, A. (2010) Splendid American: a eulogy for Harvey Pekar, *Blog: The Lesser of Two Equals*, 6 August. Available at: https://thelesseroftwoequals.wordpress.com/2010/08/06/splendid-american-a-eulogy-for-harvey-pekar/

Childs, M., Estatiev, V., Hetherington, J., Jugo, G., Richardson, T. and Walton, G. (2015) Connecting to reading: inspiring young children to read through the creation of digital artefacts and use of social media, in A. Jefferies and M. Cubric (eds) *Proceedings of the 14th European Conference on e-Learning ECEL 2015*, University of Hertfordshire, Hatfield, UK, 147-155

Childs. M. and Kuksa, I. (2014) The future of spaces; physical or virtual? in I. Kuksa and M. Childs *Making Sense of Space*, Chandos, UK: Cambridge

Fesshole (2022) I work 50/60 hours a week as a lorry driver. When I come home to relax, I love to play Scania Truck Driving Simulator, Twitter 14 August. Available at: *https://twitter.com/fesshole/status/1558942800888086540*

Howard, R.E. (1934) *'Queen of the Black Coast', Weird Tales* , 23, May 1934. Popular Fiction Publishing Company; USA; Indianapolis, pp 530 - 549

Kolb, D.A. (1984) *Experiential Learning: Experience as the Source of Learning and Development*. Prentice Hall, Englewood Cliffs, NJ.

Kolb, D.A. and Fry R.E. (1975) Towards an applied theory of experiential learning. In C. Cooper (ed.) *Theories of Group Processes*. John Wiley and Sons, New York.

Stark, C.E.L., Clemenson, G.D., Aluru, U., Hatamian, N. and Stark, S.M. (2021) Playing Minecraft improves hippocampal-associated memory for details in middle aged adults, *Frontiers in Sports and Active Living*, 3. Available at: https://www.frontiersin.org/articles/10.3389/fspor.2021.685286

Warchowski, L. and Warchowski, A. (1996) *The Matrix*, https://imsdb.com/scripts/Matrix,-The.html

Scan the QR code to listen to
the podcast episode

## CHAPTER 13:

# HOW CAN YOU MAKE CONSTRUCTIVISM AMOUNT TO MORE THAN A HILL OF BEANS?

*Mark Childs and Mike Collins*

*Mike and Markzilla are virtually back from the town of the Cyber-Elves when they find themselves in the middle of a pitched battle.*

*Apparently, someone on social media has said something stupid, and both Dwarves and Elves are up in arms about it. 'Minimal guidance doesn't work,' shouts one side. 'Who are you calling Minimal Guidance?' bellows the other.*

*The Zillas are scared, and they've become separated from Beckzilla, who's presumably still off slaying vampires somewhere. Bravely, they try to find a way through the turmoil.*

As we've seen throughout this section, two of the main schools of thought about how to approach learning and teaching sometimes find themselves in conflict. In the chapter on the ten principles of instruction and Yoda, the principles focus a lot on drill and practice, which are techniques that work, and that match closely what we know about cognitive science, how the brain processes and stores information, and what its limits are.

However, the teaching approaches that focus on how students construct learning through activity, problem-solving, putting things into practice, and reflecting on the consequences of that are core to a lot of what we see in education. Even though there is little or no empirical evidence from neuroscience to establish the validity of these approaches, experiences of direct observation of students' learning support them. And, of course, when there's no formal education available if people need to learn something, these have always been the approaches that have been called upon.

The battle (and it does sometimes get very heated) between these viewpoints is exacerbated because they are located in two very different epistemological positions – positivists like to study images of the brain and the outcomes of interventions, while interpretivists like their rich accounts of what goes on in students' minds.

Where there are two or more competing models, the truth is probably that both are correct in some situations, and we just need a model that encompasses them both. It's important to avoid false dichotomies; far fewer positions are as mutually exclusive as social media would have you believe. Just because one thing is true, doesn't mean an alternative explanation isn't. On the other hand, saying two statements are true doesn't automatically lead to the conclusion both are equally true. The path between false dichotomies and false equivalences is a broad one but, nevertheless, people often stumble away from it.

The *Pedagodzilla* ethos will flavour the discussion throughout this chapter, in which we try to resolve the debate between the cognitive science Positivism people, and the problem-based, active, and experiential Constructivism people. We do this by asking: **How can you make constructivism amount to more than a hill of beans?**

Another element of the *Pedagodzilla* ethos involves trying not to be crappy to people. Part of this stance is to have a content warning before we start whenever necessary. The example we've chosen in this chapter is a real one, involving what sounds like a pretty bad example of parenting.

## A hill of beans

Our title makes reference to the 1942 film *Casablanca* and Humphrey Bogart's line in the final scene, 'It doesn't take much to see that the problems of three little people don't amount to a hill of beans in this crazy world.'

It's also a reference to a [then] Twitter storm around a series of tweets that became known as BeanDadGate (Campanoar, 2021; Petter, 2021). The person who became known as BeanDad tweeted a story in which he was doing a jigsaw puzzle, which apparently was really important to him, when his daughter came up and asked if she could have some lunch, which he saw as a very useful teaching moment.

Instead of getting his nine-year-old child some beans, he said, 'Well, let's get the tin opener and let's see if you can work it'. She fumbled around with the tin opener, it didn't really work, and he went back to his jigsaw puzzle.

The tin became substantially battered during the first few failed attempts to open it, so it was significantly more difficult to open than it should have been. Nevertheless, the child went forwards and backwards for about six hours until she finally got the tin open.

The story and the father's account of it have subsequently been deleted, because what he originally thought was a positive story got a significantly less than positive reaction.

To be as fair as possible to the parent, BeanDad's putting his child through that torment may have come from a well-meaning place. From Markzilla's personal experience, he'd vouch for the potential to act out of fear that your child won't develop to become a functional human being by the time they leave home or, worse, that they never become a functional enough human being to leave home. For BeanDad, having a daughter who gave up trying to do something could have sounded a warning bell that she would never try, and hence would never be successful.

Markzilla had the experience in his twenties of sharing a house with a friend a few years older than him who refused to use the tin opener because she didn't know how to. Markzilla had to open the tin for her while she looked on, resentful that there could be something so alien in the kitchen.

Where BeanDad overreacted, we would suggest, is that between the ages of nine and 30, there are plenty of opportunities to learn. There's no need to panic, and certainly no need to exert that much pressure on a nine-year-old child for six hours, even if you're keeping her fed with pistachio nuts while you're doing it (Skenazy, 2021).

Where this is interesting for our wider discussion of constructivism is that not only was this a teaching moment that failed, but also some of the responses to it included references to issues around minimal guidance, specifically a paper called, *Why Minimal Guidance During Instruction Does Not Work* (Kirschner, Sweller and Clark, 2006).

So, although a stressful story it was also an insightful one, and one to which many people can relate. Particularly as, when presented with situations in which we've been expected to perform with little or no guidance – in non-formal situations like DIY for example – we've performed so badly that we've learned nothing other than that we can't do it.

## Constructivism vs cognitive architecture

To recap Chapter 6, constructivism is one of the overarching meta-concepts in teaching and learning. Under it sits a whole load of other approaches, including problem-based learning, experiential learning, and active learning.

These are all about learners who already have a schema of understanding, and a set of skills and knowledge. The teacher provides learning opportunities for students to build their own knowledge and connections on those foundations, thus creating another layer of abilities that will form the foundations of the next stage of learning.

By its very nature, constructivism is student-centred: you can't do it without starting from what the student is already capable of. It also includes a built-in assumption that the experience will be more effective if it's relevant to learners and their lives. The argument for constructivist approaches is that they're stronger and more effectively embedded than being taught something out of context in a classroom, because the links to previous knowledge have been made by the students themselves.

Constructivist approaches aren't universally accepted, however. In *Constructivism Is Like a Zombie that Refuses To Die*, Isak Skogstad interviewed Paul Kirschner, one of the authors of the paper mentioned above, and Professor Kirschner raised a lot of valid points against constructivism as an approach, the chief one being that direct instruction is the most efficient use of the time available for teaching. He's also a big proponent of cognitive load theory and how 'cognitive architecture affects how we learn and how this interacts with instruction'. Which all seems valid.

Constructivism doesn't have the same neurological basis to it, and isn't an efficient way of learning. The Kirschner, Sweller and Park (2006) paper (and, yes, that is the same Sweller we came across in our cognitive load chapter) is an analysis of the failure of constructivist, discovery, problem-based, experiential, and inquiry-based teaching. Basically, everything we've been exploring in the last three chapters. The authors' argument is that minimal guidance overloads the working capacity of the cognitive architecture of the brain (KSP, 2006). In other words, you can't learn efficiently if your brain's got too many things to think about at once.

They conclude that, 'The onus should surely be on those who support inquiry-based instruction to explain how such a procedure circumvents the well-known limits of working memory when dealing with novel information' (KSP, 2006; 77).

However, all is not lost. Kirschner and pals also acknowledge that people do learn by building on what they know already. They state, 'The constructivist description of learning is accurate.' It's just that 'the instructional consequences suggested by constructivists do not necessarily follow' (KSP, 2006; 78) and even 'the addition of a more vigorous emphasis on the practical application of inquiry and problem-solving skills seems very positive' (KSP, 2006; 77). Woo-hoo.

So what is their problem?

The teaching approach they're taking issue with is the idea of minimal guidance, which is 'the rejection of instruction based on the facts, laws, principles and theories that make up a discipline's content' (KSP, 2006; 78). Which does sound like a really bad idea. However, few people take constructivist approaches to that extreme. Showing why minimal guidance does not work is a long way from an analysis of the failure of constructivist, discovery, problem-based, experiential, and inquiry-based teaching.

There's a study presenting the opposing position that also got bounced around in the post-BeanDad storm. It's by Deslauriers et al (2019) and it advocates for active learning in classrooms rather than direct instruction. Papers in the *Proceedings of the National Academy of Sciences* (PNAS), which is where this paper appeared, don't just have abstracts, they have a significance statement, which is an excellent idea as you get the whole message encapsulated in one paragraph. To save you reading their paper, here's their significance statement:

> *'Despite active learning being recognized as a superior method of instruction in the classroom, a major recent survey found that most college STEM instructors still choose traditional teaching methods. This article addresses the long-standing question of why students and faculty remain resistant to active learning. Comparing passive lectures with active learning using a randomised experimental approach and identical course materials, we find that students in the active classroom learn more, but they feel like they learn less. We show that this negative correlation is caused in part by the increased cognitive effort required during active learning. Faculty who adopt*

*active learning are encouraged to intervene and address this misperception, and we describe a successful example of such an intervention.'*

Deslauriers et al (2019)

So, some things to unpack there – particularly active learning being recognised as a superior method of instruction (tell that to the positivists). You'll have to look up the paper to see them back up that claim (oh, looks like we haven't saved you that step after all).

However much the authors disagree with the Kirschner et al paper on that point, there's one area where they do agree: it's the extra cognitive load involved in active learning that gets in the way. In other words, students are so busy learning that they don't have the spare capacity to stand back and observe how well they're learning. Their cognitive load can't handle both cognition and metacognition at the same time.

And this is the point: behaviourism, constructivism and (to be covered in the next chapter) social constructivism aren't competing approaches, or even theories, about learning; they're complementary ones.

Direct instruction is efficient; the traditional approaches build on centuries of experience, and can be legitimised by reference to the cognitive architecture of the brain, which beats anything else. Remember our chapter on ontology and epistemology? Not all epistemologies are created equal.

The approaches where you can point to a scan and say, based on valid and reliable analysis, 'Look, that's where the learning is happening,' have more solid evidence than any number of interpretivist studies, no matter how randomised they are. From the learner perspective, students are familiar with traditional approaches, they know where they stand with them, and they recognise how learning works within them.

Constructivist approaches model real-world behaviour for most subjects. They're slower, more difficult, and involve more missteps, but they're more empowering, and they're often more fun. Learning has to be open-ended, random and playful sometimes, or who'd want to do it?

Kirschner's argument in the Skogstad interview that 'students need longer time to solve problems, to learn to solve them, they make more mistakes and also get frustrated on the way' is not a good reason for omitting problems from the curriculum. Efficiency is not the be-all and end-all of education. And we could also argue that, if you want efficiency, a 40- or 50-minute lecture isn't the best approach either.

The middle ground within both these papers (when they're not dissing the alternative approaches) is the acceptance by traditionalists that their approaches benefit from a bit of problem-based learning, and recognition by the active learning bods that active learning needs some scaffolding with direct instruction and modelling of approaches, in order for students to fully benefit from the activities. Once learners have acquired the basic schema for the subject, and have all the good facts-laws-principles-and-theories stuff bedded down in their long-term memory, then they've got the spare cognitive capacity to do all that constructivist-feelgood-empowering-and-fun farting-around-with-problems stuff without being overloaded and without the learning being too inefficient.

Then, when they've done that, teachers can show them what they've learned, because while they're deep down in the problem solving, they're too busy doing that to sort out what it is they're learning. And if they've somehow constructed the wrong schema in coming to an answer to the problem, teachers can point that out and help them to the correct solution.

So, basically, the summary of the problem is: learners don't want maximum guidance because it's boring and it doesn't teach them to be independent learners. On the other hand, they don't want minimal guidance because that means they're lost. With minimal guidance, nothing makes it into your long-term memory due to cognitive overload, because everything's in your working memory. Not only that but you also feel as if you're not learning because you're not reflecting on your learning, and you're not being shown what you've learned.

Obviously, the best, most effective learning is something that combines those two things according to a ratio that you have to determine as an educator. And that choice is determined by a variety of contextual elements, including how well your students know the subject, what age they are, and what their previous experience is.

## The answer

To answer our question, **How can you make constructivism amount to more than a hill of beans?**, let's take a look at BeanDadgate and how constructivism could have been used far more consciously to make this a good learning and teaching event.

The scenario starts with the daughter coming to her dad with a tin of beans, wanting some food. He gives her a tin opener and tells her to work out for herself how to open the tin. The worst form of minimal guidance. At the other end of the spectrum, equally bad from a learning point of view, would have been doing it for her and saying, 'There you go.' With the implicit metacognitive message being, 'Wasn't that simple? Aren't you an idiot for not being able to do it yourself?'

Though at least the daughter would have been fed and the father would have been able to go right back to his jigsaw puzzle.

Cynically, we're not convinced most universities would do it any better. Our best guess about what the university approach to tin opening would look like is: give a 60-minute lecture on the history of tins and how they have been opened, focusing on the white males who've opened tins in the past; describe how a tin opener works, including different mechanisms and the evolution of the design, possibly requiring students to buy an expensive textbook that illustrates the process in great technical detail; ask students to give presentations on tin opening and, finally, assess them by getting them to write an essay about tin opening. Enough to persuade any student they'd be better off going for a take-away. At no point though, would they actually pick up a tin opener and open a tin with it.

If BeanDad wanted to go for direct instruction, he could provide a demonstration to his daughter, explaining how to hold the tin opener, where the cutting blade is, and how the process works. She might learn how to do it in this way, but she might still not be able to open a tin, even if she could describe how the tin should be opened.

Ideally, BeanDad would scaffold the process by breaking it into three steps. The first would be to demonstrate how the tin opener works, accompanied by a description of what he was doing: 'You clip this on here and rotate this.' So far, so like direct instruction.

However, the teaching and learning wouldn't end at that point. Second step: once he'd demonstrated the process, he'd get his daughter to try it herself under his guidance, helping out if she ran into problems. Once she's opened the tin successfully with his support, he'd ask her to do it again – this time without guidance. They'd have ended up with three opened tins, but then some people like three tins of beans.

This is, incidentally, how meerkats teach their young to kill scorpions, by showing them how it's done, then giving them increasingly difficult tasks; starting them off with dead scorpions before proceeding to live ones. (Hoppitt, et al, 2008; 487).

They're not consciously providing the scaffolding that educational theorist Vygotsky suggested was helpful for learning – they're just responding to different bleating from their pups. At least their approach is student-centred, though.

With scaffolding, each stage of the process only advances the required skills by a slight amount, so there's only a minimal use of working memory at any time. Each layer builds incrementally on the layer below, and nothing falls over because at no point is the learner having to do anything unsupported. Once the learner can do something, the scaffolding (guidance) can be removed.

Assuming his daughter has the patience, once she's finished the task (perhaps when they're eating the beans), they could talk through the steps involved in learning this skill, because although she can open a tin of beans now, there will be plenty of other things she needs to work out when BeanDad's not there, or when he's busy piecing together a more difficult jigsaw.

BeanDad might even present it to her as an example of problem-based learning (see chapter 11). She's worked through the first steps by herself:

1. She examined the case and identified that the day wasn't proceeding as it should.
2. She identified the problem – she was hungry.
3. She analysed the problem – usually, someone provides food around now.
4. She drafted an explanatory model – a good solution would be to get her dad to open a tin and heat up some beans.

Her dad could take her through the next steps of problem-based learning:

5. He established a learning goal for her – learn to use the tin opener. In future, she could establish her own learning goals.
6. Instead of asking him to open the tin, she could have collected information from him on how to do this.
7. The final stage would have been to apply and discuss what she had learned by trying to use the tin opener and asking him for support if necessary.

That's probably way too much formality for a discussion over a tin of beans, especially for someone who really wants to get back to his jigsaw, but the basics can be summed up briefly. 'You did really well in making some moves towards lunch. It's helpful to learn how to do things for yourself; you can always ask me for help with this sort of thing and check back with me if you run into problems.'

BeanDad and his daughter might have talked about places to go to learn how to do things, like YouTube, or how to search for operating manuals. They could have discussed how the feel of the machine and your own proprioception are important to get right when learning practical things and how you adapt grip etc to get the right feel of something clicking into place. They could have talked about experimentation and observation leading to the correct result.

Then maybe the next time the daughter was stuck on something she might have recalled how she learned to open the tin of beans and then applied those strategies to learn for herself rather than bothering BeanDad all the time. Jeez.

We keep emphasising metacognition in this book, because reflecting on how you've learned and learning the process of learning is translatable to other situations. Give a person a fish and they eat for a day, teach them to fish and they eat for a lifetime; teach them how to learn to fish and there's no end to what they can do. If you're a vegan or vegetarian, substitute your own analogy here.

Another aspect to this process of teaching independent learning is that, as a parent, you don't know the answer to every question. As a teacher, the change in emphasis from sage on the stage to guide on the side lets you off the hook to some extent because it reduces the expectation that you'll always know the answer. The most exciting, and also daunting, moments are when your children or students surpass you in some areas.

The final lesson to take away from any sort of learning, particularly important with a constructivist approach, is that not knowing is fine. Maybe you don't know how to open tins of beans when you're nearly 30 because you've been buying those weird little plastic pots all these years. Mark's nineties flatmate had possibly just used tins with ring-pulls, or perhaps was too upper class to ever eat beans. Or perhaps had always hacked away at tins with a pen-knife or something. When faced with a tin opener for the first time, it's fine to ask how to use it. Being annoyed by and fearful of an unfamiliar tool in your shared kitchen isn't. The best thing to teach people is that not knowing is legitimate, not trying isn't. Which applies to teachers as well as learners.

While we're on the subjects of minimal guidance and cognitive load, there's another factor to be considered, building on the discussions in our cognitive load chapter, which is the role of germane cognitive load.

Germane load is basically nothing to do with the material being learned, or how it's presented. It refers to other elements in the scenario having an impact on the capacity to learn. A hugely limiting part of an excessive germane load is self-doubt. The higher their self-efficacy, the more a student is going to learn. A lot of that is because, while they're learning, their brain isn't full of messages like, 'I'm so shit at this.'

Some frustration is good, because if a learner is driven by needing to solve a problem, it can be motivating when they overcome the frustration and finally get it right. Too much frustration is demotivating. This is why the best console games adapt their difficulty levels to the player's ability. If a player fails too many times on a task they'll give up, not only on that game, but on being a potential customer for all the sequels.

Each successful task completed produces a small dopamine hit that reinforces behaviour, although how dopaminergic systems work with cognitive load is really complicated (Otto et al, 2013; 752).

Reinforcing an individual's motivation to learn is a good thing, whereas failure reinforces the message that they can't do it. This increases the germane load, making it even more difficult to do it in future.

This helps to explain why small step-changes are so successful as strategies for learning. Each small task is likely to be successful, because it makes small demands on skills or knowledge, and so learners are more motivated to try the next one. If you're bad at DIY, for example, solving a problem like an F01 error code on your washing machine can feel like a big deal and might encourage you to try something more complicated next time.

> *For anyone who's interested, it's an error with the basic input / output system (BIOS) so you need to reboot it. Just turn it off at the socket for two minutes, then turn it back on again (Whirlpool Appliances, 2020). For someone who knows what they're doing, they might then be up to replacing the drum. But replacing the drum when you have no idea about how washing machines work could go badly wrong.*

> *As a learner, you have to make those calls for yourself. As a teacher or parent, your role is partly to assess whether a learner is at the turning-it-off-and-on again stage or whether they are now able to progress to the turning-it-off-and-waiting-two-minutes-before-turning-it-back-on-again stage.*
> *~ Markzilla*

The other aspect of germane load that's relevant to our example is that learners who are hungry have much lower cognitive function, particularly children. When we were recording the original podcast in early 2021, footballer Marcus Rashford was campaigning for children in the UK to be fed during school holidays, because a lot of them rely on their school meals for a significant part of their nutrition. There have been a lot of studies linking children's hunger with poor cognition (e.g. Taras, 2005). If you're hungry, you're operating with one hand tied behind your back, cognitively speaking. Learning with minimal guidance is therefore going to be trickier, because you need to be fed in order to learn effectively.

In summary, to answer the question: **How can you make constructivism amount to more than a hill of beans?**

1. Minimal guidance isn't effective, but neither is an approach that fails to develop independent learners, so guide them step by step. Scaffold learners through the stages of opening a tin of beans, by demonstrating and explaining the process, getting them to repeat it with guidance and, once they have done it successfully, asking them to repeat the process independently.
2. Help learners to reflect on their own experience, so they understand how to learn for themselves.
3. Don't try to teach hungry kids, but do try to teach them that they can learn.

# Tips for practice

Our top tip for applying the above in your own teaching practice is that there's no specific winning formula. Don't follow the cognitive-architecture-and-behaviourism people completely; don't put into practice a full-on version of the approaches suggested by the active-problem-based-constructivism people. You don't want minimal guidance, but you also don't want complete guidance.

With minimal guidance, you'll be overloading your students cognitively because they'll all be trying to think through everything from first principles. You need to model what they need to do. You need to provide some sort of scaffolding. Build in reflective stages so the problem-solving skills they've acquired can be applied the next time they need to solve a problem. This means you can gradually step back and start giving learners problems without providing a lot of guidance. The first time through, don't just throw them in at the deep end. Teach them how to swim first, get them to practise in the shallow end. Only when you're sure they won't drown can you throw them in at the deep end and expect them to have fun there.

At the other end of the spectrum, you don't want to provide complete guidance, because then learners won't acquire problem-solving skills. If all they're doing is learning the facts, then reiterating them might be efficient. It might be an effective way to learn the content of your course. But it's not going to provide the long-term skills that learners need to interact with the world, and it's not going to be fun either.

Getting the balance between those two elements right is a matter of judgement. It's a matter of knowing your learners, knowing what they're capable of at their age and their level. It's also being sensitive as a teacher and a learner to your students' context, being sensitive to the fact that your students may not be in an ideal personal situation for their own learning, and perhaps thinking about ways of supporting them that don't just involve teaching.

And don't just enable your students to learn, but also teach them to reflect on that learning, on the processes they've tried out and how to apply them in the future. If you give people constant guidance, they don't learn to be independent learners. They may learn a lot of facts and they may learn them really quickly or effectively and efficiently, but if they're not given the opportunities to develop metacognitive skills, then once they're no longer under your direction they won't be ready to go off and do their own thing.

That's difficult, so here's our final point. While you're teaching students the reflective metacognitive skills that help them identify the process of their learning, there's another level. They need to be able to critically evaluate that process and identify the strengths and weaknesses of the approach for them as individuals. Doing this can not only help students to guide their own independent learning, you can use this approach to help you modify your approaches and take some of the guesswork out of creating the right balance. Not only does minimal guidance of learners by teachers have some major failings, so does the minimal guidance of teachers by learners.

But that's a whole other tin of beans.

# References: Dig deeper into the hill of beans

Campanoar, D. (2021) Here's why everyone is talking about 'Bean Dad', Blog post *Refinery29*, 3 January. Available at: https://www.refinery29.com/en-gb/2021/01/10248576/what-is-bean-dad-story-twitter-meaning

Deslauriers, L., McCarty, L.S., Miller, K., Callaghan, K., and Kestin, G. (2019) Measuring actual learning versus feeling of learning in response to being actively engaged in the classroom, 4 September,, *Proceedings of the National Academy of Sciences*, 116: 39, 19251-19257. Available at: https://doi.org/10.1073/pnas.1821936116

Hoppitt, W.J.E, Brown, G.R., Kendal, R., Rendell, L., Thornton, A., Webster, M.M. and Laland, K.N. (2008) Lessons from animal teaching, *Trends in Ecology & Evolution*, 23:9, 486-493. Available at: https://doi.org/10.1016/j.tree.2008.05.008

Kirschner, P.A., Sweller, J., and Clark, R.E. (2006) Why minimal guidance during instruction does not work: an analysis of the failure of constructivist, discovery, problem-based, experiential, and inquiry-based teaching, *Educational Psychologist*, 41:2, 75-86, DOI: 10.1207/s15326985ep4102_1

Otto, A.R., Gershman, S.J., Markman, A.B, and Daw, N.D. (2013) The curse of planning: dissecting multiple reinforcement-learning systems by taxing the central executive, *Psychological Science*, 24:5, May, 751-761, https://doi.org/10.1177/0956797612463080

Petter, O. (2021) Who is 'bean dad' and why does Twitter hate him? Blog: *Lifestyle, Independent Newspaper*, 4 January. Available at: https://www.independent.co.uk/life-style/bean-dad-john-roderick-twitter-b1781905.html

Skenazy, L. (2021) Remember Bean Dad? Child Protective Services was called to check on his daughter, Blog: *Free-Range Kids*, 16 February. Available at: https://reason.com/2021/02/16/bean-dad-child-services-john-roderick-can-opener/

Skogstad, I. (2019) Constructivist pedagogy is like a zombie that refuses to die, Blog: *3-Star Learning Experiences*, 26 March. Available at: https://3starlearningexperiences.wordpress.com/2019/03/26/constructivist-pedagogy-is-like-a-zombie-that-refuses-to-die/

Taras, H. (2005), Nutrition and student performance at school, *Journal of School Health*, 75, 199-213. Available at: https://doi.org/10.1111/j.1746-1561.2005.tb06674.x

Whirlpool Appliances (2020) What do your washing machine error codes mean? *Indesit: Life Proof*. Available at: https://www.indesitservice.co.uk/washing-machine-repair/error-codes

Scan the QR code to listen to the podcast episode

# PART 3

## THE BASIN OF BONDS

*In which our Zillas take the arcane secrets of the cognitivists, the dark rites of the constructivists and the sweaty prophecies of the positivists to the southern lands, to see how learning works once people start doing it together.*

**CHAPTER 14:**

# HOW DOES SOCIAL CONSTRUCTIVISM ENABLE THE FELLOWSHIP OF THE RING TO FIND THE PATH TO SUCCESS?

*Rebecca Ferguson, Mark Childs and Mike Collins*

*Mikezilla and Markzilla leave the lands of the Positivists and Constructivism, hoping that due to their intervention, combined with their general tendency to sit on the fence at every possible opportunity, they have brought about some reconciliation between the two nations.*

*They enter the land of Social Constructivism and, in need of a drink after their travels, they enter an inn. Here they're reunited with Beckzilla, who has been here all this time. She introduces them to the locals – a gregarious folk who learn through talking and sharing.*

*There's an ominous land on the horizon that could be the Zillas' next stop. Only, according to the locals (backed up by Google Maps), one does not simply walk there.*

Looking back to earlier chapters, it's evident that working things out from first principles is not an effective learning strategy. From BeanDad's daughter struggling for hours with a tin opener to Luke Skywalker staring morosely at a sunken X-wing, learners need more support than an enigmatic, 'Do. Or do not. There is no try.' Most of the successful learners we have looked at have drawn on multiple perspectives and links to support them. Scrooge amended his understanding of the meaning of Christmas in response to the different views presented to him by various ghosts and spirits. Buffy solved problems by drawing on the skills of her Scooby Gang. However, it's not enough simply to have multiple people involved. *Come Dine with Me* contestants misjudged their abilities because they drew on too narrow a range of perspectives. The entire team that Arnie led was killed horribly by the Predator (see the next chapter) because Arnie failed to provide them with ways of learning together as a group. So learning with others is important, but it doesn't always work. This prompted us to look at an example of this in action in *The Lord of the Rings*, and to ask the question: **How does the Council of Elrond use social constructivism to plan the destruction of the One Ring?**

## *The Lord of the Rings*: Council of Elrond

Let's start with *The Lord of the Rings*, the novel and film trilogy in which the Council of Elrond takes place. This is an epic fantasy that follows the travels of Frodo and his pals: Sam, Merry and Pippin. They're hobbits, little halfling people who've got great big hairy feet and like to have lots of breakfasts, which we can all relate to. They're brave and adventurous and they find themselves in possession of the One Ring, Isildur's Bane, the Great Ring to rule them all, which was created by the villainous Sauron who was (mostly) destroyed in a previous super epic war. With

## 14: SOCIAL CONSTRUCTIVISM AND *THE LORD OF THE RINGS*

a weapon of that power, there are only three options: use it, hide it or destroy it. After a long discussion at the Council of Elrond, Frodo and his friends decide on option three, then embark on a long quest to hurl it into the volcano where it was forged.

Along the way they meet old friends, colleagues, allies and enemies. These include Gandalf the wizard, cool but grumpy dude Aragorn, Legolas the elf, Gimli the dwarf, and Boromir – because one of the group has to be expendable. In this chapter, we join them at the point where they have the ring but don't know its true nature. Individuals from many lands have come to visit Elrond, one of the greatest elves, and each of them is saying in their own way, 'What's going on? I can see there's a war coming. I can see there's trouble brewing. I've got some fragments of a story, but I can't see the whole picture. I've come to Rivendell, aka Imladris, aka The Last Homely House, along with all these others, because Elrond always knows the answers.' And Elrond essentially says, 'Right, we'll gather together in a Council and we'll spend the morning sharing our stories.'

This is a part of the epic that comes between Dark Bits. The hobbits have come to Elrond through adventures. They've been attacked. Frodo's been stabbed with an evil knife and has just spent something like four days unconscious. But now he's recuperating in a blissful place. Everything's happy. The weather's nice. It's a lovely autumnal day. But soon they're going to have to set out on a dangerous and dark quest. This is an interlude with a calm-before-the-storm feel to it. And it's a period of massive exposition. The longest chapter in the whole book. Well, there's a lot to exposit.

The book itself is long – often published in three or even six volumes. However, it's only part of the much more extensive mythology created by its author, John Ronald Reuel Tolkien. Tolkien was born in Bloemfontein, South Africa, but grew up in one of the leafier parts of Birmingham, aware of the encroaching industrialisation around him in the Black Country. When the First World War broke out, he completed his Oxford degree in English Language and Literature before reluctantly enlisting in a war that killed many of his closest friends. Invalided out of the army, he began work on a mammoth project, aiming to create a mythology for England. The project grew as he worked first for the *Oxford English Dictionary* and then as a professor at Oxford. He developed whole languages, complex genealogies and detailed caste systems, inspired in part by the *Kalevala*, a Finnish epic compiled from folklore and mythology.

Tolkien's deep love of languages is apparent throughout *The Lord of the Rings*. Derivations of words are provided and the text often explains where different words come from. Key people, places and events have multiple names, depending on which elvish or dwarvish language is used. To take just one example, Aragorn, one of the main characters, is known by his genealogy (Aragorn II, son of Arathorn; Isildur's heir; Elendil's heir), his geographical origin (Man of the West), and his actions (Strider). He also has different names in the various languages created by Tolkien, including Dunadan (language: Sindarin); Estel (languages: Quenya and Sindarin); Elessar, Telcontar and Envinyatar (language: Quenya).

The mythology that Tolkien developed remained unfinished at his death but it permeates his work. More recently, much of it has been collected, edited and published – most notably in *The Silmarillion*, a collection of myths and stories about the 'Elder Days', the First Age of his imagined world. A better known book is *The Hobbit*, which introduces some of the characters who appear in *The Lord of the Rings*, and provides a detailed account of the finding of the Ring by Frodo's cousin, the hobbit Bilbo Baggins. One of the elements that made the book so successful, and created a set of belting movies, the 12th biggest movie franchise of all time, is the richness of this world – the sense that life goes on for characters even when the reader/viewer's attention is not focused on them. For example, not only does the Council of Elrond take place in a moment of calm in the book, for anyone who has read *The Hobbit*, this is a chance to re-encounter familiar characters. Bilbo is there, living in retirement. Gandalf the wizard and Glóin the dwarf are familiar faces, as is elf-leader Elrond. Legolas is the son of Thranduil, ruler of the elves who imprisoned Bilbo and his companions in Mirkwood.

In the Council of Elrond, the hobbits and their companions are about to engage in a process of social constructivism that will shape the future of their world. So, before looking at what happens there, let's introduce social constructivism.

## Social constructivism

We encountered constructivism in Chapter 10, where active learning helped Julie Andrews escape the Nazis (hoorah!). At its core is the idea that understanding is actively constructed by the learner. From the time we are born, we begin to develop our own understanding of how the world works. This understanding, and the way in which it is structured, varies according to context and the experiences that we have. This means that everyone comes to learning with their own ideas; everyone starts from a slightly different position. Constructivist approaches provide learners with activities, problems or experiences designed to add to that initial understanding and address existing misunderstandings. This is called constructivism because learners are guided to construct their own knowledge based on what they already have in their heads.

Constructivism focuses on the individual learner. You construct your own knowledge, and you build your own ideas. What social constructivism adds to the mix is that you build that knowledge with other people and that knowledge is shaped by the perspectives of other people. To some extent, this is obvious and straightforward. People tell you things, they share knowledge with you, and you add that to what you know, what you've experienced. Even for people with no interest in social constructivism, education is typically seen as a relationship between pupil and teacher. Even when you're learning alone with a book or video, you're engaging with ideas shared and expressed by others. It's not impossible to learn by working things out from first principles yourself, but it's massively time consuming and inefficient.

So the idea of sharing ideas with others is familiar. But there are also much more complex things that you can do when you work together to develop knowledge. You can challenge people's ideas, you can critique their ideas, you can expand on their ideas. You can ask them to justify or explain their ideas. Social constructivism is about coming to a common understanding in your context of what the truth is at that point for you as a group or for you as a couple of people. Throughout our lives, this is what we do. We get ideas from others, from relatives, friends, school, the media and multiple other sources and we make sense of those in relation to our current knowledge.

Some of these ideas we simply assimilate. We test them against what we already know and then we either reject them, take them on board, or take a version of them on board. Where social constructivism can help is by pushing us that little bit further, not just relying on our own sense of what we've understood, but testing our understanding against others and building on those multiple understandings.

This means that language is an important tool in learning and that teachers have an important role in facilitating conversations. These are ideas that are very closely associated with the work of Lev Vygotsky, a Soviet psychologist who worked in the 1920s and

30s. His publications weren't translated into English until the 1970s, at which point his ideas really took off and people began to build on them. He wrote about language as a psychological tool that can be used to modify the course and structure of thoughts; a tool for constructing understanding within your head and also a tool for constructing understanding with others. He saw writing as another tool, one that humans use to control their memory and to refine their thinking. He was also interested in the zone of proximal development (ZPD), the idea that you can do a bit more than you can on your own if you're working with a more experienced other who can support you to do something and then support you to do it by yourself.

Vygotsky observed that, when we talk, we transform our thoughts into words. Even if in your head you're putting phrases together, talking to yourself, or carrying on an internal monologue, talking to others is when you have to make your ideas explicit. It's at this point you may see your ideas coming together, or you may begin to notice holes in your argument. There's nothing quite like realising you don't know something when you're trying to explain it to somebody else for the first time. In your head, you think you've completely got it. But when somebody says, 'Well, now explain that to me,' you stumble and run into problems.

Social constructivism represents a shift in how people thought about learning. In the past, people considered learning to be an individual thing that goes on inside your head. Social constructivists say it's much more complex than that. Learning is an interaction. It's a negotiation. It's profoundly social. This has opened the way to new understandings – there are theories in which learning doesn't even end up with the individual. The theory of distributed cognition, for example, takes things one step further and says that sometimes knowledge is embedded in a group, team, or network. But that's a theory for another episode, another chapter and, as it turns out now we've reflected on our production schedule, another book.

If learning takes place only in someone's head, you can't see it taking place unless you have access to sophisticated equipment capable of observing a brain at work, as well as quiescent learners who are willing to be hooked up to that equipment. This is a difficulty that people have struggled with for a long time, which has led to the identification of various 'proxies for learning'. These proxies are things that indicate learning has taken place, or might be taking place. That's why educators and educational researchers are often interested in things like how engaged students appear to be, how much time they are spending looking at a screen or at a teacher, or how frequently they're accessing learning materials. It's also one of the reasons why so much time is spent administering tests, because these provide an indication of how much has been learned. Time-on-task and test results are both used as proxies for learning. Over a century ago, behaviourists were struggling with the same issue. To help them address it, they defined learning as a long-term change in behaviour, which meant they had to watch out for changes in behaviour.

Once you realise that a lot of learning takes place in conversations, especially now that a lot of those learning conversations take place online, using written text that can be preserved, you can see those moments where people change their views, change their perspective, perhaps say, 'Oh yeah, I understand,' rephrase something that they've heard before, or start using vocabulary that's specific to the discipline they're studying. This gives us a new way of looking at learning and seeing when that learning is taking place, which can be very helpful.

Even in science, although the positivist view is that there's an objective reality out there, humans are always interpreting reality. The way we come up with an intersubjective interpretation of what the world is, the way that everyone gets closer to a consensus opinion about the world, which is as close to reality as we can get, is by socially constructing that interpretation through discussion, argument, challenges, and critiques – the tools of social constructivism.

There are many pedagogies that come under the umbrella title of social constructivism. For example, communities of practice (which we'll cover in chapter 16) are very much tied up with the idea that lots of people have ideas, knowledge and skills. When you put those together, they enable individuals to expand their own skills and knowledge. The community of practice is a shared space where we establish meaning. Social constructivism also adds another dimension to constructivist approaches such as active learning, experiential learning, and problem-based learning.

Despite the advantages of this approach, as with any pedagogy, it's not enough just to employ the bare bones of the idea and expect learning to result. Putting people in groups to have conversations won't automatically lead to learning – it's more likely to lead to bad group dynamics and off-task discussion. Some of the things it's important to pay attention to when designing social constructivist activities are: use of language, group dynamics, rhetorical moves, and student understanding of the pedagogy.

## Use of language

When people try to have a learning conversation, some will have a lot of distance between them in terms of ideas. To some extent, this will be because they've got different ideas, but another problem may be that they're not using the same words to mean the same things. Part of the work involved in social constructivism is to come up with a common meaning for key words early in the process.

We've seen that in *Pedagodzilla*, where it took us a few episodes to realise that Markzilla and Beckzilla were using the same words in slightly different ways. We had to argue that out, make our points to each other and try to come to a conclusion. Our initial maps of the Realm of Pedagogy weren't the same because we didn't agree on definitions of key terms, and we saw the relationships between ideas in different ways,

> *My understanding of social constructivism has shifted since doing* Pedagodzilla. *I didn't realise at first that it's quite such an umbrella term, that it's so broad and it covers a lot of things that we've been discussing, like zone of proximal development and situative learning. I was considering it as a distinct sort of pedagogy and teaching style, whereas it's actually a whole broad way of looking at things.*
>
> *Another thing I've learnt during our conversations is that it's not the same as social constructionism. Social constructionism is the idea that a lot of the things in the world around us are socially constructed. They don't have a meaning or a value independent of human beings. Fashion is one of those. Good fashion and bad fashion only exist as social constructions. It's only because society agrees something looks good that it looks good.*
>
> *So my advice is – don't get them mixed up.* -Mikezilla

As already seen in chapter 4, if you think of something as simple as the question, 'What is one plus one?', then most of us would automatically respond, 'Two.' But that's only because we assume the person asking the question is working in a denary system which counts: zero, one, two, three, four, five, six, seven, eight, nine, ten. They might actually be working in a binary system which goes zero, one, ten, eleven, in which case one and one would be ten. The answer 'two' also assumes that both of us are talking about numbers as abstract ideas, because if we put one apple and one orange together, we still have one apple and one orange. We'd have two items of fruit, but that assumes that we've both agreed that we can abstract the idea of "orange" and "apple" to "items of fruit". If one of us doesn't see the world in that way, they won't see that there's two of anything. So, there's lots of social convention built into how we talk about things which seem obvious. And that's because we take it for granted that everybody makes the same assumptions. That's why it's important to establish what we mean by the terms we use.

### Group dynamics

To build knowledge, it's useful to have a diverse range of perspectives involved in the discussion. There's a balance to be achieved here. In most cases, you'll be aiming to construct knowledge that is useful and helpful in your context. That suggests that conversations with people who would normally be in your context will typically be the most fruitful. If you want to move further and explore new ideas, it helps to increase the diversity of the group. However, if a group is too diverse, participants will have no common reference points and will talk past each other. So setting up groups requires some thought about what you're trying to achieve.

It's also important to provide groups with some guidelines about behaviour and expectations. Some of these guidelines are likely to relate to respect for each other, listening without interrupting, turn taking, and critiquing ideas rather than individuals. Some guidelines will be more related to process – ensuring everyone has an opportunity to present their opinion, deciding who (if anyone) will take the lead and who will record the discussion. Some preparation is likely to be necessary in order to ensure that everyone feels confident to speak. Reflection after the discussion can also be helpful in pinpointing problems, finding ways of addressing them in future, and thinking about the ways in which ideas were discussed and challenged.

## Rhetorical moves

Educational researcher Neil Mercer studied multiple learning conversations and found there are three main ways in which learning discussions may go, if they stay on topic. The first is disputation. One person says, 'This dress is blue', and somebody else says, 'This dress is gold.' They restate their position in different ways (Blue! Gold!) or attack the other's position (You're wrong!). They fundamentally disagree. The conversation doesn't get them anywhere, and no useful learning takes place. Not surprisingly, these aren't the conversations you want to see taking place when you set up a social-constructivist activity.

Cumulative talk is more helpful. People keep adding pieces of information. This is useful, it moves everyone on and it's a learning discussion. It's important, though, to avoid groupthink, which occurs when a group reaches a consensus without critical reasoning and without evaluating possible consequences or alternatives. For example, a dominant student might propose an answer to the question the group is discussing, and then everybody adds information that supports that viewpoint and keeps quiet about other possible solutions.

The most valuable type of learning discussion involves exploratory talk. Students can be supported to develop and use the techniques that are necessary for this. Exploratory talk involves evaluating information, explaining ideas, asking for explicit reasoning, critiquing, challenging and justifying ideas. These are all techniques that students can be encouraged to use that will enable them to learn more deeply.

## Student understanding of the pedagogy

Students often don't like group work. This isn't necessarily an issue – most of us don't enjoy the more laborious aspects of learning such as revision, exams and skills practice. In lots of cases, problems with group work aren't connected with perceived difficulty, but are linked to experience. Most students have had experience of group work that has gone wrong, where some people have free-loaded on others, where nothing got done or nothing was learned. These issues can usually be addressed by paying attention to group dynamics and the skills associated with group work, but it's also important that students understand why they are being asked to interact with others. If they know the reason for the activity then, even if they don't enjoy it, they are more likely to appreciate what they've gained from it.

In the case of group discussions, an issue might be that students kick back and say, 'Why should I listen to six wrong opinions? I want you, as the expert in this area, to tell me what the right one is.' In situations where there's a right answer, like 'What is the mass of a boson?', that's a valid point – a social-constructivist approach probably isn't useful. However, in most subject areas, particularly those based in the social constructionist domain, there isn't a right answer to every question, and the object of the lesson may be to explore ideas rather than to settle on a single one.

If a student introduces incorrect ideas or false information to the discussion, a teacher can intervene before a group goes too far wrong. But one of the advantages of social constructivism is that people can challenge, and challenge is an important part of the approach. Justifying opinions is important. Producing evidence is important. So students who are familiar with social-constructivist approaches will be aware of techniques that can help them to identify factual errors quickly and explore alternatives.

Overall, as with other pedagogies in this book, it's worth explaining to students why you're using a social-constructivist approach, how it can help them, and what they may gain from trying it. It's also helpful to foreground possible problems and ways of avoiding them. Returning to *The Lord of the Rings*, participants in the Council of Elrond experienced both the advantages of the method and some of its downsides during their extended discussion, so let's return to the question: **How does the Council of Elrond use social constructivism to plan the destruction of the One Ring?**

## The answer

The Council of Elrond involves about a dozen participants. They've come together from different places and different backgrounds, all trying to work out what's happening in the world and what they should do next. They spend four or five hours together talking and, basically, they spend a lot of time on exposition. There's a great deal of cumulative talk as they pile fact upon fact.

Elrond, the wise elf leader, recounts thousands of years of history and stories. As he's more than 6,000 years old, much of this is based on his personal experience. And, as his account covers so many millennia, it is both detailed and complex. Dwarves and humans explain what's been happening in their lands more recently, stories they've heard, and actions they've taken. Two of the hobbits, Bilbo and Frodo, explain their connection with the Ring. Gandalf the wizard talks about the work he's been doing, the places he's visited, and the challenges he's encountered.

All the participants must be heroically bright, alert morning people, because when the Council ends, without even a coffee break, they seem to have taken all this information in. Although a lot of this information was known by many participants, only Gandalf knew everything, so a lot of information sharing was necessary.

The key thing is, they have a ring and, when they arrive at the Council, they don't really know if it's the One Ring or not. They know the dark lord Sauron lost the One Ring, the Great Ring of Power, to Isildur when Isildur cut it from his hand. But then, the story goes, Isildur was wearing it when he was killed by orcs. It seems that the ring fell into the Anduin River and was lost. So, just because Bilbo acquired a ring from Gollum in a cave under the Misty Mountains 3,000 years after those events, what evidence is there that this is the same ring? The Misty Mountains are nowhere near the Anduin. This is one of the points where the discussion shifts from cumulative to exploratory talk. The elf Galdor of the Havens asks for evidence: 'The Wise may have good reason to believe that the halfling's trove is indeed the Great Ring of long debate, unlikely though that may seem to those who know less. But may we not hear the proofs?' Boromir also has questions: 'How do the Wise know that this ring is his [Isildur's]? And how has it passed down the years, until it is brought hither by so strange a messenger?'

Prompted by those questions, Bilbo explains how he acquired the ring (correcting the false tale he told his companions in *The Hobbit*), and Frodo tells his part of the story. This still leaves a gap of several thousand years in the narrative, which Gandalf fills. To find out what happened to the One Ring, he travelled to the land of Gondor. There he found out that Isildur didn't die from an overdose of orc arrows directly after obtaining the ring, he made it back to Gondor first, a story that Boromir confirms. Before setting off up north again, Isildur recorded that, when the ring was hot, the inscription within it started glowing. Gandalf heated up Frodo's ring and found the same inscription. *Ash nazg durbatulûk, ash nazg gimbatul, ash nazg thrakatulûk agh burzum-ishi krimpatul.* One Ring to rule them all, One Ring to find them, One Ring to bring them all and in the darkness bind them.

Put together, the stories establish the ring's provenance, and Gandalf's experiment with putting the ring in the fire at Frodo's home confirms their belief that Frodo is the current bearer of the One Ring. Challenges and questions have been met with explanations and explicit reasoning. False beliefs have been corrected – Isildur didn't die immediately after leaving Mordor, and Bilbo's original tale of how he acquired the ring was untrue. All the evidence lines up, and the story aligns with what everyone knows, so they accept they now have the One Ring. This leads to the question of what they should do with it.

Various solutions are proposed. Elrond's counsellor, Eréstor, suggests handing it to the carefree ancient being Tom Bombadil because Frodo has already explained that the Ring had no power over Tom. Gandalf believes the Ring has no significance to Bombadil, who would forget it or throw it away, so that idea is dropped. Galdor of the Havens wonders if the elves have the strength to protect the Ring. Elrond says they don't – and he's in the top five most powerful elves, so he should know. Galdor's other solutions are to send the Ring over the sea or to destroy it. Glorfindel suggests they should cast it into the deep, Eréstor proposes hiding or unmaking the Ring. Gandalf and Elrond identify problems with all the solutions suggested by these elves.

In the end, there are two preferred options. Eréstor, Galdor and Glorfindel have been convinced by the arguments of Elrond and Gandalf that their suggestions will not work. Boromir is in favour of wielding the Ring and using its power to defeat Sauron, while Elrond feels the only possible solution is to send the Ring into the fires of Mount Doom in Mordor. Boromir challenges Elrond's proposal: 'Why do you speak ever of hiding and destroying? Why should we not think that the Great Ring has come into our hands to serve us in the very hour of need?' Gandalf and Elrond have answers to this – the ring corrupts, and is a danger even to the Wise. As both Elrond and Gandalf are secretly the bearers of lesser rings, they do have experience in this area. Boromir appears to concede the point but clearly remains doubtful. Ideally, they should discuss his idea further in order to reach full consensus, but time is short, and the Council appears to be in agreement. This failure of the Council to reach full agreement stores up trouble for the future because, as readers later find out, Boromir tries to take the Ring at one point because he wants to use it to defend his homeland of Gondor.

Overall, though, the Council of Elrond is an example of social constructivism working successfully. A disparate group, including humans, hobbits, elves, dwarves and a wizard share a huge amount of information from their different contexts and experiences, bring together a range of perspectives, look for justifications and evidence, offer challenge and critique, propose various solutions and together construct a shared understanding of what has happened and what is to be done. In the long term, this knowledge and the actions based upon it lead to victory. However, the Council is not a total success – the arguments that are made are not strong enough to convince Boromir and that difference of opinion has fatal consequences.

So, in an ideal world, what could the Council have done better? One improvement might have been to think more carefully about who was represented. In this case, Elrond is limited to those present in Rivendell at the time. As Rivendell is an elvish valley, elves are perhaps over-represented on the Council. Elves are immortal, so their perspective is longer term than that of humans like Boromir. In addition, Elrond is their leader, so they tend to defer to him. It takes very little argument to convince the elves that their plans for the Ring are unworkable.

More expertise might have been useful. The three elven rings are worn secretly by Gandalf, Elrond and Galadriel, so Galadriel could have been invited to attend and share her perspective. Her absence underlines the fact that the Council is entirely male. As all societies in Middle Earth appear to have been highly sex-segregated, females might have brought ideas around peace and reconciliation, trade and treaties to the table, as a counter to those related to power and destruction.

The Council also excludes some of those who were most directly concerned. In the end, nine individuals make up the Fellowship of the Ring, setting out with the joint intention of distracting Sauron and destroying the Ring. The Fellowship includes four hobbits, but only one of those, Frodo, is formally invited to the Council. Sam is there only because he sneaks in. Merry and Pippin, both of whom eventually volunteer for this dangerous mission, aren't present at the Council and so miss out on the debate that's so vital to their future.

In general, Elrond does a good job of keeping the Council on an amicable footing, because many of the attendees have reasons to be antagonistic to each other. Historically, elves and dwarves have never seen eye to eye. Aragorn appears to those who do not know him as a dusty tramp. Boromir, like others in the novel, is at first doubtful of this stranger's status. As events progress, he's inclined to be jealous of Aragorn's heritage. The hobbits are an unknown quantity, but the general feeling appears to be that they have little knowledge or status. Sam is an interloper in a secret council, and Bilbo is revealed to have told an elaborate lie to his erstwhile companion, Glóin. All these antagonisms appear to have been overcome, but the make-up of the council does mean that the voices of Gandalf (who has the trust of the three hobbits and Aragorn) and Elrond, who has the trust of the five or more elves in the room, are likely to prevail. Boromir, who is introduced as 'a man from the South' and 'the stranger' has less status and no allies.

To summarise the answer to the question: **How does the Council of Elrond use social constructivism to plan the destruction of the One Ring?** The Council participants do this by coming together, by bringing different pieces of information, by talking through what they know, by offering challenge and critique, by asking for clarification, by asking for evidence, and by reporting on investigation and experimentation. The group and the discussion aren't perfect but they achieve their aim. Without the Council, the different factions would not have been able to develop the shared understanding and purpose that were necessary for victory.

## Tips for practice

The introduction to social constructivism above introduced some of the elements that are important when using this pedagogy.

- Establish early on what terms mean and the context in which they are used.
- Provide students with guidelines about behaviour and expectations when engaging in learning discussions.
- Support students to use different strategies for exploratory talk, including evaluating information, explaining ideas, reasoning explicitly, critiquing, justifying and challenging ideas.
- Keep your pedagogy transparent – explain to students why they are having these learning conversations and what they can hope to gain from them.

In addition: be aware of the different types of learning discussion (disputational, cumulative and exploratory) and encourage your students to engage in exploratory discussions that are going to lead to deeper learning. Be aware of the characteristics of exploratory talk, introduce these characteristics to your students and support their use.

When setting up groups or conversations, find a way to include a variety of voices and think carefully about which voices may be excluded or silenced. If group members aren't included, or are actively excluded, they won't learn as much as they could and they may go off in the wrong direction

Monitor and reflect on the activity and encourage learners to do the same things. Take into account how the conversation has gone, and how information has been shared. Look for flaws in that process. Important information may have been sidelined or overlooked, or someone's view may have been given priority based on their status rather than on their arguments. Encourage learners to ask for evidence in support of information that is offered and, if there is conflicting evidence, to decide on criteria to help them establish which is most likely to be accurate. For example, Gandalf reports, based on hearsay, that the men of Rohan have been paying tribute to Sauron. Boromir, who knows these men and their priorities, challenges this story but his status in the group is low and nobody follows up on his challenge.

This connects with work on decolonising the curriculum and critical pedagogy. It's important to think about who is involved and where your decision making is coming from. You can have a very diverse set of people in the room but if you don't value the perspectives of some of those people, or their ways of thinking, then you limit the conversation rather than enriching it and challenging accepted ideas.

Although the diversity of the people in the room leads to a more enriched set of perspectives, those differences in perspective can lead to very different interpretations of the meanings of words. One of the reasons why the Council of Elrond works is that everybody's speaking a common language. Although there are age-old conflicts between the dwarves and the elves which neither side agrees on who started, there is no point at which people argue over the meanings of words. But with the podcast episode this chapter is based on, for example, if we hadn't established between us the meanings of the terms constructionism, social constructionism, constructivism and social constructivism, we wouldn't have been able to have a meaningful conversation. So, don't underrate the language. Instead, if you're facilitating a learning process make that the first step, ensuring everybody is on the same page with regards to what they're talking about. Sometimes that can just be a quick two- or three-sentence summary of a concept that means people can use it in conversation and aren't going to get thrown by the terminology.

With any form of social interaction in learning – problem-based, inquiry-based, collaborative – it's important not to assume that students know instinctively how to form a group and have a valuable conversation. It's not an innate skill to be able to engage in brilliant learning conversations. Most students have had the depressing experience of being shoved in a corner with random people and told to solve a problem. The result is that they spend most of their time trying to sort the group out rather than trying to solve the problem. This sometimes happens because teachers have been introduced to the idea that discussions and interactions are good, but haven't thought through exactly why they're good. As a result, they assign group work without knowing how to support people engaging in that work. Things go more smoothly when you help students to set some rules for group work and learning conversations, define some boundaries, decide points at which they'll check on progress, make plans for dealing with conflict, and come up with strategies for involving those who aren't contributing.

# Mathom and other references

Mercer, N. (2000) *Words and Minds: How We Use Language To Think together*. Routledge.

Tolkien, J.R.R. (1954-55) *The Lord of the Rings*, Houghton Mifflin.

Vygotsky, L.S. (1987, original work published 1934; original work written between 1929 and 1934) Thought and Word. In: *The Collected Works of L S Vygotsky, Volume I*, edited by R. W. Rieber and A. S. Carton, Plenum Press.

## CHAPTER 15:

# HOW DOES ARNIE KEEP HIS SKIN ON THROUGH SITUATIVE LEARNING IN THE MOVIE *PREDATOR*?

*Mark Childs and Mike Collins*

*Having learned some of the ways of Social Constructivism, the Zillas travel deeper into the land. This place really does seem to have a lot of useful stuff dotted around, but Markzilla is starting to get a bit whiny.*

'Can we go and visit the Deep Elves now?' he pleads.
'Well…' says Mikezilla.
'It is just up the road, after all,' agrees Beckzilla.
Markzilla trots happily ahead. 'Most of my friends are here,' he tells them.
'They've got some cool stuff. I'll show you Activity Theory and maybe later we could look in on Communities of Practice.'

In the chapter about mapping the Realm of Pedagogy we mentioned how, when writing this book, we discovered we had different models of how the various pedagogical theories can be divided up. Those models overlapped a lot but didn't quite match up.

One thing we agreed about when writing this book was that we'd make it straightforward for the reader to locate different theories within their overall context. Without some sort of map, it's difficult to see how the theories are connected; which are the larger overarching concepts and which are subsidiary ones; which are closest to each other and which are furthest apart. So when we started putting a map together, we ran into some problems.

Beckzilla, who's studied history and inclines to an interpretivist view of the world, was working with a chronological account, which divides and arranges theories chronologically, depending on when they were first adopted. On the other hand, Markzilla, who's studied both natural science and social science but as separate degrees that have very different ways of viewing the world, was approaching them from how they drew on different epistemologies. Although they both had three overarching terrains for how we looked at the theories, they were drawing the boundaries in different ways and using different labels for the same things (and sometimes the same labels for different things).

After heated discussions, the Zillas created a map that divides pedagogic theories into four main categories (see Chapter 6), and in our descriptions of social constructivism and situative learning we've emphasised the dialogic elements of social constructivism and the environmental elements of situative learning, so they at least look like separate categories. This is why you're unlikely to see a framework quite like ours. It worked for our purposes for this book, which is all that frameworks need to do. Our recommendation is: don't worry too much about how these theories fit together. Pick a map that makes sense to you (pick ours!) and stick to it. Just be aware that if you're communicating with anyone else about these things they may have a different map in their head. If you're writing anything up, make it clear which map or framework you're using.

We're going to venture into the long grass as we explore the model that Mark had in his head when he started learning about pedagogical theories, partly because it includes some useful ideas, and partly to model how you can mix and match others' theories to make something that works for you. If you're not interested in that, just skip ahead to 'What exactly is situative learning'.

But before that we look at one of our favourite movies, *Predator*, and ask: **How does Arnie keep his skin on through situative learning in the movie *Predator*?** In order to stay focused on the task at hand, we've cut out the fan theory about all Arnold Schwarzenegger's movies being linked, so for that you'll have to listen to the original podcast.

## *Predator* (1987)

The original *Predator* movie came out in 1987, was directed by John McTiernan, and starred Arnold Schwarzenegger (Arnie) as the lead character, Dutch. There have been loads of movies in the series since, but none of them have really captured the feel of that original movie, although Markzilla likes *Predator 2* a lot ('It's got Gary Busey in it!') – but it's best not repeating the argument about that here.

The 1987 *Predator* film follows a team of elite commandos on a mission in Central America. They've been tricked into doing this by CIA agent Dillon, who tells them they'll be rescuing hostages. Actually, there are no hostages, it's a ruse to get them to take out a rebel camp after some Green Berets Dillon's already sent in there have mysteriously disappeared.

The elite commandos wipe out the camp anyway, and take captive one of the rebels to play the role of token female in the movie. As they make their way to the extraction point, they're hunted by a technologically advanced extraterrestrial creature that bumps them off one by one in fairly gruesome ways. For the Predator it's a ritual hunt. It's customary to land on a planet, kill the local wildlife, then take trophies and return home. Or lose to the local lifeforms and then commit suicide by setting off your Yautja wrist bomb.

The Predator has a neat camouflage technology, making for some great visuals, as the victims catch only glimpses of it in the trees. It also only targets people who carry weapons, which becomes more obvious in *Predator 2* (released in 1990), which is set in a crime-ridden future Los Angeles (so like our past now). In 2010, *Predator*s was released as another direct sequel to the original film, featuring a group of individuals who are dropped onto an alien planet and hunted by Predators. In 2018, a direct sequel to the original *Predator* was released called *The Predator*. This was directed by Shane Black, who had a small role in the first film. This movie introduced a new group of soldiers and a more evolved Predator, but ended up with a script that hadn't evolved at all. Disney acquired the rights to the *Predator* movies when they bought 21st Century Fox in 2019, and their first entry into the franchise was a prequel to all the others. It was set in 1719, titled *Prey*, was the first-ever feature film to have a version entirely in Comanche, and was a bit of a return to form.

There have also been a couple of crossover films featuring the Predator creature. *Alien vs. Predator*, which was pretty good, and *Aliens vs. Predator: Requiem* which was so bad it simultaneously killed off both franchises for quite a while. We summarise the movies in the table below, together with their imdb ratings out of 10, which we are a pretty good guide to how good they are.

| Movie | Year | IMDB rating |
| --- | --- | --- |
| *Predator* | 1987 | 7.8 |
| *Predator 2* | 1990 | 6.3 |
| *Aliens vs Predator* | 2004 | 5.6 |
| *Aliens vs Predator: Requiem* | 2007 | 4.6 |
| *Predators* | 2010 | 6.4 |
| *The Predator* | 2018 | 5.3 |
| *Prey* | 2022 | 7.1 |

*Table 15.1 The Predator movies rated*

That's basically it. The plot structure is your standard Best Man's Fall[1] but with Arnie doing what Arnie does best against a kick-ass monster-in-the-shadows. The only survivors are Anna (the rebel) and Arnie. Anna basically survives by running away while Arnie defeats the monster. How he does that using situative learning is what we'll be looking at in the rest of the chapter.

---

1. A playground game, also known as Best Man's Drop, where one kid stands at one side of the playground and pretends to machine-gun everyone else – they compete by pretending to die in as dramatic a way as possible – this was in the days before the Gameboy was invented, obviously. We're using that as our name for the subgenre of movies where the storyline is basically a series of deaths which aim to top the previous ones in their inventiveness.

# Situative learning

## The model situative learning comes from

The model of pedagogy we're looking at in this chapter identifies three perspectives on learning (Mayes & de Freitas, 2004: Conole et al, 2005). If we mapped this model, it would have three lands: associative, cognitive and situative. The **associative perspective** focuses on learning through association and reinforcement – operant conditioning (see the chapter on *Pokémon Go* and behaviourism) is one example. This sort of aligns well with the Positivist Land of the Dwarves in our shared map. The **cognitive perspective** is the 'outcome of an interaction between new experiences and the structures for understanding that have already been created' (Mayes & de Freitas, 2004) and aligns pretty much with the constructivist and social constructivist areas in our map. Finally, as we'll explore later, the **situative perspective** looks at how learning is influenced not only by its context (such as its cultural and social setting), but also by the environment in which it's located.

Associative perspectives include a variety of different theories that are empiricist in nature. They link tasks to behavioural models of how the brain works, and then focus on the instructional design of the content in order to make best use of these empirical findings. Martin Oliver (n.d.) wrote a follow-up to the 2004 report by Mayes and de Freitas, in which he looked at how different perspectives use different types of evidence. When Markzilla was building up his map of pedagogies in his head, he used Oliver's work as the basis for dividing the pedagogies. Behaviourism, cognitive architecture, cognitive load and so on are all investigated by measuring things, so they can all be grouped together as **positivist approaches**.

What this framework calls 'cognitivist perspectives' include 'communication, explanation, recombination, contrast, inference and problem solving' (Conole et al, 2005). From an epistemological perspective, a lot of the evidence here is based on learner reflection, so these approaches are within the **interpretivist** domain.

Consolidating our whole mapping exercise a bit more, it's possible to view these differing perspectives as analysing learning at different levels of aggregation.

- Analysis from an associative perspective is concerned with empirical observations. It analyses overt activities and the outcomes of these activities for individual learners.
- Analysis from a cognitive perspective attempts to describe the detailed structures and processes that underlie individual performance, either with resources or with other learners.
- Analysis from a situative perspective aggregates at the level of groups of learners, describing activity systems in which individuals participate as members of communities. (Mayes & de Freitas, 2004).

For any learning situation you can a) examine the learner in a positivist way by direct observation of what they do or what their brain's doing, b) ask them, in an interpretivist way, how they or the group are learning and how they're building up ideas in their heads or c) look at what the group produces, the record of how they've interacted, and our interpretations of that, using a combination of epistemologies.

*Markzilla's brain, observed here thinking about old Kaiju movies*

Although we found the division into approaches by their epistemologies useful, we also found the labels confusing. In our map in Chapter 6, the 'assimilative' category includes theories based on empirical observations of how the brain works, and these observations inform the design of content that aligns with these observations, so we've dropped the word 'assimilative' and replaced it with 'positivist'.

We also dropped the word 'cognitivist' because it confused us by sounding as if it applied to the brain-focused studies (as in cognitive science) rather than the social-focused approaches. Also with this category, when we put our map together, we took into account the fact that the literature often looks at these as separate approaches, we separated the constructivist theories into those that are solely constructivist and those that are social constructivist. Constructivist perspectives tend to be interpretivist because they draw on accounts by learners of how they've built up their learning.

So: with positivist, constructivist, and social constructivist as our first three categories, we then have situative learning as a fourth category, which we'll get into now.

### What exactly is situative learning?

Situative learning emphasises that learning is always situated in a context. The idea is a bit broader than situated learning, which is a group name for theories about how learning can unintentionally be acquired from culture and practice. This definition of situated learning comes from Lave and Wenger of communities of practice fame (see the next chapter for details). For a summary of situated learning we like, see *New Learning* (Kalantzis & Cope, 2022), a book that's not only comprehensive on a range of pedagogical theories, but also available free of charge on the authors' website.

> *I see what you mean about Lave and Wenger claiming situated learning, and situative learning being something different but I wonder if the two got mixed up somewhere along the way. There's not much written these days about situative learning, but there's a lot written about situated learning, using it in a way that is the same as situative used to be. It's like social learning, which was a massively well established positivist theory, and then people got mixed up with learning via social media and groups, and it now means something completely different.* ~Beckzilla

Situative learning includes both intentional and unintentional learning and it's a perspective that looks at elements including the context of the classroom, the design of the environment, how the students interact within that environment, and so on. Checking in on Martin Oliver (n.d.) again, he sees the data about situative learning coming from direct observations of the environment, as well as interpretations of social interactions, and the developing identities of learners. It includes measurable stuff we can see from things like virtual learning environment (VLE) data, as well as observers' interpretations of what learning is taking place based on reviewing discussion forums, or watching videos of classroom activity. Epistemologically, then, this is a mixture of positivist and interpretivist viewpoints.

A situative learning perspective is particularly useful in conversations around online learning. One reason for this is that the other perspectives are essentially unchanged when you switch from in person to online. The behaviourist and cognitive architecture stuff in the brain is the same, because it's the same brains doing the learning (don't get us started on digital natives – an idea that belongs in the Quagmire along with learning styles). The experiential and active learning stuff builds on personal knowledge creation, so that's the same (check the *Matrix* chapter for our justification for this). What changes online are the environment, the ways in which people connect with each other, and how communities are formed. All of these fall within the scope of a situative perspective.

Situative learning can be broken down into the interplay of three areas: **environments and contexts** in which social practice takes place, processes that support **learner identities**, and **dialogue** that facilitates learning (Oliver, n.d., 5).

## 1. Environments and context

**Context** provides a framework for use of the product or results at a specific time, place and situation in these social, psychological, and material environments. So we could look at how different classroom designs have an impact on the dynamics between learners. If the learning is taking place online, we can look at how different ways of using discussion boards impact on engagement.

We can also get into discussions of sociomateriality, which is the idea that the stuff we use – technology, spaces, objects, and so on – can't be understood or assessed in isolation, but the ways people interact with them have to be taken into account too. This is partly because we each approach these things in different ways, and also because what the technologies represent has been socially constructed. In *An Entangled Pedagogy*, Tim Fawns (2022) discusses many of the models of sociomateriality, if you want to know more. These include Activity Theory, Actor-Network Theory and quite a few others. We won't go into detail about them here, but the key thing for educators is that they present a range of different ways to slice up what's going on for analysis. So, for example, you could use Activity Theory to look at interactions in a community of learners using a specific tool. This would lead you to examine how those interactions change depending on whether you then look at a different community using the same tool, or the same community using a mixture of tools. Alternatively, you could look at how the interactions differ, or the contribution of different roles within the group, depending on what the object of your study is.

The Five Stage Model (Salmon, 2022) is another model classified by Conole et al (2005) as situative learning. The Five Stage Model is a process for encouraging online learning; mapping learning activities to where the learners are in a growing familiarity with the platform, and linking this to an increasing level of participation in an online community. It's situative in that it makes explicit the links between context (not just the platform but how easy people are finding it to use), community (the more you use it the better you get to know each other, and vice versa) and learning (the more developed their use of technology and sense of connection with each other, the more the students can learn).

## 2. Identity

One of the aspects these models don't really include is learner identity, which is a big omission as an individual's identity will not only affect how they interact with a community, it will also have an impact on the degree to which they choose to engage with a technology, for example if they have an ideological opposition to a specific platform.

For more on the specifics of learner identity, take a look at Markzilla's chapter in a book on digital identity (Childs, 2011). It could be argued that identity is so firmly embedded in society that it doesn't need a separate category, it's just more context. Or it could be argued it's another tool we create for interacting with others. As it's so contested, it makes sense to add it as another separate category for analysis, which Mark did when coming up with an extension to Activity Theory in a 2010 paper (Childs, 2010).

## 3. Dialogue

The main driver for learning within communities is dialogue. This overlaps with social constructivism (which we looked at in the previous chapter). On our map, the difference between the two is that the social constructivist perspective looks at the individual constructing internal mental models as a result of their interaction with others, while situative learning looks at the knowledge that is being co-created *externally* through the interactions. So ... same activity, but the focus is on different things. Obviously, both are happening simultaneously but few models encompass both (for one that does, see Chapter 17 on constructionism and Apollo 13).

From a researcher perspective – particularly researchers reviewing asynchronous online discussions where emergent social construction is easier to capture than spoken dialogue because it's recorded as text – this is fascinating, as you can see the interactions emerging on whatever platform you're using, rather than relying on what the learners report is happening in their heads. From an experimental point of view, you don't need fancy scanners to look in on what the brain is doing, and you're not dependent on learners reporting what they're feeling. You can also then relate this to which teaching approaches and platforms support this process effectively and which don't.

*A hat is better than a brain scanner if you're communicating that you're feeling dapper.*

Ultimately though, as a researcher it's still your own interpretation of those observations that you're working with. Even if you're applying learning analytics, they may be positivist in terms of bare numbers like drop-outs from a course, but working out why people have dropped out? That's an interpretation. Even so, epistemologically and methodologically, doing research from the situative perspective by examining the context for learning is a nice midway point between cognitive science's hard data and the reflective interpretation of the constructivists.

## The answer

The key elements of situative learning are: context and connection to the environment (tools, platform, that sort of thing), identities of learners, and the social construction of knowledge that occurs through the dialogue and interactions. Now we'll use these elements to answer our question: **How does Arnie keep his skin on through situative learning in the movie** *Predator*?

To start with the social construction of knowledge by the commandos in *Predator*, it's only by pooling their knowledge that they start to form an idea of what's going on. The first person who picks up and works out they're being preyed on is the scout, Billy. He senses that something's out there. He's able to do that partly because he's more connected with his environment than the others. He's more of a jungle tracker than they are so, because of his immersion in the environment, he's a faster learner, and he senses a disturbance more quickly.

In contrast, CIA agent Dillon is way behind on the learning curve. He trips, and is nearly stung by a scorpion. In lots of small ways, the film indicates how unfamiliar he is with the space and shows that he's not functioning properly within it.

Because of this, he's not able to make decisions effectively, and he learns more slowly than the others. On the other hand, Anna, the female rebel they have (sort of) kidnapped, is a local and has her own knowledge about the environment. She's aware of the Predator from folklore and knows it's a demon that collects men as trophies. Her cultural knowledge is added to the mix; for her this is a real thing that her people have known for generations.

In the middle of all this is Dutch, the Arnold Schwarzenegger character, whose real expertise lies in putting together disparate pieces of information. His role is commander, and we see from situative learning models such as Activity Theory how role plays into the dynamics of a learning situation. At first Dutch dismisses what Billy is saying because he thinks it's not plausible. But they also have evidence that people are being hunted because they saw, skinned and hanging from trees, the Green Berets commando group that went in before them.

A key transition point in their perspectives is when the first of the group is killed. This is Hawkins, played by Shane Black. Anna sees something in the woods immediately afterwards, so they're aware that something is there. One of your colleagues being killed is a hell of a learning incentive.

That's when Dutch starts taking a more concrete role in their learning because, as the leader, he's the guy synthesising the information and choosing which bits are absorbed. He prioritises the information presented by Billy and Anna because they both have specialist knowledge. Dillon is still resistant, however, because he's not really part of their community.

Identity plays a strong part in how the members of the group adapt to their new situation. The initial identity of the team is that they're commandos with a moral code. They're a rescue squad, not assassins. During their journey through the jungle, their identity changes bit by bit; the ones who survive the longest are the ones who recognise their new identity as prey. This is where Dutch succeeds, because his whole way of functioning in response to the Predator is by acting as prey and using that identity against his opponent.

A couple of the commandos can't cope with this new identity. Mac chases the Predator into the jungle in a doomed attempt to shoot it on his own. Billy can't adapt either. Even though he's the first person to recognise that they're prey and even though he's immersed in the environment, his identity isn't one that can encompass being hunted. He challenges the Predator on his own, standing on top of a tree trunk, and dies immediately.

Dutch, on the other hand, effectively synthesises the knowledge acquired from the group, but also from observations in the environment. When he's covered in mud, the Predator can't detect him, so he realises it tracks by heat. As he learns from his environment, he's also learning to use the environment. He's learning to adapt the tools around him because he's now fully immersed in the space, both psychologically immersed and also literally immersed, because a big part of his environment is smeared all over him.

We see the same thing happening with learners, particularly online, only with less mud. Situative learning theories are great at deconstructing online learning, because considering all the separate elements helps us see that the technology itself is not key. It's the learners' relationship with the technology that is important; learning to use the technology effectively is crucial for them to learn with it. The more they can use the technology, the more invisible it becomes to them. The more they can be immersed in the technology, the less it acts as a barrier to their learning, and the more it can promote their learning.

For Dutch in *Predator*, the environment is not just to cover himself, he starts drawing on elements he sees within it to use as part of his adaptive strategy. He stops using metal weapons, because the Predator can detect them. Instead, he creates bits of spiked wood that swing backwards and forwards to crush his opponent. Once a learner is fully immersed in a context, they can more effectively see ways to create and further their own learning.

In summary, Arnie keeps his skin on through situative learning for several reasons.

- The commandos, Anna, and Dillon all learn at different rates because of the degree to which they are immersed in the environment. Dutch is one of the most immersed.
- They succeed to different extents because of their ability to adapt their identity to accommodate what they have learnt (that they are prey) and modify their behaviour accordingly. Of all of them, Dutch and Anna are the only ones who adapt to the new identity fully.
- Dutch is effective at synthesising the information provided by the others within the group so, from that perspective, he's a great leader. Not so effective at helping the others adapt, otherwise the others would have survived too.

Epistemologically, we're not dependent on interpretivist data to draw conclusions about the development of individual learning. We can see Dutch immersed (literally) in the environment, and we can see the artefacts Dutch builds that demonstrate the principles he's acquired. Or we could, if they hadn't all been blown to shit by a small nuclear explosion at the end.

## Tips for practice

A key principle is to give your students a chance to become immersed in the use of tools before employing those tools for learning. If they're studying online, give them opportunities to learn how to use the tools, because if they feel connected to the online space, they're in a better position to learn from it.

As with social constructivism, give your learners opportunities to form a community. The effectiveness of the social aspects is very important. In situative learning, social and technological elements are closely intertwined. If you can build familiarity with the platform alongside familiarity with other learners, you'll find the two reinforce each other.

The final key thing to learn is to create a space or a scaffold for students to work through their change in identity as the learning changes who they are. One of the problems that Billy and Mac have is that there's no way for them to recontextualise who they've become as a result of what they've learnt. We see this frequently, and it's often overlooked – learning changes students. We rarely prepare students for the changes in who they are that result from their learning.

Also, as we learnt when recording the episode that became the basis for this chapter, ensure your environment isn't on fire, as that can severely limit the extent of your learning.

# We begin finding our references. We found them sometimes without their ISBN numbers... and sometimes much, much worst

Childs, M. (2010) A conceptual framework for mediated environments, *Educational Research*, 52: 2, June, 197–213

Childs, M. (2011) Identity: a primer. In: A. Peachey and M. Childs (eds) *Reinventing Ourselves: Contemporary Concepts of Identity in Virtual Worlds.* Springer Series in Immersive Environments. Springer, London. Available at: https://doi.org/10.1007/978-0-85729-361-9_2

Conole, G., Littlejohn, A., Falconer, I. and Jeffery, A. (2005) Pedagogical review of learning activities and use cases: *LADIE Project Report*. Available at: https://oro.open.ac.uk/52378/3/52378.pdf

Fawns, T. (2022) An entangled pedagogy: looking beyond the pedagogy – technology dichotomy. *Postdigital Science and Education*, 4, 711–728. Available at: https://doi.org/10.1007/s42438-022-00302-7

Kalantzis, M, and Cope, B (2022) *New Learning: Elements of a Science of Education*, Cambridge University Press, UK: Cambridge. Available at: https://newlearningonline.com/new-learning/chapter-6/supporting-material/lave-and-wenger-on-situated-learning

Kawamura, Y. (2012) *Fashioning Japanese Subcultures*. London, Berg.

Mayes, T. and de Freitas, S. (2004) *Review of E-learning Theories, Frameworks and Models*, London: Joint Information Systems Committee. Available at: https://core.ac.uk/download/pdf/228143942.pdf

Oliver, M. (n.d.) Stage 2: *Assessing The Relevance of the Review of E-Learning Theories, Frameworks and Models and the Mapping Table to Evaluators*, London: Joint Information Systems Committee. Available at: http://www.jisc.ac.uk/whatwedo/programmes/elearningpedagogy/outcomes.aspx

Salmon, G. (2022) *Five Stages Model*. Available at: https://www.gillysalmon.com/five-stage-model.html

Scan the QR code to listen
to the podcast episode

**CHAPTER 16:**

# FROM N00B TO L33T. HOW COMMUNITIES OF PRACTICE PROVIDE A ROUTE INTO *WORLD OF WARCRAFT*

*Rebecca Ferguson, Mark Childs and Mike Collins*

*The Zillas continue their exploration of the different areas of Social Constructivism, making lots of interesting discoveries along the way. This time, they've made their way to one of its more commercial areas, a place called Communities of Practice, situated within the wider Landscapes of Practice.*

*As with their previous sidequest, when they explored the virtual world of* The Matrix *as an example of experiential learning, Mike and Markzilla have wandered off into a virtual space, that of the* World of Warcraft. *On hand to rein them in this time is Beckzilla.*

As we saw in Chapter 14, during the longest chapter in *The Lord of the Rings*, participants in the Council of Elrond take on board and make sense of a huge amount of current affairs, recent events, plus ancient and modern history. Perhaps you felt that coming to grips with so much content before lunch without drinking even one cup of coffee was evidence of the preternatural skills of participants in the event. Perhaps you felt Tolkien was pushing the bounds of credibility by piling so much exposition in one place. Yet today, as our fictional worlds expand in size and scope, newcomers to games must come to grips with even richer, more complex settings. If you arrive in the *World of Warcraft*, with its backstory built up over three decades and elaborated by millions of players, what are the chances you will ever understand what is going on? The Zillas reckon that becoming part of a community of practice is key. So, **how do communities of practice provide a route into** *World of Warcraft*?

## *World of Warcraft*

These days, *World of Warcraft* (which has the snappy acronym, WoW) is best known as a massive multi-player online role-playing game (a genre which has the far more cumbersome acronym of MMPORG). It has its origins, though, in a series of real-time strategy (RTS) games of which the first was released in 1994. This drew on the conventions of the multi-user dungeons (MUDs) that had been popular in the mid-Seventies, together with role-playing games (RPGs) such as *Dungeons and Dragons* (D&D), all of which had their roots to some extent in wargames brought to life with a liberal sprinkling of characters and conventions familiar from fantasy fiction and its multiple sources.

The specific mythology of WoW was introduced in 1994 in the *Warcraft: Orcs and Humans* RTS. Unlike board games where players take turns, in an RTS all players can be active at once. In this case, players could take on the role of the human inhabitants of Azeroth or the invading orcs (the influence of Tolkien's work is clear to see) from the world of Draenor. They then had to build a settlement, create an army, and defeat the opposing side. In the process, they might collect the gold and wood necessary to make progress, go to the aid of besieged towns, put up some magical buildings, or summon mythical creatures. The game was already developing a complex back story, which was developed further in the sequels, *Warcraft II: Tides of Darkness, Warcraft III: Reign of Chaos* and *The Frozen Throne* expansion pack.

So, by the time *World of Warcraft* was launched in 2004, new players found themselves in a complex world with well-established mythology, history, locations, allegiances and characters. Not only did they have to get to grips with the relatively new concept of a MMPORG, in which they were playing online with characters controlled by individuals all over the world, they also had to find their place within the gameworld, and get to grips with a complex set of game controls, not to mention wade through a quagmire of acronyms.

In fact, there is so much to come to grips with in WoW that Mikezilla had played for 300 hours before he realised that this game, unlike the others he was used to, didn't simply involve acquiring objects and working hard to level up. The real game, the meta game, was about forming allegiances, players banding together in guilds and taking on missions together that might involve multiple hours of continuous game play. What's more, his original choice of role as a hunter had been great for solo play but limited his options within a guild because other players were looking for tanks to protect them from attack, or healers to bolster spirits and heal the wounded. Highly frustrating to find these things out after so long! So, how could Mikezilla have made these discoveries earlier on? Perhaps by linking up with a community of practice.

## Communities of practice

Back in the 1980s, cognitive anthropologist Jean Lave and her doctoral student Etienne Wenger studied how people pick up a practice in areas where training is hands-on and often informal. They looked at various examples of apprenticeship, including meat cutters, naval quartermasters, tailors, midwives, and non-drinking alcoholics. Wenger carried out a detailed study of people working on processing insurance claims. Putting these studies together, they identified the profoundly social and situated nature of learning and, in their 1991 book *Situated Learning: Legitimate Peripheral Participation*, they introduced to a global audience two terms that have been taken up widely – the 'legitimate peripheral participation' of the book title and 'communities of practice'.

Wenger significantly expanded on these ideas in his 1998 book *Communities of Practice: Learning, Meaning and Identity*. Since then, he has carried on this work, married and become a Wenger-Trayner. Together with his wife, Beverly, he has worked on refining and developing the concept, expanding it into landscapes of practice.

Getting back to the basics, though, what are communities of practice? Well, the Wenger-Trayner website defines them as 'groups of people who share a concern or a passion for something they do and learn how to do it better as they interact regularly'.

It's worth unpacking that terminology, because not every group of people is a community, and not every community is a community of practice. Simply putting a group of people together in a classroom or a virtual learning environment doesn't turn them into a community of practice. From an educational perspective, there are lots of ways of grouping people. Some are largely practical: learners are put into a year group, a cohort, or a class. This makes them into a manageable administrative unit. At the other extreme are networks, loose groupings of people who can share skills, knowledge, or useful contacts with others.

Communities are found in lots of places and form for many reasons. As a result, they have multiple definitions. In the past, these definitions usually focused on place, with communities forming around streets or villages, for example. When the Internet emerged there was initially a lot of resistance to the idea that a community could develop online, but that debate died away as social media grew in importance and online communities became increasingly important in people's lives.

One of the crucial elements of a community is that it has criteria, however informal, for membership. Mikezilla's drinking mates, Markzilla's virtual golf group, and Beckzilla's daughter's boyfriend's ex-boss may have absolutely nothing in common but they are, nevertheless, very loosely linked into a network by their connection with those three Zillas. On the other hand, the Zillas can be seen as a community because they have a shared commitment to the *Pedagodzilla* podcast. The membership aspect of community can be elaborated as a sense of belonging, or expressed more negatively as a way of excluding others. A community also has some sense of structure, perhaps containing leaders, founders, or experts. Community members feel they gain something from membership and, over time, are likely to create things together.

In terms of pedagogy, three types of community have received a lot of attention: the communities of learners sometimes known as learning communities, communities of inquiry, and communities of practice. First are the communities of learners/

learning communities. These terms have different, sometimes highly specific, meanings in different contexts. Basically, though, as their names imply, they're communities that have some connection with learning or with education. Typically, they're presented as an improvement on a group set up purely to make administration easy. Classes, year groups, schools, teaching staff can all benefit from becoming a learning community, and there are lots of ideas online about how to shift them in this way.

Communities of inquiry (CoI) are usually seen as a way of learning in online or blended settings. Within them, groups engage in discourse and reflection in order to construct and agree meaning together. They involve three main elements, or types of presence. Social presence is the ability of members to present themselves as real people, even though they may only interact with others online. Cognitive presence is their ability to communicate in order to come to a deeper understanding together. Teaching presence involves an educator designing and facilitating what goes on within the community in order to support the development of this deeper understanding. CoIs are useful when you're running classes online, but less so when you're struggling with the Swamp of Sorrows and attempting to re-imprison a demon for all eternity, or trying to find a way of breaking Marshall Windsor out of his prison in the Blackrock Depths.

None of these types of community would be particularly helpful when you take on the specific challenges associated with a particular practice, whether those involve interpreting an insurance claim form, adding the correct robot voice to an episode of *Pedagodzilla*, or searching underwater for the body of a dwarven soldier. A community of practice helps in those cases because all its members have a connection to that particular practice and can draw upon knowledge, skills, experiences, connections – all sorts of resources that can help to solve a problem, whether it's completely new or one that everyone in the community faces at some time or another.

Communities of practice have three main elements: domain, community and practice. The domain is a shared interest – community members have some commitment to the domain, some competence related to it, and some understanding of what expertise looks like. The community is the grouping within which they interact and learn from each other. That learning is important. People aren't members of a community of practice solely because they sit next to each other, have the same role, or face similar problems. It's interaction and learning that establish their connection. The final element is practice – members must be practitioners, not simply people with a shared interest or theoretical knowledge.

So that's a community of practice. What about legitimate peripheral participation, which sounds a whole lot more complex? Well, you can see a community of practice as concentric circles. There are outer circles of people who have various levels of involvement and an inner circle of people who are the most involved – often the founders or the leaders. Then there are people moving in and out of those circles. Let's concentrate on the ones coming in from the outermost circle and moving towards the centre. They're on an 'inbound trajectory'. If this is a workplace community of practice, like the insurance brokers Wenger first wrote about, people become members by getting a job, turning up to work, getting on okay with the people in the office, and then staying with the organisation for a while.

Whether you're trying to establish or strengthen a community of practice, it's useful to consider the stages by which people get inducted into that community and what helps them do that. Legitimate peripheral participation is part of the process that enables newcomers to become experienced members of the community. It's a first step that enables them to get used to the language and practices of the group before becoming an active member. Peripheral participation might involve observation to find out what is involved in being a member of a community. For example, an apprentice might be expected to spend some time observing an expert before taking any active part. Or peripheral participation might involve having a very junior role – for example, as a young child growing up aware of the family business but without any formal responsibilities within that business.

The 'legitimate' aspect of the participation has two elements. First, community members have accepted, perhaps through some membership programme or initiation experience, that the participant is a legitimate part of the community. The participant has made the shift from spectator or outsider to someone who has begun the journey towards expertise, and existing members of the community have accepted their right to be there. Second, it's legitimate for the new participant to be contributing nothing, or to be undertaking only small, fringe actions. Community members recognise that newcomers are peripheral, and they're okay with that. Lack of engagement is accepted if you are a peripheral participant. This contrasts with a much more negative attitude towards 'lurkers', who watch but have no intention of contributing, and 'free-loaders' who benefit from the contribution of others while doing little or nothing themselves. Lurkers and free-loaders are unpopular because they are perceived to be a drain on the community, whereas legitimate peripheral participants have indicated that they intend to become contributing members.

Another important element of helping people progress within a community of practice is the knowledge broker (not to be confused with the insurance brokers mentioned above). They have the role of helping to introduce people to the community. They show newcomers the ropes and take them around. This usually goes beyond a formal induction process. Over time, knowledge brokers introduce the ideas, the tools, the people, and the history of the community. This usually isn't a formal role, but the more people who are willing to act as knowledge brokers, the easier a newcomer will find it to get to grips with the complexity of the community.

Finally, there are boundary objects, the various concepts, pieces of information, and resources that help someone progress through the various levels of participation of the community. Boundary objects help people feel part of the community, participate in it, and do this effectively. Every community of practice will have its own language – terms, acronyms, and abbreviations that are used by members. These can feel alienating at first, but once you have acquired them, by learning what they mean, they become your own special language. And that special language helps you create a coherent feeling of unity within the community.

At the same time, there may be tools, resources, a dress code or uniform, which help to mark out a member of the community. These boundary objects may have subtle differences between them – different colour shades on a jacket, a stripe on a sleeve, a small badge on a hat – which mark out differences in skill and experience in ways that can be understood fully only by community members. Each boundary object you acquire, each nuance you recognise takes you further from being an outsider and closer to the centre of the community.

## The answer

So, with their knowledge brokers, boundary objects, and legitimate peripheral participation, just how do communities of practice provide a route into *World of Warcraft*? Let's take the example of Fictional Fiona. Fiona signs up and logs into *World of Warcraft* for the first time. She has no idea what she is doing – it's different from all the other online games she has tried. But here she is, and she has a pop-up text tutorial pointing her to her first quest. A whole new world for her to discover.

Fiona is a newcomer, a newbie, within the game. But what sort of newbie? Higher-level players make distinctions between these newly arrived players. A newb (pronounced either nyoub or new-b) is someone who has just arrived and is starting to learn. Newbs are aware they don't know what's going on. As a result, they're likely to tread carefully, keeping their ears and eyes open until they learn some of the social rules. If Fiona is a newb, she'll gradually learn some of the cues and the clues, and she'll begin to grasp the social norms. She'll actively try to learn in a positive way.

On the other hand, Fiona might be the sort of person who is unaware of how little she knows. She'll go in, she'll talk across other people, and she'll make glaring errors because she isn't sitting back and trying to learn before doing anything. She's the sort of person who can't even pronounce newb properly. In fact, she's a noob (pronounced as it looks) or n00b. 'N00b' is a term in leetspeak, a modified spelling system developed on the Internet that combines numbers and letters. The term leet (which may also be spelled l33t or 1337) means 'elite', and the l33ts are at the other end of the scale to the n00bs. As one game player said (quoted in Calka, 2006) 'a noob is someone who should know what they're doing, but do not: someone careless, pigheaded, and inattentive, who often causes ruin to others via their actions'.

In terms of a community of practice, a newb is someone engaged in legitimate peripheral participation. They're willing to learn, and they recognise the expertise of others. They're on an inward trajectory and are likely to be able to get some help from more expert players. N00bs, on the other hand, are a drain on the community. 'The "n00b" is the player who is utterly hopeless both in manner and in skill' (Calka 2006). Their very name is an insult and a joke. Part of the problem n00bs have is that they are so unaware of what the WoW environment involves that they may not even be aware there are social norms and social cues. They therefore don't put the time in to learn what these are before really, really winding people up.

Luckily for our demonstration of an inward trajectory, Fictional Fiona is a newb. She's entered the domain of the community of practice (that domain being the *World of Warcraft*) but is not yet a part of the community. Because she's a newb, she appreciates that she's in a peripheral situation. She sees that she's got a lot to learn, but she's determined to learn it. She recognises that she's facing problems. She's got to learn the ropes and get to grips with the available tools, which could be difficult. She wants to be part of the community, which could take time. She's got to make friends, which isn't going to happen immediately. She's got to establish her role in the community and her value to it. All those activities take time in the physical world. They're going to take time in the virtual world too and it's important for Fiona, like any newcomer to a community of practice, to see that's a normal, legitimate peripheral stage.

However, it's difficult at first. Fiona may struggle to make friends. She may struggle to understand what's going on and feel marginalised. If she begins to think, 'This isn't for me. I can't get this. This is too difficult', she's likely to drop out. But she doesn't in this case. She remains as a peripheral member of the community who needs to get to grips with the practice. The practice in WoW isn't quite what it appears on the surface, as Mikezilla finally realised after hundreds of hours of play. On the surface, it seems to be simply about playing the game and levelling up. However, community members have all learned that practice in *World of Warcraft* is the end-game content. The entire metagame of the game and the community revolves around everything that happens when you have ostensibly finished the game. As far as members are concerned, that's when the game actually starts.

The WoW game is just something you do in order to meet the challenge and be part of the community. Once you realise this, you transition into another part of the community because you've got the key, you've understood that there's a metagame going on. That knowledge is a boundary object, because once you've got that idea in your head, you've transitioned to a different part of the community.

Fictional Fiona begins as a peripheral member of the WoW community of practice, on an inbound trajectory. She may meet a knowledge broker in the form of a guild recruiter. 'We're recruiting for a new guild,' they say, and sign her up. Or perhaps she's gone in with a friend who's been playing for longer. The friend starts to show her the ropes and introduces her to the boundary objects, both objects within the game and game lore. Things like knowledge of the actual game, the metagame that's going on, the goals within that, and the need for Guild cooperation. Things like what your Hearthstone does (it reduces travel time significantly). Things like the realisation that the game isn't really about low-level tasks such as killing and skinning boars, it's about gruelling six-hour raids during which you take on titanic opponents.

So Fiona gets into WoW by following an inbound trajectory within the community of practice, avoiding acting like a n00b, and instead moving from newb to a raid participant. She leaves the periphery and meets knowledge brokers, who introduce her to boundary objects and guide her deeper into the practice, learning as she goes. It's a social participative learning experience. Fictional Fiona advances from her initial 12 hours of play to 312 hours. She joins a 50–100 person guild. She understands the context. She's actively engaged in the practice itself, the end-game content.

During this process, her identity changes because she's connected to other people, learned the language, accessed the boundary objects, and developed her role. She may bring in knowledge and experience from her day-to-day life, or she may decide that her identities in WoW and in the physical world will be completely different. One aspect of communities of practice is that they allow you to develop different identities. Fiona may have a professional role in the physical world as an accountant, a family role as a single mother, a social role as a talented cellist, and a WoW role as a night elf. Each of those identities will be associated with different qualities, different vocabularies, different ways of speaking, different knowledge brokers, and different boundary objects. Even within her WoW guild, her identity will not be the same as it was outside the guild.

At the start, Fictional Fiona knew nothing. She had no idea what she was getting herself into or what lay ahead. If she hadn't engaged with the community of practice, if she'd remained a n00b, she would never have got anywhere. She'd have rubbed other players up the wrong way, interrupted them, disrespected them, and never begun an inbound trajectory. But by engaging as a newb with the community of practice, by paying attention, by recognising she had much to learn, by interacting with and learning from others, she gradually made her way up to l33t status. She'll never know everything about the game – it's too vast, too densely populated for that. But she'll know enough to mark her out as a leader, to be able to assign specialised roles, to maximise efficiency, and to locate resources inside and outside the game world.

## Tips for practice

Fictional Fiona's communities of practice covered different aspects of her personal, professional and gaming life because such communities support learning in many situations. However, it's worth noting that the classroom is rarely one of those situations. For one thing, the practice that pupils have in common is being pupils. They're not practising historians, mathematicians, scientists, or linguists. They may be becoming aware that those practices and their associated communities exist, but they haven't committed to any of those domains as a practitioner, and they're unlikely to be interacting with a range of experts in one of those communities on a regular basis. At higher levels of study, the situation may be different, particularly in the case of apprenticeships or courses that involve work experience. A community of practice may also apply at school for sports teams, orchestras, drama groups or brass bands, but in most cases these will be practices situated outside the classroom and the formal timetable.

Outside school, most things we engage with and learn about are practices, so communities of practice are common and largely informal. However, adding some structure and formality may make them more effective ways of learning. Learning to bring up children can be done through an informal community of friends and relations, but regular meet-ups at birthing classes, or parent-and-toddler groups provide an extra layer of value. Discussing plants with neighbours or the people who pass your window box may be useful, but developing your expertise as a member of a gardening club is likely to offer more value.

Wenger (2011) identified five types of value that can be created in a community of practice, and it's worth bearing these in mind when forming or developing a community. Let's return to the example of Fictional Fiona. She gains immediate value from her WoW community of practice when she enjoys community activities, makes a new friend, or spends a happy evening forgetting her miserable day at work. As she engages with the community, she gathers things that are of potential value. These might be artefacts, weapons or potions, perhaps new skills, or a powerful ally. She has no immediate use for any of these things but can see potential uses for them in the future. At some point, she does make use of them and experiences their applied value – she uses her mystical brew to avoid damage and is guided by the wisdom of the jade snake. However, simply applying her skills and resources is not enough. Do they benefit other community members? If so, then they have produced realised value and benefited her guild. Finally, does her activity shift her guild's goal or values? If so, the community of practice has had reframing value that has benefitted all its members.

In less fantastic settings, these five types of value: immediate, potential, applied, realised and reframing are just as important and it is worth considering how each type of value applies within your own community and how it can be applied to learning. In particular, it's important to relate them to the aims of the community, and to have a clear idea of what those aims are. Is the focus on learning as a community, providing peer support for individual members, or collectively developing practice? It's also useful to think about the types of interaction within a community of practice that might be applied. The wide range of possibilities includes increasing the confidence of members, visiting other practitioners or relevant sites, building an argument for change, documenting projects, or problem solving.

Consider the different elements of a community of practice and think about how they apply in your own community. Who are the knowledge brokers and how do people access them? Are there enough of them for a community of your size? Would it be helpful to train more, or to develop the skills of your existing brokers? What are your boundary objects – how easy is it to recognise and acquire them? Are new members able to adopt an incoming trajectory easily, or do many leave discouraged because they can't find a way in? Reflecting on a community of practice in this way helps to identify steps to improvement that will support more learners.

In particular, it is helpful to think ahead about the key things community members need to know. Enabling people to see barriers or transition points, to recognise what these are and identifying ways to help them through those transitions are all key. Think about how people's identities may change as they become community members, and support that shift. Make explicit the difference between marginality and peripherality. Watching and learning when you join the community are often good things to do – they don't mean you are excluded, they mean you are having the opportunity to prepare for further progress. Legitimate peripheral participation is a key part of that process – you are not expected to jump in and be active immediately. Making explicit to learners that these are the steps that everyone takes when becoming part of a community of practice contextualises the experience for those learners, making it seem a bit less daunting.

Communities of practice are everywhere; we join many of them without thinking. Like so many of the pedagogies in this book and on the podcast, becoming aware of them, seeing what they can offer, where and when they work best, can increase their value to you and all the learners you support.

# References of Warcraft

Calka, M. (2006) *Beyond Newbie: Immersion in Virtual Game Worlds*. Masters Dissertation. Ball State University. Available from: https://www.researchgate.net/profile/Michelle-Calka/publication/238103400_THESIS_Beyond_Newbie_Immersion_in_Virtual_Game_Worlds/links/53e02fa90cf2a768e49f5cac/THESIS-Beyond-Newbie-Immersion-in-Virtual-Game-Worlds.pdf

Lave, J.. & Wenger, E. (1991) *Situated Learning: Legitimate Peripheral Participation*. Cambridge, Cambridge University Press.

Wenger, E. (1998) *Communities of Practice: Learning, Meaning and Identity*. Cambridge, Cambridge University Press.

Wenger, E., Trayner, B. and de Laat, M. (2011) *Promoting and Assessing Value Creation in Communities and Networks: A Conceptual Framework*. Heerlen, The Netherlands: Ruud de Moor Centrum, Open University of the Netherlands.

Wenger-Trayner, E. & Wenger-Trayner, B. (2015) *Introduction to Communities of Practice*. Available at: https://www.wenger-trayner.com/introduction-to-communities-of-practice/

Scan the QR code to listen to
the podcast episode

**CHAPTER 17:**

# HOW DID THE APOLLO 13 CREW USE CONSTRUCTIONISM TO RETURN SAFELY TO EARTH?

*Mark Childs, Mike Collins and Becky Cohen*

*Beckzilla decides to stay a little longer in the land of Social Constructivism, so the others agree on an excursion to a nearby area, the Vale of Constructionism.*

*'Constructivism and Constructionism – easily confused,' notes Mikezilla. 'Nonsense,' says Beckyzilla of the clan Cohen, as she joins them on their trip. 'After all, you wouldn't confuse me with Beckzilla just because our names are similar.'*

*While exploring, the Zillas make some discoveries, the first being that this is possibly the place where they have had the most fun. There are robots, LEGO, and coding, oh my.*

*There's also a fair bit of inner mental building of the mind to go along with the outer building with the hands, so it's not much of a surprise to see people from neighbouring lands hanging out here as well. This place keeps the constructivists happy, as well as the social constructivists, and they're all building things together.*

*Isn't it great when people get along?*

In our tour around the various forms of constructivism, we've saved constructionism until last because it brings together a lot of the other theories. With constructionist approaches there's a bit of building, a bit of talking, and a bit of constructing schema in your mind. It's also best to make sure constructivism is thoroughly bedded in as a term before looking at constructionism, as it's quite easy to get the two words mixed up.

This chapter also talks a lot about Apollo 13 (the mission) and *Apollo 13* (the movie) though, obviously, there's a lot of overlap. This is one of our rare forays into reality, so we make the most of it by talking about the real-world space mission, which is useful in setting the scene for the events of the movie. If nothing else, you'll come away with a good idea of how the Moon missions were supposed to go. Moonnobbers[1] and welwalas[2] can skip this first part, but read on if you want to find out the answer to the question: **How did the Apollo 13 crew use constructionism to return safely to Earth?**

# Apollo 13

For many born in the sixties and earlier, the Moon missions were a vision of the future. There were 12 guys (all guys, all white, all American but ... ahem, moving on) who showed us that space was something that could also be colonised by white people. That by 2001 there really would be moonbases, and people living on space stations, and missions to Jupiter. A formative memory for Markzilla was being ushered into the hall at Princes End Infant School in Tipton and the whole school sitting together watching footage of Neil Armstrong stepping onto the lunar surface. It's

---

[1]. A pejorative term introduced by Professor Brian Cox to describe people who do not believe in the Moon landings.
[2]. See https://expanse.fandom.com/wiki/Welwala

difficult to capture that excitement now. Even by Apollo 13 (the third mission to the Moon) in 1970 there was waning interest in the Apollo programme – then everyone was gripped once again when the mission went wrong.

If you're not familiar with the Apollo rocket configuration, it's basically a huge cylinder topped by a truncated cone, topped by a smaller cylinder, topped by a smaller truncated cone, topped by a smaller cylinder, topped by a tiny cone. The tiny cone at the top is where the three guys sit. That's the command module. The cylinder underneath that is the service module, and the truncated cone below that is where the lunar module (the bit that lands on the Moon) sits. Everything else is just there to get those three modules into space.

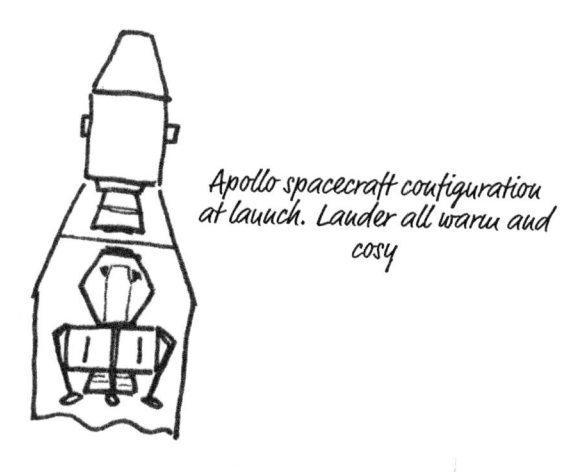

*Apollo spacecraft configuration at launch. Lander all warm and cosy*

The key to understanding what went wrong with Apollo 13 is that, just after the top section (the top cone, the top cylinder, and the truncated cone below that) leaves Earth orbit, the truncated cone where the lunar module is stored falls away. There's then a manoeuvre during which the lunar module joins onto the front end of the command/service module (see illustration). That's when Apollo 13 ran into problems.

In Apollo 11, the lunar module and command/service module were joined together as they travelled to the Moon. Then Mikezilla's namesake, Michael Collins, stayed in the command module, Buzz and Neil climbed into the lunar module and went down to the Moon. Only the top section of the lunar module came back, it reconnected with the command module, Buzz and Neil climbed back into the command module, the lunar module was jettisoned, then the remaining command/service module came back to Earth. The whole trip ended when the tiny cone that had formed the tip of the original craft splashed down in an ocean somewhere. Simple. Apollo 12 ditto. Apollo 13 – not so much.

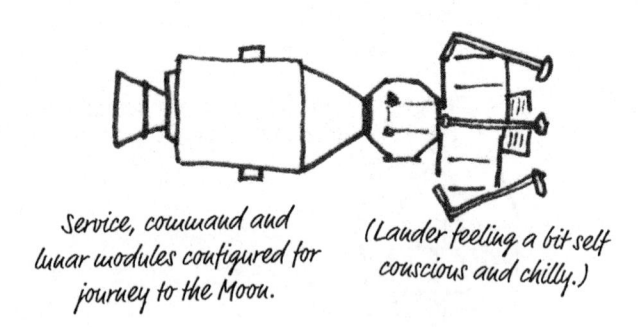

*Service, command and lunar modules configured for journey to the Moon.*

*(Lander feeling a bit self conscious and chilly.)*

The movie *Apollo 13* is based on the events of the Apollo 13 lunar mission. For astronauts Jim Lovell, Fred Haise and Jack Swigert, everything is going according to plan after they leave Earth's orbit. But then disaster strikes and an oxygen tank explodes. The movie explores the subsequent tensions within the crew and the numerous technical problems that threaten the astronauts' survival and their eventual safe return to Earth.

Some comments on the film: it's a Tom Hanks movie, he plays Jim Lovell, who is not only the commander of the mission, he wrote the book the movie is based on. With Kevin Bacon playing Jack Swigert, it's a double whammy of movie legends. Gary Sinese (another legend) plays Mattingly, an astronaut who's been bumped from the mission. It's Jack Swigert who stirs the oxygen tanks of the service module, presumably to prevent the oxygen from getting a skin on the top like custard. This should be a routine task, but the stirring causes an explosion, due to some wire in the tanks that has damaged insulation. This explosion leads to the oxygen venting into space. There's still enough oxygen to breathe, but as it's also used for fuel by the fuel cells, with no oxygen the astronauts seem doomed to end up running out of power before they get back to Earth.

Initially, crew members weren't sure whether or not it was just a pressure indicator inside the tank that was faulty and misleading them by showing there was no oxygen pressure or whether they were really losing oxygen. They worked out which of these interpretations was true by looking out of a window and seeing that – yes, they were venting oxygen. One of our top tips in relation to constructionism is that it's sometimes useful to look out of the window.

To preserve power in the command and service modules, the astronauts climbed into the lunar module. The plan was altered. They would skip the Moon landing. Instead, they would all hang out in the lunar module, which had been designed for two people for three days. If they didn't use the lunar module to land on the Moon, it would have enough power to fly everything back to Earth. So that's what they did, saving the command module and service module until they absolutely had to use them for the final stage of the journey. Another problem was that they weren't sure whether the command module's heat shield had been damaged in the explosion, so they had no idea whether they would get back down to the surface without burning up in the atmosphere.

An additional problem, once they'd decided on this course of action, was that the command module guidance system that was to be used for steering the craft back was never supposed to be turned off, but in this case it had been turned off completely. The astronauts therefore had to use the guidance system on the lunar module to do the job. This meant entering all the calculations onto the lunar module computer, which had less computing power than the average phone has today.

As an aside, we note a *Pedagodzilla*-style fact connected with these events. Judith Love Cohen was one of the software engineers who wrote the code for that guidance program. She was pregnant at the time and completed her part of the coding as she went into labour, actually taking a printout of the program to the hospital to finish it off there. Your trivia question is: who was the baby she gave birth to? Our clue is: this is not the greatest trivia question in the world, no, this is just a tribute. See the end of the chapter for the answer.

Yet another problem they had to deal with, which led to one of the most dramatic (and for our purposes here, useful) scenes of the film is that, as there were 50% more people in the lunar module and they were spending considerably more time there than intended, far more carbon dioxide had to be scrubbed from the air than the equipment could handle. Avoiding $CO_2$ poisoning became a key issue. The astronauts could get the carbon scrubbers out of the command module, but they didn't fit in the lunar module. This meant the astronauts had to jury rig a solution using what was available to them in their spaceship, this being in the days before Amazon deliveries. In the movie scene, the staff at Mission Control gather together a set of equipment identical to that available in space and try to replicate the solution on the ground in order to be able to advise the astronauts.

A final problem arose because all these systems were so finely interconnected. Turning off the fuel cells meant there wasn't enough water to drink, because the cells produced water as a by-product. So the astronauts were dealing with the situation while becoming increasingly dehydrated.

But they all made it back safely to Earth, and there was a brief rekindling of the interest in the Apollo programme, enough to last for four more missions, the final trip being Apollo 17 in 1972. In the half-century since then, no human has returned to the Moon (though, as we write, NASA has announced Artemis II, a crewed mission around the Moon that is planned as preparation for a Moon landing).

## Constructionism

Before moving to construct**ion**ism, let's recap on construct**iv**ism. Constructivism is the whole collection of approaches based on the view that learners build ideas in their heads. So, what you're doing when you're teaching people is helping them build their own ideas by providing experiences, problems to solve, activities, and support along the way that will enable them to do that building. Social constructivism is the idea that learners build those ideas in their heads by interacting with others. Situative learning is concerned with the ways in which learners interact with their environment and how that influences the ways they construct their ideas.

Constructionism blends these concepts by focusing on how learners build an understanding by building artefacts. The approach is basically constructivist because it views learning as a process of individuals building ideas in their heads. It's also situative, because it involves learner interactions with their environment. The proponents of constructionism argue that it's also social constructivist, because the building process is fundamentally a social activity. Looping back to our discussion of reality in the chapter on *The Matrix*, the artefacts that are built can be constructed in physical or virtual environments, or a combination of both.

For a popular culture introduction to constructionism, take a look at *The Toys That Made Us: LEGO* (Stern and Frost, 2018). This covers how LEGO took on the ideas of Seymour Papert's *Mindstorms* (1980, 2020) to develop the toy in the educational arena.

Papert is a key figure in the development of constructionism. He worked with the psychologist Jean Piaget, who was a founding figure in constructivism, and went on to add some nuances to Piaget's work. Essentially, Piaget argued that constructivism is about building up models in the heads of learners. They are 'builders of their own cognitive tools, as well as of their external realities. For them, knowledge and the world are both constructed and constantly reconstructed through personal experience' (Ackermann, 2001).

Constructionism proposes doing this by *actually* building things so that ideas are 'formed and transformed when expressed through different media, when actualized in particular contexts, when worked out by individual minds' (Ackermann, 2001, 88). And it's even more effective if you allow learners to 'invent for themselves the tools and mediations that best support the exploration of what they most care about' (Ackermann, 2001). These quotations are taken from an excellent text that explores the differences in these approaches, *Piaget's Constructivism, Papert's Constructionism: What's the Difference?* (Ackermann, 2001), which is one of those 'does what it says on the tin' papers.

Edith Ackermann's paper is an example of how academic writing should be – straightforward accessible language, with the various elements neatly laid out. She neatly sums up the distinction between Piaget's constructivism and Papert's constructionism:

> *Piaget's ... theory emphasizes all those things needed to maintain the internal structure and organization of the cognitive system (symbols standing for objects, abstraction of rules etc). And what Piaget describes particularly well is precisely this internal structure and organization of knowledge at different levels of development. Papert's emphasis lies almost at the opposite pole. His contribution is to remind us that intelligence should be defined and studied in-situ; that being intelligent means being situated, connected, and sensitive to variations in the environment*
>
> (Ackermann, 2001: 91)

This is why we've placed constructionism as a continuation of the situative learning models, as the approach is so fully embedded in the environment. It overlaps a lot with Krathwohl's (2002) reconceptualisation of Bloom's taxonomy (Krathwohl had been one of the original authors of that taxonomy, but Bloom's name came alphabetically first in the list and so he tends to get all the credit). The revised taxonomy includes a hierarchy of overlapping activities under the headings: Remember, Understand, Apply, Analyze and Evaluate. The final element of the taxonomy, Create, involves 'putting elements together to form a novel, coherent whole or make an original product' (Krathwohl, 2002). Mention of the taxonomy gives Mikezilla another chance to ring his metacognitive bell, because the revised taxonomy has a knowledge dimension, which includes factual knowledge; conceptual knowledge (the relationships between those facts); procedural knowledge (how to do things in a subject area); and concludes with metacognitive knowledge, 'Knowledge of cognition in general as well as awareness and knowledge of one's own cognition' (Krathwohl, 2002, p214),

We should also fold into our mix (we did a lot of breadmaking during Covid) Kafai and Resnick's ideas on learning by design (2011). They point out that, although design theorists have traditionally concentrated on the final products and learning theorists have emphasised the process of constructing ideas, there are strong connections between design and learning. The two fields are converging to some extent, as the focus in design is now much more on the process, including ways of understanding objective constraints and subjective meanings. At the same time, learning theorists, particularly constructionists, have begun to concentrate on the roles played by products and artefacts that learners produce.

So, for example, the LEGO robotics and coding *Mindstorms* sets do what they do so well, which is getting people to learn to code, by showing them immediately the results of their coding with little robots crawling around on the floor and doing things. And, of course, making robots in the first place helps learners to understand and acquire the principles of engineering. Other products, like the Logo Turtle developed by Papert, work on the same principles (Barnett, 2017). The Turtle robot responds to the commands programmed into it – providing immediate feedback on what has worked and what has gone wrong. It's worth noting that, although constructionism seems to be a long way from behaviourism, the immediate reward of success and the disappointment connected with failure align well with the principles of operant conditioning described in Chapter 7.

Building things that are tangible and shareable is typically a social activity, so constructionism draws in a lot of the ideas around social constructivism. People don't just make a LEGO robot and instruct it to move, they do this individually or as a group, they draw on what they know of the robots that others have created, and they show off their results to other coders or to friends and family. Sharing ideas and negotiating meaning are as important as the process of constructing the artefact.

The map in Chapter 6 is a good example of constructionism at work. Markzilla came up with a sketch that laid out the domains of pedagogy as he saw them, Mike and Beckzilla proposed changes, added the elves and dwarves metaphor, and pointed out inconsistencies in the domains. Between the three of them, a common ground was created. Creating a map, rather than simply discussing ideas, helped focus discussion and led to decisions about which ideas should go into the design, and where domains should be located.

In Lave-and-Wenger speak (see Chapter 16), the object enables reification[3] – or making concrete – things so they can be worked on and designed further (Farnsworth et al, 2016, 9), which is a core part of how communities of practice function. Wenger's idea of reification goes back to Papert's idea that 'building knowledge occurs best through building things that are tangible and shareable' (Barnett, 2017). So, for example, *Mindstorms* (the LEGO product) synthesises *Mindstorms* (the Papert book) and, in a meta way, is a concrete representation of the concepts in the book, while Wenger makes the point that writing a book is an act of reification in itself.

As an aside, talking about *Mindstorms* in the podcast on constructionism was also an act of constructionism, because the podcast was a reification of our various concepts around

---

3. Reification has lots of fancy definitions, but the one we like best is 'thing-ification' – turning something abstract into an object. You see this a lot on the TV around Christmas when advertisers try to persuade you that concepts such as freedom, love and teen spirit can be distilled and stored in scent / deodorant bottles.

constructionism, informed partly by having watched people using *Mindstorms* on TV. Our podcast was therefore constructing something from our abstract ideas about the TV show; the show reified the uses made of *Mindstorms* the kit (since people worked together and negotiated what that meant when creating the programme); and the kit was a concretisation of the principles expressed in the book; which was itself a product in which Papert coalesced what was in his mind.

And writing this book chapter about the podcast is a concretisation of the ideas formed by reflecting on the podcast …. ahhh, this could be an infinite regression of building concepts by building things. Let's stop before we go down that rabbit hole and instead answer our question.

*Getting a bit confused so building a shed out of concretisation and metabricks. Still a good shed.*

## The answer

In the description of the issues associated with three men moving into the lunar module for the flight home, a space that was designed for two men for a shorter period, we highlighted carbon dioxide build-up as one of the key issues. There were carbon dioxide scrubbers in the command module, but these couldn't easily be used in the lunar module, because the housing wasn't compatible.

Cue one of the most dramatic scenes in the movie (and the reason for choosing it as our example of constructionism). The specialists in Mission Control back on Earth cleared a room and collected together their own set of the equipment available to the astronauts in the spacecraft. Between them they had to build something, using only the available materials, that would enable the command module scrubbers to fit into the lunar module housing. They did this while in continuous dialogue with the astronauts.

What makes this a great example of constructionism is that the thinking about the design is done entirely through interaction with the objects; there's no purely abstract conceptualisation, the thinking is enacted through building and through the engineers expressing their ideas to each other by interacting with the objects in the room with them. They're collaboratively building knowledge, literally and metaphorically. Once they have a process developed, they then have to recreate that process in a step-by-step guide for the astronauts.

What helped in this process was that one of the people on the ground, Mattingly, had trained with Lovell and Haise. He had been intended to be on Apollo 13, but had to be scratched from the mission. All these space missions had a prime crew and a back-up crew, but one of the back-up crew (Duke) caught rubella. He could have infected all five other astronauts, but the others were immune – except Mattingly. Normally, if one astronaut was scratched from a team, the whole trio would be replaced, but with one scratched from the prime crew and one from the back-up, this was a rare example of NASA having to mix and match.

Looking at this process through a social-constructivist lens, this mixing and matching may well have helped with the working together. Mattingly would, presumably, have formed a shared group identity with Lovell and Haise, and a group identity helps enormously with collaborative learning (this is sometimes called the congruity hypothesis – Rogers and Lea, 2005, 156), but is particularly difficult to enact with remote collaboration. Here, though, the group identity would have been formed by them working closely together and developing a shared understanding of each other – which we previously mentioned in the 'Tips for practice' section of the Council of Elrond as helpful in social constructivism. Of course, Mattingly (and the others) would also have been motivated by trying to save the Apollo 13 crew, but we wouldn't recommend 'solve this or your friends die' as a valid teaching approach. It's not exactly a low-risk assessment.

For our final example of constructionist principles, there's the act of looking out of the window to see whether or not they are dealing with an instrument failure or if there really is an oxygen leak. It's Papert's idea that 'being intelligent means being situated, connected, and sensitive to variations in the environment' encapsulated. The environment in question here is a command module, but the idea applies anywhere.

So, to answer our question: **how did the Apollo 13 crew use constructionism to return safely to Earth?** Well, it was actually the Mission Control engineers who did this, but the constructionist principles they used for learning were:

- using design and construction of actual artefacts to develop an understanding of how to make the command module $CO_2$ scrubbers fit in the lunar module by replicating the materials available to the crew;
- pooling, testing and checking knowledge with each other, using these materials as a collaborative space;
- collaboratively creating a physical artefact they could share, which encapsulated the conceptual output of their learning process;
- drawing on social identity formation within the Lovell-Haise-Mattingly team to convey information and work collaboratively at a distance.

- Through these, they found a solution that enabled the three astronauts to breathe more easily and survive the trip back to Earth.
- In short, they initially didn't know what to do, they made something and, by making something, they understood the answer. Which is, basically, what constructionism is.

*(also duct tape)*

## Tips for practice

For an example of using constructionism in learning activities, take a look at Walton, Childs and Jugo (2019). This paper describes a research project that encouraged schoolchildren in five European schools to develop an interest in their national literature by creating videos, comic books and playing cards based on the books they were studying in school. Students had to remain engaged longer with the books in order to create the artefacts, and they stayed interested for longer, which meant they dug deeper into understanding the books. They also had to engage more deeply in order to re-present the content to other students. By drawing on skills not normally demanded of schoolchildren, some students found they had acquired higher status amongst their peers (by being able to edit, perform, speak English etc) and through that gained self-confidence they'd not been able to acquire through standard academic work.

All these findings backed up the claims of constructionism: get students to create something together and they will be more engaged with the content of the course, talk to each other more and find the end results more fulfilling.

The key thing is not to do this in an unstructured BeanDad (Chapter 13) kind of way. What the teachers did in the project wasn't just to set the students off to create something, they all (independently across the five schools) found that the process which worked best was:

1. talk about the book;
2. talk about the artefact they wanted to make;
3. teach students the skills (where needed) to make the artefacts;
4. talk about what the students found out about the book in the process.

So they brought in the Papert principle of making sure students 'invent for themselves the tools and mediations that best support the exploration of what they most care about'.

They pupils didn't just build things – their teachers integrated these activities within a cycle of instruction, collaboration, reflection and the next stage in the creation process. Ultimately, it's the reflection that consolidates the learning. The collaboration itself has to be structured, learners need to be taught the skills to work together effectively and how to create an artefact together. They also need to be able to create meaning not just from the content they are studying, but also from discussing the multiple interpretations that arise from considering that content. Constructionism requires a single output as an artefact, which requires synthesis of these multiple perspectives[4], which is why, in the revised version of Bloom's taxonomy, 'synthesise' is renamed 'create'.

---

4. Or at least a mechanism for displaying multiple points of view, for example how we've occasionally fractured the narrative into multiple points of view and peppered the text with call-out boxes and footnotes like this one.

So our major learning tip is that MAKING STUFF IS EXCELLENT. It requires learners to think about things from different perspectives and codify their thinking into a tangible output. Essays count here, but consider mixing it up a bit for variety.

So do it, do it all the time, do it loads. Every course, every module that you teach should have some elements of making stuff in it.

There is a danger (again we refer you to the Walton/Childs/Jugo paper, we're not biased) that the students who are considered more academically able, and who can think academically, may be alienated by this approach. Often it's the learners who aren't very good at making stuff or who aren't very good at sharing or working with others who excel in conventional lessons. When they're asked to work with other people to create things, suddenly they're not the ones at the top of the class. You need to find ways to reassure them that they still have an important role to play, even in a situation where the less academically oriented are able to shine.

Constructionism has to be managed to some extent. There's a danger that some students will get too deep into the creation and lose their way. They may not focus on the things to be learnt and, instead, become sidetracked by the process. If you've asked your students to make a film about the book they're studying in order to learn more about the book, steer them away from experimenting with expressionist cinematography and lead them towards talking about the text.

The process also has to be scaffolded. Provide instruction in the skills learners will need, not just the technical techniques but also the collaborative techniques. Maybe one of the students just wants to crochet; support the others to find ways either to incorporate that idea into their final product or to convince the student that another approach would work better. Maybe someone isn't great at pushing their ideas; the group as a whole needs to be taught how to find a mechanism for communication that includes all voices. Ideally, you'll include some activities to build a group identity first, but also give people opportunities that don't involve group work, because it doesn't suit everyone. For those who have had bad experiences of group work in the past, perhaps because of free-loaders in the group, discuss what went wrong and which strategies they could use in the future.

Crucially, develop a balance and comfort levels between the more traditionally academic skill set and the skill set associated with creating artefacts. Provide opportunities for the academics to be successful, but don't let them rely entirely on their normal ways of doing things. There are benefits to rethinking something conceptually as a physical, tangible thing that a group can all work on; doing this generates possibilities that otherwise wouldn't have been apparent. Anxieties around stepping into unfamiliar territory can be lessened by 1) explaining the pedagogic rationale for the activity and 2) assuring learners that they won't be judged on the quality of the artefact, but on the quality of the learning that emerges from constructing the artefact. And, from an assessment perspective, make sure you really are judging learners on the learning they display and not on the use of chiaroscuro in the mise en scène, or whatever.

Finally, making things together can be fun, not only for learners, but for educators as well. In the research project mentioned above, teachers reported there was more conversation going on in the classroom, there was more engagement, and the activity broke down barriers, because for once the teachers weren't the experts on everything taking place in the school. The students could do things the teachers couldn't, which led to a flattening of the different statuses, which produced a type of environment in which people learn well.

And, even if sometimes they don't learn well, isn't it better to spend your time doing something that's fun rather than miserable? There's always going to be some dreary thing to bring you back down to Earth, which (unless you're stuck out in space) is rarely a good thing.

## Houston, we have a citation

Ackermann, E. (2001). Piaget's constructivism, Papert's constructionism: What's the difference? In *Constructivism: Uses and Perspectives in Education*, Volumes 1 & 2, Conference Proceedings (85-94). Geneva, Switzerland: Research Center in Education. Available at: http://www.sylviastipich.com/wp-content/uploads/2015/04/Coursera-Piaget-_-Papert.pdf

Barnett, M. (2017) Exploring Turtle Art on the pi-top, *Blog:MakerMark*, Medium, 24 April. Available at: https://medium.com/@maker_mark/exploring-turtle-art-on-the-pi-top-f89919d81ff7

Farnsworth, V., Kleanthous, I. and Wenger-Trayner, E. (2016) Communities of practice as a social theory of learning: a conversation with Etienne Wenger. *British Journal of Educational Studies*, 64:2, 139-160.

Kafai, Y. & Resnick, M. (2011). Introduction to constructionism. In Y. B. Kafai & M. Resnick (Eds.), *Constructionism in Practice: Designing, Thinking and Learning in a Digital World* (1-8). New York, NY: Routledge

Krathwohl, D. (2002) A revision of Bloom's Taxonomy: an overview. *Theory into Practice*, 41:4, 212-218, DOI: 10.1207/s15430421tip4104_2

Papert, S. (1980, revised 2020) *Mindstorms: Children, Computers and Powerful Ideas*. Basic Books. USA: New York

Rogers, P. and Lea, M. (2005) Social presence in distributed group environments: the role of social identity, *Behaviour & Information Technology*, 24:2, March-April, 151-158.

Stern, T. and Frost, B.J. (2018) *The Toys That Made Us*, LEGO 2:3. Netflix, USA: Los Gatos, California

Walton, G., Childs, M. and Jugo, G. (2019) The creation of digital artefacts as a mechanism to engage students in studying literature. *British Journal of Educational Technology*. 50:3, 1060-1086.

*Answer to the trivia question is: Jack Black. You gotta believe me.*

Scan the QR code to listen to the podcast episode

**EPILOGUE:**

# JOURNEY'S END *OR* THERE AND BACK AGAIN

*Mike Collins*

*And so, leaving learners from many lands happily playing (and learning) together in the Vale of Constructionism, the Zillas bid adieu to the Realm of Pedagogy for the time being and head back towards their day-to-day reality, thinking about the ideas they've encountered and the friends they've met along the way.*

Mike(zilla) here, breaking the style convention in the rest of the book of having our little personal observations in neat little callouts, because this one is a bit big for a Zilla-based callout.

*big thoughts for smol brain*

Remember the chapter on transformative learning? It's close to my heart. *Pedagodzilla*, as both a podcast and now, as a book, has been a transformational experience for me in many ways.

Shortly before starting the podcast in 2019, I was a trained if inexperienced Learning Designer, and had my first disorienting dilemma. I'd written up a piece of guidance for academic authors, submitted it for review, and then was knocked on my bum when I received the feedback, 'Where is the pedagogy?'. I looked through the guide again – it wasn't there. I'd come up through a technical, production and coaching route – and suddenly realised I didn't have the vocabulary or confidence to engage in a pretty significant part of my role, and the deeper I dug in to it the more I realised that the knowledge I thought I'd acquired up to that point was little more than damp paper towel over a yawning chasm of my own ignorance. It was, to put it bluntly, a bit of a shocker.

After a lovely bit of flap and panic I looked around for ways to plug the gap. Books on 'pedagogy for dummies' weren't forthcoming but an early infographic on Learning Theories that has long since disappeared from the internet gave me a hitlist of esoteric and mysterious terms to unpick and learn. I don't have a naturally academic mind, but had recently gotten back in to podcasting – so figured I could have a go at talking through some of the theories with myself (and/or a pot plant), and that perhaps in editing and listening back to it some of it would sink in.

This was a dreadful idea, and would have resulted in something stilted, embarrassing, and boring, particularly for the pot plant. Fortunately, on my way to the recording booth I ran into Mark(zilla), who was taking a coffee break, and explained my plan to him. Mark offered to be the fauna to replace my flora, and after that initial recording I never looked back.

Since then we've recorded a lot of episodes, covering (as far as I know) most of the pillars of pedagogic theory and the design of learning.

Like a five year old's living room fort, we've tacked the sheets of pedagogies and practice over familiar toys and conceptual cushions, and in doing so I've built up a strange structure of understanding just enough of what the theories are to apply them in my own practice, see them out in the wild – and help folk design learning to draw on their advantages. It's also given me a way to have a bit of fun while talking about it all with Mark, the best collaborator a fella could ask for – and some absolutely incredible pedagogues from across the industry, whose expertise and good humour I have in no way deserved but massively appreciated.

I've also gradually learned that pedagogy isn't a set of neat theories and models in boxes, but instead a confused winter soup, where the parsnip of constructivism disintegrates within the broth of behaviourism, and bobs up against the partially dissolved brussels sprout of situative learning – ready to be soaked up by the crusty roll of applied practice and research. It's a mental toolbox (some would say metacognitive toolkit) of stories that helps you articulate and understand different facets and perspectives of the same messy tangle that is 'learning'.

As a field it's as wide as the ocean, as deep as two oceans stacked, and as interesting as three oceans made of little fiddly LEGO bricks. I've found learning about learning has transformed me both professionally and personally – from the sort of person who describes themselves as 'not academic' to the kind of person who can describe what ontology and epistemology are using Winnie the Pooh memes, and have fun doing it. I hope this book has shared a bit of that fun with you, and left you feeling similarly equipped to blag these theories and stories in your own life and practice. If you want more of it, then why not head on over to the podcast itself? It's a lot like this book, but with a whole lot more rambling, nerdiness and sniggering.

*The Zillas' ruminations on their experiences come to an end. They exit the portal but – they're not back in day-to-day reality at all. They appear to be on the starting square of a huge game board. Above their heads, a large sign tells them they have entered the realm of Learning Design. Underneath that is the legend, 'You've taken your first step into a larger world.'*

*They look at each other warily, then move onto the first square. A voice commands them to answer a question before proceeding further. That question is:*

*'How does critical digital pedagogy help Starfleet boldly go where no one has gone before?'*

*The Adventure is Just Beginning...*

Coming soon (ish) *Pedagodzilla Volume 2: The Design of Learning*

Printed in Great Britain
by Amazon